BRUNEL'S CORNISH VIADUCTS

The
Construction and History
of his Timber Railway
Viaducts

by

John Binding

1993

PENDRAGON BOOKS

TRANSPORT Atlantic PUBLISHERS

THE HISTORICAL MODEL RAILWAY SOCIETY • 1950 •

For
Nicky, Dee, Chris and Rich

Frontispiece. A charming setting for Treviddo viaduct, taken in 1895, viewed from the south. It will be seen that this Class A2 structure has been shored on all seven piers while the difference between buttressed and plain piers can be easily distinguished. Note that both the landward spans comprise queen post trussed balustrades and incorporate cross timbers which provide additional support for the centre carrying beam. Similar support was later to be added to the linking spans. *L G Booth Collection*

BRUNEL'S CORNISH VIADUCTS

by

John Binding

A PENDRAGON BOOK FROM ATLANTIC TRANSPORT PUBLISHERS

IN ASSOCIATION WITH

THE HISTORICAL MODEL RAILWAY SOCIETY

SOURCES & ACKNOWLEDGEMENTS

The considerable help of many individuals contributed to the completion of this investigation and I gladly acknowledge the interest and assistance which have been so freely given. The Bibliography lists works already published which provided background information and of these, MacDermot's *History of the Great Western Railway Vol 2* and L G Booth's Chapter on Timber Works in Pugsley's *Works of Isambard Kingdom Brunel* were invaluable; as were previous articles on the subject by Gibbons (1899) and Whitley (1934).

However, as far as possible, I have drawn my information from original papers and in this respect, I am particularly grateful to Mr D J Harris, Regional Civil Engineer of Western Region, British Railways Board, for permission to reproduce extracts from Brunel's original drawings of the timber viaducts still held in the BR Archives at Swindon, and to use photographs which originated from Great Western Railway days. I should like to thank his staff at Swindon and Exeter for their ever willing help and interest in accessing the relevant records that are still available within BR.

The painstaking work of my Record Research Agent, Mrs Betty Thomson, at the Public Records Office at Kew, with the help of their staff, contributed details from Minute books and Margary's extensive reports, together with the valuable contemporary information given in the Arbitration Hearing. N A Lee of the Brunel Archive at Bristol University assisted in furnishing relevant information contained within that valuable collection. Further contemporary details emerged from my reading local newspapers.

I owe a special word of thanks to Dr L G Booth, late of Imperial College, for his continual interest and assistance in dealing with the technical aspects of the subject, the loan of photographs from his collection and for kindly reading an early draft manuscript. The work has benefited from his many helpful suggestions.

My thanks are also due to Derrick Beckett of the School of Land and Construction Management at Thames Polytechnic who very kindly checked my calculations and provided much helpful guidance. Likewise, I am indebted to the Trustees of the Science Museum for permission to consult the unpublished records of the late S. J. Crispin on the subject of the Cornish viaducts, and thank Robert Sharp and John Liffen of the Museum for their interest and help. Regrettably, the National Railway Museum was unable to furnish copies from its extensive collection of original Great Western Railway negatives.

I am particularly grateful for the assistance provided by the following: Roger Penhallurick, Senior Curator of the Royal Cornwall Museum, Truro (which is administered by the Royal Institution of Cornwall) and for permission to include a number of photographs from its extensive collection (R.I.C.); Terry Knight and his staff at the Local Studies Library, Redruth; the Staffs at the County Records Offices at Truro, Plymouth and Exeter; Peter Gilson of the Royal Cornwall Polytechnic Society, Falmouth; Chris Childs of Brunel University Library, Pendon Museum, and P W Elkin of the City of Bristol Museum & Art Gallery.

To David Jenkinson and Dr Alan Earnshaw my grateful thanks for all their kindness and help, particularly, their editorial expertise, which finally brought this work to fruition.

Of the many others who have given assistance in several ways, includng the loan of photographs from their collections, I should like to acknowledge the following:
John Beckett, Theo Beckett, David Bearne, J D Blyth, G J Biddle, Tom Bowden, R Carpenter, M M Chrimes, David Crocker, Miss J M Elton, Tony Fairclough, Dane Garrod, L T George, Keith Hickman, G W Knight, Peter Laws, Ian Leith of the RCHME, Michael Messenger, T B O'Loughlin, Bill Peto, John Pomroy, John Rapson, Jack Slinn, P Stanier, John Slate, Alan Smith of the Newcomen Society, P H Tangye, Chris Trevan, L Waters and S J Woodward.

Finally, this work owes much to the encourgement of my family and everything to the ever-present support of my wife, Val, who made it all possible.

Rock
Cornwall April 1993

'Pendragon Books' is an imprint of Atlantic Transport Publishers, 'Trevithick House', West End, Penryn, Cornwall TR10 8HE. All rights reserved.

Set in Galliard 9pt by Ian D. Luckett Typesetting, St. Austell

Layout and Design by Barry C. Lane.

Colour and Black and White photographic reproduction by The Amadeus Press Ltd, Huddersfield, West Yorkshire.

British Cataloguing in Publication Data.
A catalogue record for this book is available from the British Library.

ISBN 0 906899 56 7

Contents

Courtesy Trustees, Science Museum

INTRODUCTION

Isambard Kingdom Brunel (1806–1859) was one of the outstanding Victorian engineers, renowned for many achievements, including the building of the Great Western Railway, the steamship *Great Britain* and the design of the Clifton Suspension Bridge. Few would dispute that he was also the greatest engineer in timber during the nineteenth century; many were the structures built for the railways under his direction. This is the story of the design and construction of a particular group which, because of their unique format and location, have always held a particular fascination for engineers and railway enthusiasts alike. On no other main line of railway in the United Kingdom were there so many viaducts per mile as those on the 80 miles between Plymouth and Penzance — a total of 43 spanning in aggregate a distance of nearly five miles — while on the branch between Truro and Falmouth, there were a further eight.

Harsh financial constraints combined with the geography of Cornwall to test Brunel's skill in the design of cheap but effective structures, to carry his broad gauge railway across the many tidal creeks and deep river valleys which intersected the route. It was probably this combination of the wild yet attractive Cornish landscape as the setting for these slender yet graceful timber structures, often built on a sweeping curve and at heights of up to 150ft, which gave them their peculiar fascination.

Agreed, timber had been widely used by Brunel for the many bridges and viaducts involved on the Great Western Railway and the other Companies where he was Engineer, while their basic engineering design had been applied at an earlier date in South Wales and South Devon. But it was in Cornwall, by virtue of their number and longevity, that the name of Brunel and timber viaducts became inextricably linked. For, without his vision and courage to resort to the use of timber in novel and distinctive form, it may not have been possible for Penzance and Truro to have been linked by rail with Plymouth at that time. This is particularly important to bear in mind since economic conditions, in the aftermath of the second railway mania, were then very much against completion of the route.

That many of his viaducts lasted in service into the twentieth century, despite the known limitations of timber as a structural material, is ample tribute to his original design conception. While, with the benefit of hindsight, we may criticise some aspects of his designs, that should in no way detract from our admiration of the handsome structures which he created. They may have severely tried the nerves of passengers in the 19th century, but there was never an accident with one of them.

The story of their spectacular contribution to the railway in Cornwall, is seen against the background of the economy of the mid nineteenth century, the fragmented construction of the routes and the then prevailing level of design technology. It is also the story of the people involved. Undeniably, Brunel was the central figure of this saga, with his clear perception of what was required, his ceaseless strive for perfection and his intimate grasp of detail. Nevertheless, the final execution of the works depended on the skill and efforts of many others. Sadly there were occasions when, in his absence on other duties, some of his site engineers could have exercised greater diligence in ensuring that his high standards were, in fact, achieved in practice.

That said, due acknowledgement must be paid to the significant part played by his assistants, like W Bell, of whom Brunel wrote in one of his letters:

> '...a very well informed young man in his profession and particularly also in those branches requiring mathematical knowledge which are too often neglected'.

He went on to become eminent in his own right in developing the theory of structures. Then there was R P Brereton, who joined Brunel in 1836 and as his chief assistant was deeply involved in much of his work. After Brunel's death, he assumed responsibility for a number of unfinished projects including, as we shall see, the completion of the Falmouth branch.

H S Bush was one of the other assistants engaged in the construction of the Cornwall Railway and in 1858 Brunel recommended his appointment as Resident Engineer of the line at a salary of £350 pa, writing:

> 'I have not been able to think of a better man...for the purpose...and I have great confidence in his steady attention to his duties'.

Bush held this office until his death in 1868.

However, the protegé most deeply concerned with the timber viaducts during the greater part of their lifetime was Brunel's young assistant, Peter John Margary (1820–1896). In his early years he had been engaged, under the direction of his Chief, in the building of the South Devon Railway and then, on Brunel's death, succeeded him as that Company's Engineer — a post which he held until he moved to a similar appointment with the Cornwall Railway in 1868, following the death of Bush. From that date, until his retirement in 1891, he is constantly involved in our story. We shall see how he struggled, in the face of the obstinacy of the Cornwall Directors, to replace Brunel's handsome but frail structures, with designs more suited to the demands of the heavier traffic of the latter half of the 19th century.

In considering the work of the other personnel involved, we must also recognise the contribution of the bridge site engineers — H G Cole (sadly killed in an accident) and his successor, T H Gibbons, who was closely involved on a day to day basis, in the routine maintenance of these many structures and played a significant part in their replacement. He subsequently became Divisional Engineer at Plymouth and in 1899 presented a Paper on the subject of the Cornish viaducts to the Institution of Mechanical Engineers.

Finally, of course, tribute must be paid to the immense contribution of the hundreds of workmen, from humble labourer to skilled woodworker, stone cutter and trowel mason (as they were called in those days), who were engaged in the building of these fifty one viaducts. Despite their obvious limitations, some of these structures saw service for nearly 75 years, while others had their original piers incorporated in the viaducts which still carry the main line into Cornwall — eminent testimony to the quality of their workmanship. Today, at other locations alongside the route, stand redundant, gaunt stone stumps, defying the hazards of nature, all that is left of Brunel's masterpieces. But, they stand in tribute to the memory of a brilliant engineer, lofty and lonely as the granite remains of the engine houses that dot the landscape, and also form part of the heritage of Cornwall's industrial past.

1. A Falmouth branchline train crosses Collegewood Viaduct, en route to Falmouth, in the 1890s. Hauled by one of the ubiquitous Metro class tanks of the 1491–1500 group, which had their dome set on the front boiler ring, the stock comprises a pair of brake 3rds, constructed to Diagram D.3 in the early 1880s. This view should be compared with the illustration of this same viaduct in Fig.140A, a photograph taken in its final years, that shows a 4575 Class Prairie tank hauling an unusual collection of coaches, also Falmouth bound. It is perhaps significant that, up to the date of its replacement, this structure was carrying locomotives over 20 tons heavier than the 40 ton Metro tanks which latterly handled most of the passenger traffic. Collegewood was the last of the Cornish timber viaducts to be replaced, in July 1934, following a life of 71 years. Built after Brunel's death, the masonry piers are all buttressed while the Class A2 superstructure follows a smooth curve throughout its length. Note the landward span, incorporating queen post truss balustrades, in the absence of a masonry abutment, is supported on a timber platform seated on the embankment. ***Courtesy Trustees, Science Museum***

Chapter 1

HISTORICAL BACKGROUND

As the 10.50pm train for Truro steamed out of Falmouth station on Saturday 21st July 1934[1], probably hauled by a Metro Class tank engine, an era of Cornish railway history was coming to an end. A few minutes later the train slowed for the speed limit, believed to be 15 mph, which had been imposed on the branch line timber viaducts. As it crossed Collegewood, near Penryn (Fig.1), the last of Isambard Kingdom Brunel's famous and picturesque timber structures in Cornwall ended its career. The following day, traffic was routed over the more permanent if less artistic looking structure in masonry, brickwork and reinforced concrete, recently completed as a replacement for its timber predecessor which had been in use since 1863. Thus ended the era which had been instituted by Brunel over eighty years earlier when, because of his great love of timber as well as financial necessity, he selected wood as the main material to be used in the construction of the 51 viaducts required on the West Cornwall and Cornwall railways.

Brunel's love of timber, coupled with his talent for artistic design, are reflected in the structure and proportions of the splendid train shed at Bristol, Temple Meads, which still stands today as a tribute to his engineering genius. Two other examples of his many architectural achievements in timber were the elegant roof of the engine house at Swindon and his remarkable 102ft timber arch bridge across the River Parrett in Somerset. Sadly both are now just memories. Although Brunel adapted well established principles for his designs, it was in their application (with meticulous attention to detail) that his works attained the stature which they enjoyed for so many years.

Of equal significance, but evolved under the imposition of severe financial constraints, this same genius was exemplified in the graceful timber viaducts which he designed for Cornwall in the 19th century. Accordingly, the story of their history and development which follows, needs to be considered in relation to the peculiar economy and the physical geography of the County, and the then current level of technical knowledge available as a basis for design. All these factors played a part, thus influencing the final shape and form of the 51 structures for which Brunel was initially responsible. There were in addition, timber bridges across rivers at Lostwithiel and St Erth, which also merit consideration.

A chronological study of Brunel's West Country timber viaduct designs, as finally built, shows that they can conveniently be divided into five quite distinct groups identified as follows:

1. The five structures built for the South Devon Railway, opened in 1849, intended to carry the relatively light loads of the atmospheric trains. Subsequent strengthening by the addition of a substantial timber parapet was introduced to accommodate locomotive working, followed in 1861–4 by the addition of wrought iron girders, before they were replaced in 1893.

2. The nine viaducts of the West Cornwall Railway, opened in 1852, which followed either a simple strut formation for those of around 35ft in height or, for the higher structures, a light type of three leg fan construction. Both were all timber and incorporated the concept of laminated horizontal beams to support the decking, with special cast iron seatings to locate the main component members in their respective planes.

3. The thirty four viaducts of the Cornwall Railway, opened in 1859 where, no doubt, drawing from his service experience of the West Cornwall line, Brunel introduced a combination of simple masonry piers to carry a four leg fan type of timber superstructure for the taller inland viaducts. Only where the line crossed tidal creeks, with the need to employ timber piles in the interest of economy, did he retain an all timber formation. These latter designs owe their origin in part to the earlier South Devon structures, and incorporated two trussed timber beams to support the decking, in place of the three simple laminated horizontal beams of the fan type structures. All these main line viaducts were replaced between 1879 and 1908.

4. The six structures on the Tavistock branch of the South Devon Railway, opened in 1859, which were generally similar to the Cornwall Fan types, and were replaced over the period 1893 to 1910.

5. The eight viaducts on the Falmouth branch of the Cornwall Railway, built by Brereton after Brunel's death and opened in 1863, which were a strengthened version of those on the main Cornwall line. They were not finally replaced until the period 1923 to 1934.

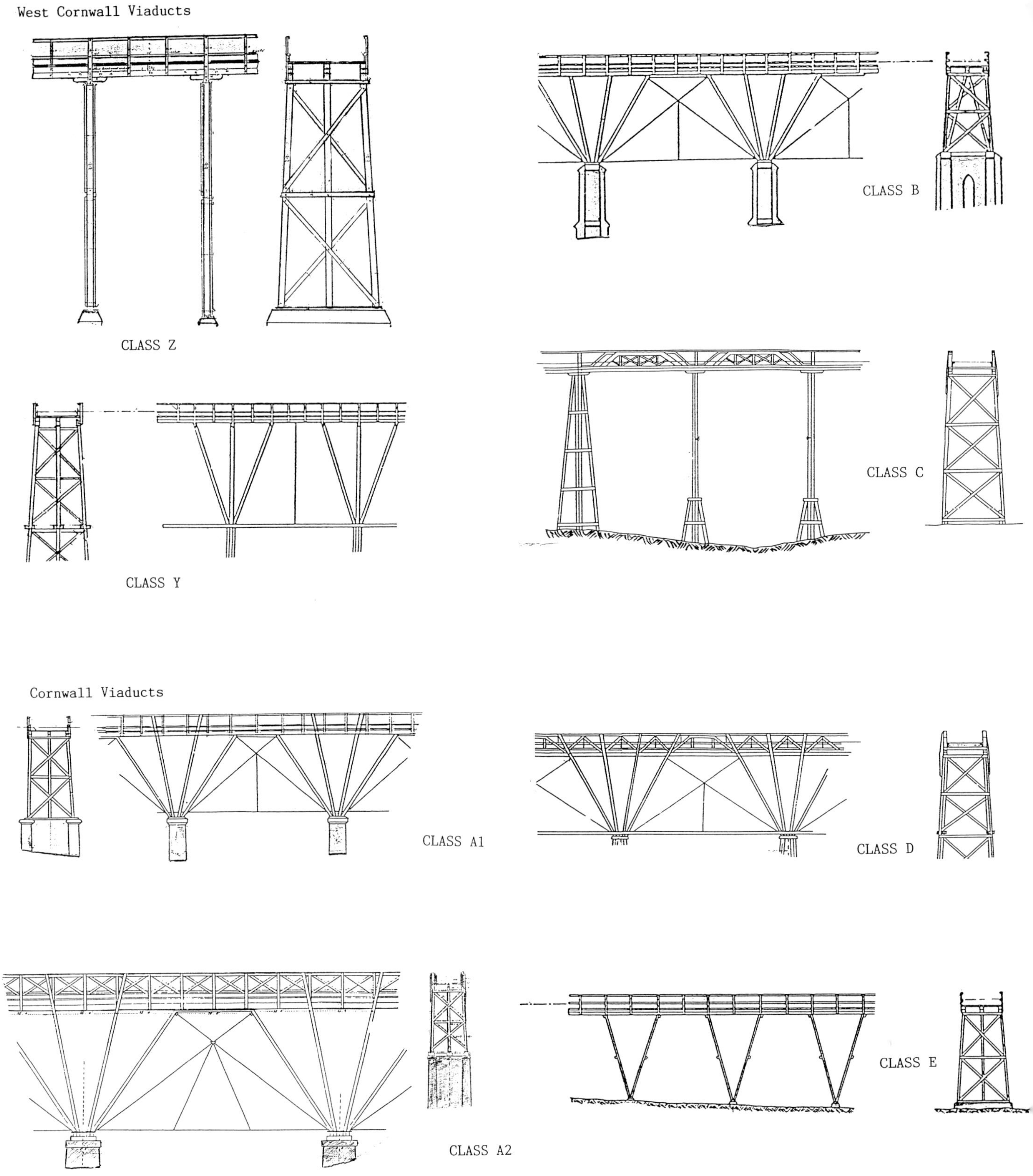

2. Outline sketches of the eight Cornish viaduct Classes, based on the Margary notation with author's additions (see Chapter 5) — not to scale. Because St Germans was unique it is not included.

In this study we are concerned with the viaducts involved in groups 2, 3 and 5, although reference is made, where relevant, to certain aspects of the structures in the other groups.

It is believed that Brunel's original intention was to have a series of standard designs, using interchangeable components. However, because of different conditions at each location, he had to resort to variations in this basic concept, and introduce different viaduct Classes, which we shall consider in more detail in a later chapter. For ease of understanding, Fig.2 shows an outline sketch of each of the eight Classes which he built in Cornwall, using a standard form of identification letter which will apply throughout this book.

Common factors in all his designs were the use of material in large cross-sections, with the object of reducing the risk from decay and fire, and the avoidance of intricate details. This allowed relatively unskilled labour to be employed, both in their construction and subsequent maintenance, in that replacement of faulty timbers in service could be carried out with the minimum interruption to traffic. In effect, Brunel can be considered to have initiated a new regional craft, ideally suited to the craftsmen of the West, with their long experience in the boat building industry.

However, the concept of easy replacement in service of decayed timbers proved to be of doubtful benefit, since by the very nature of the operation of removing a structural member, the strength and interrelation of the other members in the structure was disturbed[2]. Over the years, this led to a gradual deterioration in the stability of the overall framework of a viaduct and emphasised the need for complete replacement by a new structure built in more durable material.

The well known routes of the Cornwall and West Cornwall Railways, together with the main stations and the location and names of the viaducts concerned in this story, are shown in Fig.3. Under the subsequent management of the Great Western Railway, these structures were numbered sequentially, as shown, from Plymouth, westwards. The accompanying Table lists all the viaducts in numerical order with details of location, Class, length, and maximum height (based on information from MacDermot[3]), together with their dates of construction and replacement, insofar as it has been possible to establish these from available records. As we shall see, MacDermot's dimensions do not always agree with those given in drawings and reports but they at least form a consistent base to start an investigation.

In his 17th century *Survey of Cornwall*, Richard Carew of Anthony described the County as '...a demi-island in an island...' — a situation which had changed little by the 19th century. It was for the most part separated from the rest of the country by the River Tamar which, rising on its north east border, flowed southwards across the county to discharge into the English Channel, through the estuary of the Hamoaze at Plymouth, and thus created a barrier to easy communication with the rest of the United Kingdom. The terrain of the County comprised wild moorland in the north while the southern flank was intercepted by numerous deep river valleys and inlets from the sea — the overall region presenting a daunting prospect for any civil engineer planning a rail link through the County.

3. This map dates from the late 19th century and was prepared to show the identification number, location and names of all the viaducts in Cornwall at that time. It includes the bridge across the Hayle River at St Erth (No. 51) but omits a similar structure across the Fowey at Lostwithiel. Although built of timber, neither of these structures were viaducts in the true sense. ***Proc I Mech E***

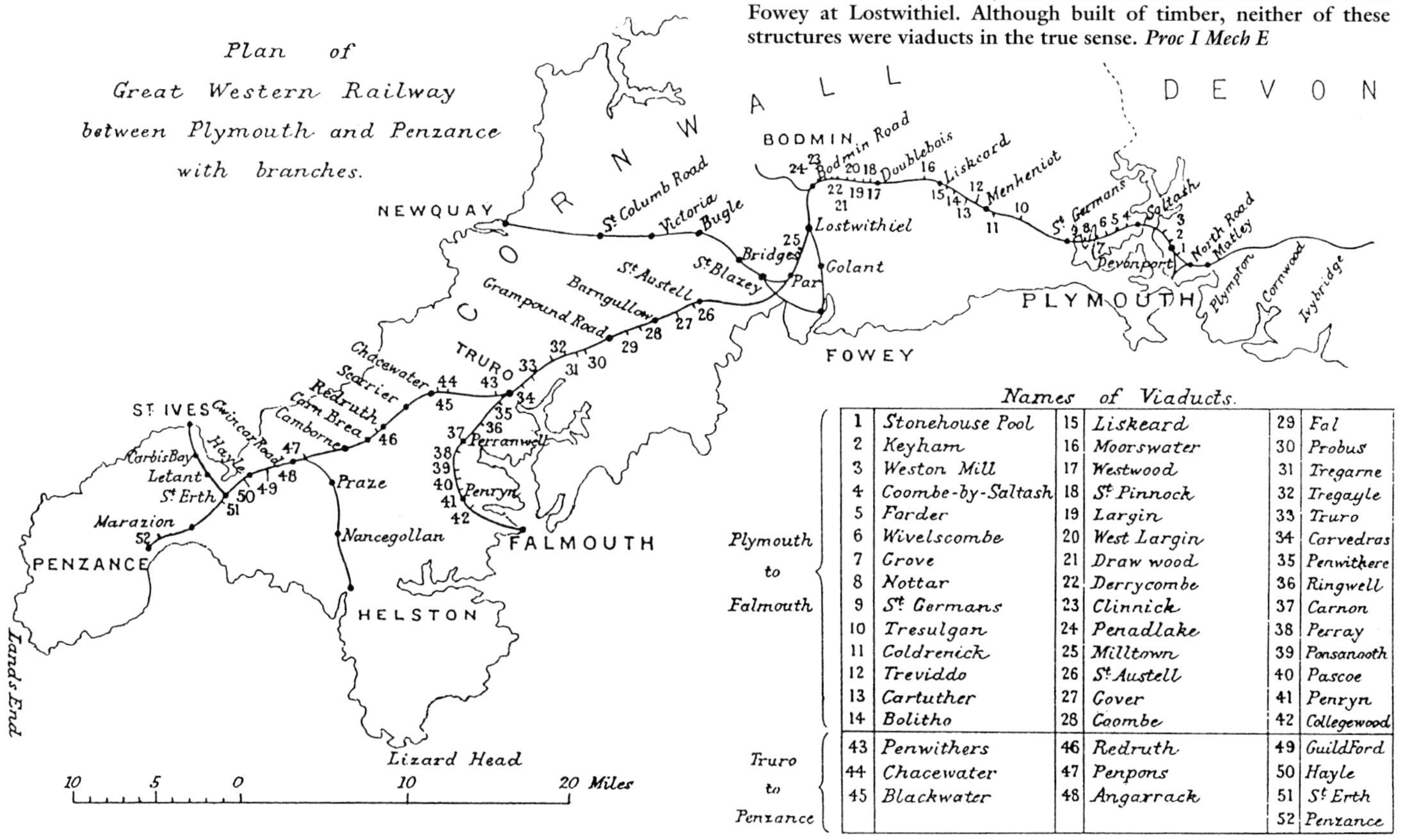

Names of Viaducts.

Plymouth to Falmouth	1	Stonehouse Pool	15	Liskeard	29	Fal
	2	Keyham	16	Moorswater	30	Probus
	3	Weston Mill	17	Westwood	31	Tregarne
	4	Coombe-by-Saltash	18	St Pinnock	32	Tregayle
	5	Forder	19	Largin	33	Truro
	6	Wivelscombe	20	West Largin	34	Carvedras
	7	Grove	21	Draw wood	35	Penwithere
	8	Nottar	22	Derrycombe	36	Ringwell
	9	St Germans	23	Clinnick	37	Carnon
	10	Tresulgan	24	Penadlake	38	Perray
	11	Coldrenick	25	Milltown	39	Ponsanooth
	12	Treviddo	26	St Austell	40	Pascoe
	13	Cartuther	27	Cover	41	Penryn
	14	Bolitho	28	Coombe	42	Collegewood
Truro to Penzance	43	Penwithers	46	Redruth	49	GuildFord
	44	Chacewater	47	Penpons	50	Hayle
	45	Blackwater	48	Angarrack	51	St Erth
					52	Penzance

SCHEDULE OF PRINCIPAL DIMENSIONS, TYPES, DATES									
No.	Name	Locat'n[1]	Class	Length[2] (feet)	Height (feet)	No. of Piers	Date Built	Date Replaced	Replaced by
Plymouth to Truro — Opened 1859									
1	Stonehouse Pool	247/31	A2	321	57	5	1858	1908	Iron Girders on alignment
2	Keyham	248/68	A2	432	90	6	1858	1900	Steel Girders on alignment
3	Weston Mill	249/45	C	1,200	46	29	1858	1903	Steel Bridge on downside
4	Coombe by Saltash	251/38	D	603	86	9	1859	1894	Masonry viaduct on up side
5	Forder	252/54	C	606	67	16	1859	1908	Masonry viaduct on new alignment
6	Wivelscombe	253/43	C	198	25	4	1859		Cut out by deviation on new alignment
7	Grove	255/12	E	114	29	2	1859		Cut out by deviation on new alignment
8	Nottar	255/31	C	921	67	27	1859	1908	Masonry viaduct on new alignment
9	St Germans	255/74	Spec.	945	106	16	1859	1907	Masonry viaduct on downside
10	Treslugan	260/72	A2	525	93	8	1857	1899	Masonry viaduct on downside
11	Coldrennick	261/42	A2	795	138	12	1857	1898	Steel Girders on alignment
12	Treviddo	262/49	A2	486	101	7	1857	1898	Masonry viaduct on up side
13	Cartuther	263/74	A2	411	89	6	1857	1882	Masonry viaduct on downside
14	Bolitho	264/21	A2	546	113	8	1857	1882	Masonry viaduct on alignment
15	Liskeard	264/49	A2	720	150	11	1858	1894	Steel Girders on alignment
16	Moorswater	265/38	D	954	147	14	1858	1881	Masonry viaduct on up side
17	Westwood	269/12	A1	372	88	5	1857	1879	Masonry viaduct on downside
18	St Pinnock	269/40	B	633	151	9	1856	1882	Iron Girders on alignment
19	Largin	269/69	B	567	130	8	1856	1886	Iron Girders on alignment
20	West Largin	270/21	A1	315	75	5	1857	1875	Masonry viaduct on downside
21	Draw Wood	270/39	E	669	42	17	1857	1875	Retaining Wall & Embankment
22	Derrycombe	270/75	A1	369	77	5	1857	1881	Masonry viaduct on downside
23	Clinnick	271/46	A1	330	74	5	1857	1879	Masonry viaduct on downside
24	Penadlake	272/20	E	426	42	10	1857	1877	Masonry viaduct on downside
25	Milltown	278/49	A1	501	75	7	1858	1896	Masonry viaduct on up side
26	St Austell	286/60	A1	720	115	10	1858	1898	Masonry viaduct on up side
27	Gover	287/37	A1	690	95	10	1858	1898	Masonry viaduct on downside
28	Coombe St Stephens	291/16	A1	738	70	11	1858	1886	Masonry viaduct on up side
29	Fal	291/59	A1	570	90	8	1858	1884	Masonry viaduct on up side
30	Probus	295/30	E	435	43	11	1858	1871	Embankment
31	Tregarne	296/52	A1	606	83	9	1858	1902	Masonry viaduct on downside
32	Tregagle	297/07	A1	315	69	4	1858	1902	Masonry viaduct on up side
33	Truro	300/09	A1	1,329	92	20	1858	1904	Masonry viaduct on up side
34	Carvedras	300/39	A1	969	86	15	1858	1904	Masonry viaduct on up side
West Cornwall Line — Opened 1852									
43	Penwithers	302/03	Y	372	54	7	1852	1887	Masonry viaduct on downside
44	Chacewater	305/46	Y	297	52	6	1852	1888	Masonry viaduct on downside
45	Blackwater	305/68	Y	396	68	8	1852	1888	Masonry viaduct on downside
46	Redruth	309/79	Y	489	61	9	1852	1888	Masonry viaduct on alignment
47	Penponds	314/49	Z	693	45	32	1852	1900	Masonry viaduct on downside
48	Angarrack	317/52	Y	798	100	15	1850	1885	Masonry viaduct on up side
49	Guildford	318/25	Y	384	56	7	1850	1886	Masonry viaduct on downside
50	Hayle	319/39	Z	831	34	36	1850	1886	Iron Girders on alignment
51	St Erth	320/35					1850	1883	Steel Girders
52	Penzance	326/10	Z	1,041	12	44	1852	1871	Rebuilt
								1921	Granite faced Embankment
Falmouth Branch — Opened 1863									
35	Penwithers	301/43	A2	813	90	12	1863	1926	Embankment
36	Ringwell	304/01	A2	366	70	5	1863	1933	Embankment
37	Carnon	304/26	A2	756	9	11	1863	1933	Masonry viaduct on downside
38	Perran	305/70	A2	339	56	5	1863	1927	Masonry viaduct on downside
39	Ponsanooth	306/74	B	645	139	9	1863	1930	Masonry viaduct on up side
40	Pascoe	307/19	A2	390	70	6	1863	1923	Embankment on new alignment
41	Penryn	308/69	A2	342	83	5	1863	1923	Embankment on new alignment
42	Collegewood	309/32	A2	954	100	14	1863	1934	Masonry viaduct on downside

Notes: [1] Miles/Chains from Paddington via Bristol and Millbay.

[2] Dimensions are taken from MacDermot, so as to provide a consistant source. However, from the examination of other records, there are instances where these data should be questioned and the dimensions used by the author in his analyses are probably more accurate.

The population, of Celtic origin, was fiercely independent, inward looking and steeped in the traditions of the sea, mining and, to a lesser extent, agriculture. Practically isolated, as it therefore was at the beginning of the 19th century, communication with the rest of the United Kingdom was mainly by sea, for the export of the Duchy of Cornwall's extensive mineral wealth and the import of coal and supplies for the working of the mines. As a correspondent wrote[4], those persons who did venture to travel by road from the western parts of Cornwall into Devonshire:

> '...must have had a lively recollection of the long and wearisome coach journey — the cramping of limbs, jolting and bruising of body and cruel shaking of bones — [that had to be endured for some eight hours]'.

Thus, poor internal road communication provided the impetus, firstly, to introduce railways to facilitate transport between the mines and the coastal ports and, eventually, to link Cornwall to the railway network of the rest of the United Kingdom.

The earliest known line was the mineral tramway between Scorrier and Portreath, which dates from 1809, followed by the Redruth & Chasewater Railway of 1825, and the Bodmin & Wadebridge Railway of 1834. More pertinent to this account, was the standard gauge Hayle Railway, opened for mineral traffic in June 1838 — to link the Tresavean Mine near Redruth with the port of Hayle — some two years before trains were running between London and Bristol over the Great Western Railway.

Over the next few years, in order to develop rail transport in the western extremity of the County, the West Cornwall Railway was projected, to form a link between Truro and Penzance. As finally approved in 1846, it was to take over the Hayle Railway, including the realignment of part of the latter's route so as to avoid the cable worked inclines at Angarrack and Penponds. Projected as a single line of broad gauge construction, Brunel was to be its Engineer. In the final route of 26 miles between Truro and Penzance, there was a total of nine viaducts with an aggregate length of just over one mile. The highest was at Angarrack, (100ft) and the longest at Penzance (1,041ft), and all were of timber construction. In the event, economic necessity determined that the line should retain the standard gauge of the original Hayle Railway and the new route, although built to accommodate the broad gauge, was opened for this traffic in 1852. The Act incorporated power to lay in a broad gauge rail on receipt of six months' notice from a connecting broad gauge company, but this was not implemented until 1866 when the Company, through lack of the necessary finance, had been taken over by the GWR and the other Broad Gauge Companies — the Bristol & Exeter and the South Devon.

In turning to all timber designs for the nine viaducts Brunel sought to keep initial costs as low as possible, even at the expense of incurring ongoing and increasing maintenance charges in subsequent years. These structures were designed in the late 1840s and while by the late 1880s the majority had been superseded by masonry viaducts, quite remarkably Penponds, with some modification, saw service into the year 1900 and Penzance until 1921.

Coincident with the development of the West Cornwall Railway, plans were being prepared to link Falmouth and main centres of population of the County with the South Devon Railway, which was to reach Plymouth in 1849. In the days of the sailing ship Falmouth enjoyed considerable importance as the first home port to be reached by the regular world wide packet services — in 1839 no fewer than 341 vessels called at Falmouth. With the coming of railways, the Government was anxious that these services should first call at a port having good rail connections with the capital. There was thus a growing threat to use a port, other than Falmouth, which was more easily accessible from London, and this lent impetus to the merchants and bankers of Cornwall to support the projected rail link between Falmouth and Plymouth. Clinker[5] outlines in some detail the background to the various factors and opinions relating to this project and the reluctance of some parts of the populace to face the inevitable march of progress. After much deliberation the Cornwall Railway was formed to build a broad gauge route from the South Devon's terminus at Plymouth, Millbay, to cross the Tamar at Saltash and continue down through Cornwall to Truro and on to Falmouth. Although Captain Moorsom had carried out an initial survey, the route as finally incorporated was the work of Brunel, who was appointed Engineer. The project received Royal Assent in 1846, but not until 1859, with the completion of the line and the opening of the Royal Albert Bridge across the Tamar, was it possible to travel between London and Penzance by rail; and then only with a break of gauge at Truro.

A further four years were to elapse before trains reached Falmouth, the original terminus projected for the Cornwall Railway. What had been conceived as a bold and imaginative project to build a double broad gauge line of railway between Plymouth and Falmouth had, after some thirteen years of delays and frustration, at long last been completed as a single line. The major factor contributing to such slow progress was the reluctance on the part of the merchants and business people of the County to subscribe the necessary finance. MacDermot recounts the financial difficulties faced by the directors of both the Cornish companies during these years, and the part played by the other broad gauge companies in contributing to the satisfactory completion of the overall broad gauge link between these centres. Under the arrangements as finally established, in 1855, the Cornwall Railway was leased to them, with its management being exclusively in the hands of a Joint Committee. This comprised four Cornwall, two South Devon, two Bristol & Exeter and two Great Western directors, appointed under the terms of that lease. The subsequent development and growth of railway traffic in Cornwall is covered in an excellent account by Professor J Simmons[6].

The 53 miles of railway between Plymouth and Truro included not only the magnificent structure of the Royal Albert Bridge, at Saltash, but in addition, a total of 34 viaducts. Having an aggregate length of approximately four miles, the highest was St Pinnock (151ft), and the longest, Truro (1,329ft).

However, the intervening years had been a period of a false start and endless frustration as the Directors struggled to raise the necessary finance. Progress on the building of the line faltered and then ceased altogether for three years for want of money. During that time, in a desperate attempt to effect economies, Brunel revised his overall plans. The projected double line was changed to a single track, while he evolved designs for the inland viaducts to incorporate plain masonry piers, built up to within about 35 feet of rail level, which in turn supported a simple timber superstructure, to carry the decking and permanent way. Using his practical experience, combined with the then current level of theoretical analysis and backed by his earlier test work, Brunel attempted a cheap yet effective design, of which the viaduct at Gover (Fig.4) was a typical example.

4. The viaduct at Gover, completed in 1858, and here photographed in 1895, was among the early structures to be ready to receive the permanent way. It was built on a curve to the Class A1 design and of the eight masonry piers, only two were buttressed while the fan at each end sprang from the embankment slope. During its life, a shore was introduced on each pier, which can be seen in this photograph. In spite of its age, it remained in service until 1898 when the line was diverted across a masonry viaduct built on the down side. ***L G Booth Collection***

Rolt aptly describes the resulting construction in his remarks that:

> '...so nicely was the proportion of each beam and truss adjusted to the load it would have to bear that the effect was one of lightness and fragility so remarkable that it looked incapable of supporting the weight of even the lightest of locomotives'.

These comments, while descriptively true, imply a refinement of design which was, perhaps, more accidental than intentional. Investigation reveals that while scientists had evolved the theoretical analysis to determine the loadings in the main members to achieve such a result, no evidence has survived to show that these calculations were carried out. Bridge design still depended very much on empirical precedent although, as we shall see, Brunel, while approaching these problems from a practical standpoint, did much to bridge the gap between available theory and practice. Nevertheless, these structures became endemic to the Cornish landscape, and their low initial cost facilitated completion of the route within the limited cash resources available.

However, Brunel's original warning that after the first ten years or so their maintenance and repair could cost upward of £10,000 per annum, was unhappily proved right in practice[7]. From the details included in Appendix 2 it will be seen that over the period from 1860 to 1882, the total cost of repairs for the thirty four viaducts between Plymouth and Truro amounted to just over £98,000 — in an ongoing situation. Little wonder that the engineer, P.J. Margary, who had been appointed to that office in 1868, pressed for their replacement in more durable materials[8]. Timbers decayed and had to be replaced while it was found that in those viaducts built on a curve there appeared an inherent weakness in design, of insufficient lateral strength to resist the outward force from a passing train. This led to the distortion of the timber structure and, in some instances, affected the stability of the masonry piers.

As early as 1869[9] work had commenced on replacing some of the lighter structures with more durable materials, to be followed in subsequent years by the progressive replacement of several viaducts which exhibited distress in service. These new constructions were built to accommodate a double line of standard-gauge tracks (which the Great Western always referred to as narrow-gauge). The works were authorised by the Joint Committee with the tacit consent of the Cornwall Board, half the cost being charged to revenue and half to capital.

By the end of 1883, work was in hand or had been completed on a total of twelve viaducts, when the Joint Committee gave instructions for the replacement of Coombe St Stephens and Largin viaducts, both of which urgently needed attention. The Directors of the Cornwall Railway then sought to establish that this work should only be put in hand on their instruction and not by that of the Joint Committee. This was, of course, disputed and the matter went to arbitration — a more detailed report of which is given in a later chapter.

The outcome of that sorry event was to restrict work to these two viaducts, and delay all subsequent replacement for a period of five years. In fact no other rebuilding was undertaken during the lifetime of the Cornwall Railway, which was finally dissolved in 1889, the railway then becoming an integral part of the Great Western Company. While this unfortunate decision delayed work on the viaducts of the original Cornwall Railway, no such embargo related to those on the West Cornwall line. In fact, it is surprising to note that, although the latter were of lighter design than the Cornwall structures, it was not until the mid 1880s that work started on their replacement.

These interruptions delayed until 1908, with the rebuilding of the viaduct at Stonehouse Pool, Plymouth, the completion of the replacement of all the original viaducts between Plymouth, Millbay and the outskirts of Penzance. On the Falmouth branch they remained in use until the 1930s, the last being taken out of service in 1934. As Booth[10] says — 'An era had ended.' However, in passing it should be noted that two timber viaducts, similar in design to the West Cornwall structures, remained standing on the original Vale of Neath Railway until 1947.

5. A lithograph of Hayle, c1852, including the viaduct. This is the only illustration of the structure showing the two leg timber pier supports which has come to light. Besley made a number of lithographs around Cornwall at that time and while he was generally accurate in his reproductions, he obviously took some license with the handrailing. ***Besley-Tangye Collection***

Chapter 2

CONSTRUCTION OF THE LINES

THE LENGTH of time involved in completing the railway through Cornwall (from 1846 to 1863) was a period longer than that required for the construction of any railway of comparable importance anywhere in England. The Parliamentary Bills authorising both the Cornwall Railway and the West Cornwall Railway which, as already noted, formed the basis for a broad gauge line from Plymouth to Falmouth and Truro to Penzance, received the Royal Assent on 3rd August 1846, in the aftermath of the 'Railway Mania'.

There the similarity ended, for each company had a different Board of Directors. While the original Acts had prescribed both lines to be broad gauge, the West Cornwall, by a later enactment, was initially constructed to the narrow gauge, although it was later converted to mixed gauge. However, as one common factor, both companies had appointed Brunel as their Engineer.

Because of the problems of raising finance, construction work for the West Cornwall Company did not commence until the end of 1850. At the half-yearly meeting of 21st February 1851, reported in the local press[1], the directors stated that:

> '...a contract has been entered into with Mr Ritson for the construction of the works from Hayle to Penzance pier for the sum of £29,100, the line to be handed over to the company in a complete state ready for traffic, with exception of stations only'.

In addition, he was to carry out the alterations and deviations necessary to avoid the Angarrack and Penponds inclines on the original Hayle Railway — 'by far the most difficult and expensive part of the line, in consequence of the viaducts and cuttings' — for £31,000.

With regard to the line between Redruth and Truro, as the compulsory powers under the original Act would expire in the following August, the directors had no alternative:

> '...but to order the purchase of the requisite land forthwith, and having taken into consideration the great desirableness [sic] of completing as early as possible the main line, have entered upon a negotiation with persons for its completion, at an amount very considerably within the original estimate'.

In the early part of 1851, a further contract was let to the same contractor for the construction of this latter portion. In August, Brunel was able to report completion of the work between Hayle and Penzance, including the timber viaduct at Hayle (Fig.5), ready to receive the permanent way.

Although he had only limited experience of the new track system patented by William Barlow in 1849, and claimed to cost only 60% of other systems[2], Brunel recommended its adoption for the West Cornwall line. It comprised an enlarged wrought iron

6. Down train crossing Penponds viaduct in the 1890s. This was one of the earliest of Brunel's structures, having been completed in 1852, and is identified as Class Z. It was built on part of the embankment of the original Hayle Railway; strengthened in the 1860s and despite its frail appearance, it remained in service until 1900. ***R.I.C.***

bridge-rail section having extended bottom flanges seating directly on the ballast. The rails were in 15ft lengths, supported at their joints in cast iron chairs linked by a wrought iron angle to keep the rails to gauge. Apparently Barlow had not designed points and crossings to match his rail section and thus special transition pieces would have been required at such locations. In addition, the rails would have had a high resistance to lateral bending so that we must question how smooth were the curves en route and, in particular, across the curved viaducts. No information on this intriguing aspect has come to light.

Initially there was a delay in supplies of rail being delivered by sea to Penzance. However, from February 1852, track laying started on the ten miles of new railway from Penzance to the junction with the old line near Trenowin Farm (not far from the village of Angarrack) together with the deviations to avoid the Angarrack and Penponds inclines. This section included the timber viaducts at Guildford, Angarrack and Penponds.

Traffic was stopped on the original Hayle Railway from 16th February to 10th March, whilst the new junctions, the relaying of the track and other conversion works were arranged. At the same time, Penponds viaduct (Fig.6) was completed on the formation of the Hayle Railway. According to a local report[3], the stability of the works:

> '...have been tested by passing over the line heavy loads of ore and ballasting, [sic] and trial trips have also been made with passenger carriages'.

Over the 8th and 9th March, Captain Laffens[4] inspected the line on behalf of the Board of Trade, and expressed his perfect satisfaction with the state of the works. The line was opened to traffic between Redruth and Penzance on 11th March 1852.

By August of that year, the 9 miles of new line from the junction of what now became the Tresavean Branch at Reduth to a temporary terminus at Truro Road, which was situated on the outskirts of the city, had been finished. This work included construction of the viaducts at Blackwater, Chacewater and Penwithers. Then, with the completion of the timber structure across the town centre of Redruth (Fig.7) the two separate sections of railway, Penzance/Redruth and Redruth/Truro, were linked to form a main line of 25 miles 12 chains between Penzance and Truro.

Captain G Wynne inspected the new extension on 7th August and his report[5] stated that:

> '...the works are substantially constructed and of sufficient strength...for the conveyance of passengers'

The opening day, 25th August 1852, saw a multitude foregather in Penzance to welcome the first train from Redruth. Quoting from a local report[6]:

> '...it was propelled by three engines, and had forty waggons crammed with passengers as closely as they could ride in them. The train arrived in safety, but about an hour after its usual time. A train left Penzance for Truro in the morning, to convey some of the directors to that town where a board meeting was held, and about twelve o'clock, the chairman and directors of the company, and gentlemen connected with the Cornwall Company left Truro for Penzance. At Camborne they were detained for a long time waiting for three up trains to pass; and consequently the directors, who were expected at Penzance at half-past one o'clock, did not arrive until more than an hour afterwards. [The train's] progress from Hayle to Penzance was at a rapid speed, and its arrival at the latter station was signalled by the firing of a cannon.'

The report went on to say that Penzance was crowded, as never before with a 'profusion of evergreen arches...the very number of which renders it impossible to particularise the whole.'

It was estimated[7] that the contract for the whole line from Truro to Penzance amounted:

> '...to about £105,000, for a single line on the narrow gauge; whereas the estimated cost by Mr Brunel in 1848 was £292,000, a great reduction having since that period been made in the cost of railway construction'.

The Cornwall Railway had also experienced similar difficulties with regard to raising finance but in 1847 a local report[8] noted that G W Findlater, the contractor for the first part of the line from Truro, had dug the first sod:

> '...in a field belonging to Mrs Paul, near Buck's Head in the parish of St Clement, and about a mile from Truro, where a shaft is to be sunk for a tunnel under the Bodmin old turnpike road...There were about two hundred persons present who, after the sod was turned, gave several cheers for success to the undertaking.'

By the end of that year a good deal of the land towards St Austell had been purchased and work begun on the two tunnels and adjacent cuttings.

However, available cash soon became exhausted and work was stopped for a period of some three years until February 1851, when Brunel reported that if only a single line of rails were laid, he could arrange contractors to complete the whole line from Plymouth to Falmouth, including the Saltash bridge and all station buildings, for under £800,000. After much deliberation, contracts were let in August 1852 to Messrs. Sharp & Sons[9] 'at very moderate prices' for the 15 miles eastward from the West Cornwall junction at Penwithers and, later in the year, for the further 22 miles on to Liskeard. Nineteen viaducts were involved in this distance.

A number of landowners agreed to accept part of the payment for their land in shares and some of these lengthy and protracted negotiations were undertaken by Brunel himself who, in general, seems to have enjoyed good relations with the country gentry. However, it appears that in his discussions with the second Lord Vivian, with regard to the land needed through the Glynn Valley, the latter gentleman took a dislike to Brunel[10], referring to him as a 'shifty personage, without any high sense of fair dealing'. Equally, it must be said that while the Cornwall Railway had its financial difficulties, those of Lord Vivian were hardly less, since his estate had become heavily overspent in previous years, so that both parties were striving to strike a hard bargain.

7. An early 1860s view of Redruth viaduct, built across the centre of this busy town, showing the all timber Class Y construction. Note the longitudinal tie beams crossing the roadway at cill height, the timber pier adjoining the roadside and the additional shoring incorporated in the right hand fan. Masonry piers were substituted in 1866 but the structure continued in service until 1888, when the existing masonry viaduct was brought into use, built on the same alignment. *R.I.C.*

The proposed route cut through his Lordship's extensive tree plantations and exposed them to a risk of fire from the streams of cinders likely to be discharged by locomotives struggling up the 1 in 70 incline. He was naturally anxious to have precise details of the line the railway was to take. Both parties were looking for an early settlement — the Company because they had let the contract for construction and needed the land; his Lordship because he was desperate for the money. Eventually, following several exchanges through solicitors , agreement was reached. A composite contract, to include settlement of a £20,000 claim made by Lord Vivian relating to the Newham branch near Truro, and £9,000 for the purchase of land in the Glynn valley, with the realignment of the route to meet his objections, brought the sparring to an end.

Construction thus having been restarted in Cornwall, these contracts were followed by a separate one with Messrs. W & H Drew for the line between Devonport and the Saltash bridge, which included three viaducts. Early in 1853 the contract for the bridge itself was let to C J Mare of Blackwall for £162,000, and by the autumn it was reported[11] that the quiet location, known as Saltash Passage, had been converted into a:

> '...place of bustle and business. Extensive workshops and smithies have been erected. Steam machinery of every description for planing, rolling into shape, cutting, drilling, and punching the masses of iron to form parts of the bridge, is in full operation. The smiths' shop contains eight forges, worked upon the principle of exhaustion, of what is commonly called fan bellows, driven by steam. A long slip, similar to that used for ship-building, has been laid down, for the construction of the cylinders, intended to be sunk in the river, for raising the centre pieces of the bridge. The one now being built is to be thirty-six feet in diameter, and eighty feet deep; when completed it will be launched and sunk into its position, and being closed at about thirty feet from the top, will, in fact, be a huge diving bell, and the men working within it supplied with air, on the same principle as that adopted with the ordinary bell.'

In his report[12] of 15th June 1853, to the Directors of the Cornwall Railway, Brunel also recommended that a further contract should be let to S. Garrett for the line from Truro to Falmouth, stipulating that work was not to commence until after the harvest. For the first twelve months, activity was to be limited to tunnelling, earthworks and to building the masonry piers for some of the viaducts. These conditions were imposed with a view to preventing undue competition between S. Garrett and Messrs. Sharp & Sons (the contractor who was already engaged on a considerable extent of the line) for the available labour in the rather remote districts involved. This same report urged the directors to proceed with the works between Liskeard and Saltash:

> 'If not commenced shortly they will not be completed so soon as the Saltash Bridge and we shall thus have a large capital expended at both ends of the line with an intervening piece intentionally omitted'.

Later that year[13] Brunel summarised the overall contract position to the effect that:

> '50 miles out of the entire line to Falmouth including all the tunnels and most of the principal works of any magnitude are contracted for in a satisfactory manner'.

Work was in progress over the greater part of this length, with arrangements in hand for the timely inauguration of the remainder of the line:

> '...so as to secure their completion at the proper time without needlessly advancing the expenditure of Capital'.

However, in September of that year[14] a warning was given by the Chairman:

> '...that in consequence of a want of labour, we have not progressed so rapidly as was anticipated; but we find now, by pressing the engineers and contractors, they are getting more men, and proceeding more vigorously than for some time past'.

Brunel's progress report[15] of 23rd February 1854 confirmed the completion of two thirds of the works between Truro and St Austell and forecast that, given a favourable summer, some 15 miles of the line would be ready to receive the permanent way. Apart from problems in Treverin Tunnel, 'where it will be necessary to provide steam power for subduing the water', the works between St Austell and Lostwithiel were proceeding to plan. Operations were also being extended throughout the Glynn Valley, a location which involved the construction of eight viaducts, including the 151ft high structure at St Pinnock, within a length of three miles. However, no work had yet commenced east of Liskeard towards Saltash, although a contract was under negotiation, while work between Truro and Falmouth and between Plymouth and Saltash was proceeding.

Sadly, by the end of 1854, the Falmouth contractor had run out of funds and, in the light of this overall situation, the Directors decided to concentrate all their resources on the Plymouth to Truro section. The workings on the Falmouth branch, comprising two tunnels and the partially completed piers of some of the viaducts, were temporarily abandoned.

In the early months of 1855 there were signs that the contractor for the Saltash Bridge was in financial difficulty[16], but by 2nd August 1855 Brunel gave an encouraging report[17] of the state of progress on the line from Truro to Liskeard; the bulk of the earthworks had been excavated, the masonry of the viaducts was in a forward state and only the tunnels at Treverin and north of Lostwithiel were incomplete. Between Plymouth and Saltash, excavations had proceeded and work would shortly commence on the viaducts. In spite of his difficulties, the contractor had maintained slow but steady progress in the construction of the Saltash Bridge.

That same report then outlined the arrangements for the completion of the line, between Saltash and Liskeard, having regard to the involvement by then of the Joint Companies in the project. The Liskeard to Coldrennick section was let to Messrs. Sharp & Sons and that from Coldrennick to Saltash to Messrs. Ritson. However, despite these optimistic comments, it appears that Brunel had cause to complain regarding the quality of workmanship of the masonry piers on some of the viaducts, a subject which is considered further in Chapter 8.

Then, in October 1855, the contractor for the Saltash Bridge failed, at a most critical time in its construction, resulting in a hold up in the contract. Brunel took possession of the works on behalf of the Company, and at the half yearly meeting in March 1856[18] reported that:

> '...to the zeal and unremitting exertions of Mr Brereton, of Mr Gainsford the Resident Engineer on the works, who is now laid up by a severe accident, and of my invaluable foreman and assistant George Whitting, and the men engaged with him, whom I must not omit to mention, we are mainly indebted for the success which has attended each stage of this difficult work.'

8. The viaduct at Coldrenick was unique since it incorporated trussed timber beams below the conventional Class A2 superstructure, introduced to raise the rail level and ease the sharp gradients at each end. This timber construction was replaced in 1897 by lattice steel girders. The original masonry piers were similar to those at Liskeard but they were later encased in granite, and today give a much more solid appearance than similar piers still in use at Liskeard, St Pinnock and Largin. ***Old Cornwall Society/J Rapson Collection***

During 1857 Brunel's reports continued to express optimism with the progress of the works. However, his involvement in other major projects is reflected in his inability to submit his usual report to the Board[19] for their September meeting. He sent a letter stating that he was 'so much more engaged than I had anticipated... that I have really been unable to sit down and write a report'. He left it to Brereton to advise the Board of progress.

Towards the end of 1857, thought was being given to the preparations for the laying of the track and permanent way. Brunel recommended[20] that the Company should purchase all the materials — timbers, rails etc — and engage the services of a Mr Eassie, at a salary of £500 pa, to organise and supervise the work on behalf of the Company. This gentleman, who had recently gone out of business, at no discredit to himself, was one of the 'largest and best of the Contractors for Permanent Way and Timberwork' and was held in high esteem for his integrity and ability for managing such work. Brunel's estimate for the quantity of materials required for the permanent way amounted to:

Rails	6,000 tons
Small ironwork	600 tons
Timber	10 or 12,000 loads.

No mention was made of the size of a load.

As part of this overall plan, he suggested that there should be one central establishment, preferably at Lostwithiel, for the conversion of the timber. Some idea of the eventual scope of this operation may be inferred from the range of plant subsequently offered for sale, on completion of the line, as reported later in this chapter.

In its issue of 23rd January 1858, the *Cornish Times* was able to report that:

> '...the permanent way from Truro to the viaduct on the western side of Liskeard is completed, and being ready for the laying down of the rails...On the eastern side of Liskeard, the permanent way is also completed as far as Coldrennick, where the balustrade is being added to the viaduct [Fig.8]. From hence across the valley near St Germans to Saltash, some of the works remain to be finished'.

Brunel's report to the Cornwall Board, dated 23rd February 1858[21], stated that:

> '...little beyond the superstructure of the Liskeard Viaduct and the Timber Viaducts between Plymouth and St Germans and the piling and superstructure of the St Germans Viaduct, remains to be completed. The laying of the Permanent Way is now about to be commenced...Arrangements are being made for the conversion and preparation of the timber at Lostwithiel, as a central point, and in a few weeks we shall be ready to commence the work'.

9. A view of Moorswater from the north west, c1860, soon after the opening of the Cornwall Railway. This illustration clearly shows the formation of the masonry piers with their gothic openings, the 2ft square sets of timber struts in each corner and the horizontal tie beams linking each pier at cill level. With a maximum height of 147ft this massive structure, 954ft long, was built on a sweeping curve at the foot of two gradients. The embankment in the foreground is free from vegetation while the sightseer is sat on the alignment of what will become the new viaduct, brought into service in 1881; giving this impressive timber structure a life of only 22 years. *Howarth-Loomes Collection courtesy the RCHME*

However, both of these statements should be considered in the light of an internal report[22] issued by Brunel's assistant, H S Bush, dated 3rd June 1858; this seemed to indicate that Brunel, understandably, was not in such close day to day contact with the state of the works as he implied, and relied heavily on the reports of his site engineers. Bush advised that the timberwork had been fixed over ten of the fourteen piers of Moorswater Viaduct (Fig.9) while the timbers for the Liskeard viaduct (Fig.10) were presently being 'hauled from Lostwithiel to the viaduct'. This would have involved carriage of over 500 tons of timbers over a distance of some 12 miles, on the inadequate Cornish roads of that time.

Bush also reported that excavation work was in progress to form the embankment up to the west abutment of St Germans viaduct. A further relevant comment related to the supply of rails; a total of 1,458 tons had been received at Fowey and Par, while the sailing vessel *Brilliant,* with a further 130 tons, was on her way from Newport to Truro.

With such an overall level of activity reported at that time, it may be inferred that many hundreds of men were employed over an extensive area, in many different trades, in the construction of the line. The supervision of all this work over the distances involved, bearing in mind the poor communications, must have severely tried Brunel's site engineers and could account for the differences in the detail design of some of the viaducts and the poor quality of workmanship which was later to become apparent.

In December of that year, the GWR broad gauge locomotive *Argo* was landed at Par. Its first arrival over the line at Lostwithiel caused great excitement, the occurrence being reported[23] in the local press, as:

> '...the welcome visitor was greeted with hearty cheers, and ringing of bells and the crowds of all classes made holiday'.

Work was proceeding on the final stages of the completion of the Saltash Bridge, while by early 1859, Brunel was able to report[24] that the permanent way was laid throughout the 45 miles of route between Truro and St Germans. The *Argo* was used to operate ballast trains of up to 160 tons over the line between Liskeard and Truro, where many of the principal viaducts were situated. The running of these trains, together with the rains that had latterly prevailed, were very beneficial in consolidating the heavy embankments occurring at the ends of many of the higher viaducts on this stretch of railway. In particular, in February, under the supervision of R P Brereton, the Moorswater viaduct was tested by the passing and re-passing over it of a ballast train of 250 tons; the result was perfectly satisfactory[25].

By the end of February 1859, the line across the Saltash Bridge from Plymouth Millbay into Saltash had been completed[26]. The only unfinished portion was that between Saltash and St Germans, where some of the viaducts awaited their superstructures; in particular, completion of the viaduct at St Germans (Fig.11 A) had

10. The second highest viaduct in Cornwall at 150ft was Liskeard, seen in this late 1890s view from the north west. It was built on nine fully buttressed piers, similar to those at Coldrennick, with the fan at each end springing from a plinth on the embankment. It was not replaced until 1894, when the original piers were built up to carry lattice steel girders. However, it will be noticed that the fan on the central pier includes an additional shore, while each of the linking spans incorporates a cross timber support for the centre carrying beam. ***P G Laws Collection***

been delayed by unfavourable weather. It is interesting to note that the major engineering structure of the whole line, the Saltash Bridge, was completed several weeks before the line between Saltash and St Germans. Eventually, on Monday 11th April 1859[27], the first through train ran from Plymouth to Truro, passing over the Royal Albert Bridge. It consisted of three carriages, drawn by one of the South Devon locomotives, and conveyed Mr Woollcombe, Chairman of that Company, together with other officials from the South Devon and Cornwall Companies. The train returned to Plymouth that same evening.

Over the period 18th to 20th April, Colonel Yolland carried out his inspection of the line on behalf of the BoT. His Report[28] covers a detailed examination of the route and notes the use of bridge rails weighing 62½ lb/yard, laid on timber baulks of section either 13in × 6½in or 10in × 8½in, in lengths varying from 22ft to 40ft; with transoms 11ft apart. However, his report mentions that:

> '...over the viaducts and portions of the line T rails are employed, weighing 66 lb/yard, the joints being fished, thus making a very superior road'.

The Royal Albert Bridge was tested by a train of:

> '...two heavy engines and a number of trucks...loaded with ballast...making up an aggregate weight of 384tons, or as large a weight as can possibly be brought on the viaduct, unless the train is made up of a large number of locomotive engines'.

With the above loading, the eastern span deflected 1.14in and the western span 1.20in. He then attempted to register the deflections caused by passing the whole of this load over the Bridge at a speed of 30 mph but the vibration was such that it was not possible to register any measurements. However, he considered:

> '...these results as highly satisfactory and so far as my knowledge goes, I believe them to be greatly superior to anything of the kind that has been attained elsewhere and accomplished at less expenditure of money and materials'

With regard to the timber viaducts, these were tested with a load averaging about 1 ton per ft lineal with varying deflections and his results are further discussed in Chapter 7.

Apart from some detail criticisms and, in particular, the need to include man refuges omitted from some of the viaducts, the line was passed by the BoT on 30th April 1859 and opened for Public Traffic on 4th May. HRH Prince Albert had come down on 2nd May, formally to open the great Bridge, to which he had given his name, having left Windsor at 6am that morning and arriving at the Devon side of the Tamar by noon.

Contemporary accounts[29] report that the weather was fine, with a vast crowd gathered on both sides of the River to witness this colourful spectacle. Following the presentation of local civic dignitaries to the Prince, the train moved forward and on passing the eastern pier, the blue ensign was hoisted; on reaching the centre pier a royal salute was fired and the Royal Standard was

11A. An impressive view of St Germans, taken from the south east. The all timber trestles, spaced at either 64ft or 66ft centres, carry the composite timber and wrought iron trussed girders at a height of 106ft above low water, with the landward spans being supported on masonry piers. Although this was the last link to be completed between Plymouth and Truro (the Saltash Bridge had been finished several weeks earlier) little is known about how it was built.

displayed and, on passing the western pier, the St George's.ensign was unfurled. The train then passed through Saltash station, His Royal Highness bowing most cordially to the occupants of the station platforms, in response to their enthusiastic cheers, which were re-echoed by the crowds gathered on the surrounding hill-sides. Following inspection of Coombe viaduct, he returned to the west end of the bridge and then walked across to the opposite side, accompanied by Brereton, Brunel's principal assistant, and various other railway officials. In passing, he examined the structure in great detail and on reaching the east end, his Royal Highness declared the Bridge to be opened; an announcement that was hailed by loud cheers from the bridge and shore.

However, the festivities of the day were marred for the visitors travelling from Cornwall, through the unfortunate failure of the locomotive *Argo*. Their train had left Truro at 8.35am and en route stopped to collect visitors invited to the opening ceremony. On restarting from Liskeard at 10.07am, one of the engine's connecting rods broke and although an urgent message was sent to Plymouth for a replacement engine, this did not arrive until 12.03pm. The driver obviously made a sterling attempt to reach the Bridge before the Royal Party but he was stopped at St Germans at 12.21pm, the Prince by then being at Saltash. As the local report[30] went on to say:

> '...this intelligence and delay had the affect of completing the disappointment previously felt, and many were the expressions of annoyance and chagrin in which both directors, officials and the general company indulged'.

11B. A 1907 view of its masonry replacement, nearly completed, with the original timber viaduct visible through the arches at the lower level. *Courtesy Trustees, Science Museum*

Sadly, through illness, Brunel was not present at this spectacular ceremony. It was not until later in the month that he was conveyed slowly across the bridge, by special train, to view his completed masterpiece. Nevertheless, despite his failing health, he duly presented a formal report[31] to the Directors, dated 20th August 1859, regarding the completion of the line and the then state of the work remaining to be done. He was also able to report that:

> '...since the opening of the Railway the Works and Permanent Way have stood well and the Viaducts are in a very satisfactory condition.'

A few weeks later, on 15th September, 1859 Brunel died.

With the line now open, the Company took prompt steps in September 1859 to dispose of much of the surplus equipment used in its construction. *The West Briton & Cornwall Advertiser* of 9th September carried two advertisements; one for the sale of the machinery of the Saw Mills at Lostwithiel and the other for 'Plant and surplus material remaining from and used in the construction of the Royal Albert Bridge', at Saltash; both lots Messrs. Fuller and Horsey being instructed to sell by auction.

At Lostwithiel, apart from 'two nearly new very powerful rack-saw benches, with iron tables and saws complete', the plant on offer included other woodworking equipment, four portable high pressure steam engines by Clayton, Shuttleworth, & Co, complete with boilers and a 30 hp horizontal steam engine with two Cornish boilers. However, perhaps the most significant items for disposal were:

> '...four large kyanising tanks, 97 feet long, 12 feet wide and 6 feet deep, strongly braced; a wrought iron cylindrical burnettising tank, 75 feet long, 6 feet diameter, with pressure pump; five lärge lead and wood cisterns'

together with sheds, engine-houses, and other temporary buildings connected with the site. It would appear, therefore, that the preparation of significant quantities of timberwork ceased at Lostwithiel from this time.

At Saltash, the equipment advertised for disposal included:

> '...six powerful hydraulic presses used in raising the tubes, two with 22-inch rams and four with 10-inch rams, made on improved principle by Messrs Easton and Amos, and used only for the tubes at Saltash'

as well as two sets of hydraulic pumps and a considerable collection of other engineering plant and materials which had been used in the construction of the Bridge.

The railway was single line throughout, with passing places at all stations. However, by June 1860 the first mile and a quarter from the junction with the South Devon Railway to the west end of Devonport tunnel had been doubled; this stretch included the unique double track viaduct at Stonehouse Pool (Fig.12).

12. Situated immediately adjoining the junction of the Cornwall Railway with the South Devon, Stonehouse Pool was the only timber viaduct built to carry double track broad gauge. In the background can be seen the masonry structure linking North Road with the Cornwall line. Apart from Penzance, Stonehouse Pool was the last timber viaduct to be replaced on the original Cornwall line. *Devon CRO*

13. A 1913 view of Ponsanooth on the Falmouth Branch, showing the fully buttressed piers, similar to those at Liskeard, and the combined Class A2/Class B superstructure. Part of the balustrade has been removed over fan No 6 in preparation for repair work to be carried out. With a height of 139ft it was the fourth highest in Cornwall and continued in service until 1930 when it was replaced by a fine masonry structure. The original piers still stand alongside, first built with gothic openings, which were later infilled. *R. I. C.*

The route to Falmouth had lain dormant since 1854, but in 1861, with Brereton as engineer, a contract was let for the eight miles between Penwithers and Penryn and, following agreement on rerouting the line into Falmouth, the remaining three miles to the new terminus was let to the same contractor by the end of that year. Construction of eight viaducts formed part of these contracts, including the completion of some masonry piers which had been part built by the original contractor, Garratt. Their overall design was based substantially on Brunel's original proposals, and included the structures at Collegewood (Fig.1) and Ponsanooth (Fig.13), the fourth highest in Cornwall. Their aggregate length was in excess of three quarters of a mile. Following satisfactory examination of the route by the BoT Inspector, the line was formally opened for passenger traffic on 21st August 1863. The special train[32], which had originated from Plymouth, was enlarged at Truro and, drawn by the locomotives *Antelope* and *Wolf*, comprised thirteen carriages crowded with some 700 passengers; the gross weight was estimated at 210 tons. Goods traffic commenced in the following October.

The construction of the broad gauge main lines in Cornwall was completed in 1866 with the laying of the third rail over the West Cornwall route. The scope of the work involved proved quite beyond the resources of the original West Cornwall Railway, and arrangements were therefore completed for the GWR to acquire the Company and assume responsibility for the conversion to mixed gauge. Apart from the complete relaying of the trackwork, and the replacement of the Barlow rails with double-headed rails in chairs on cross sleepers, cuttings and embankments needed widening while the viaducts and bridges required strengthening. A report[33] by Bush to the Joint Committee detailed the state of the conversion and the estimated cost involved which, after allowing £11,500 for the value of scrap materials, amounted to a total of over £70,000. Of this sum, the alteration to bridges and viaducts was expected to amount to £16,157.

This then was the environment in which Brunel built his timber viaducts. He applied his flair for unusual design, using cheap and available timber in combination with masonry and wrought iron, to carry his railways across the Cornish landscape. Throughout their life the structures, while initially sound, attracted criticism and anxiety from the public, perhaps best summed up by the remarks of Mr Pendarves MP, when he attended a meeting of the West Cornwall Railway on 28th August 1851[34]:

> 'I have great confidence in Mr Brunel as an engineer; but I confess that some of these bridges appear rather frightful. (Hear and laughter) I mean the height and narrowness of some of them. I have no doubt that Mr Brunel can satisfy us and the public at large that they are right. I felt the same with regard to another work of his at Ivy Bridge, when I looked at it when it was in progress; and my wife, who was with me, said 'I will never go over that'. (Laughter) I said, 'Don't you say that'. She has been over it fifty times since. I therefore repeat that I trust your engineer. (Hear)'.

Chapter 3

DESIGN CONSIDERATIONS

FROM A STUDY OF the history, it seems it was not before the middle of the 19th century that the subject of structural analysis had received the level of attention and understanding to enable it to make a positive contribution to the design of complicated structures. However, it must be remembered that, even now, structural design is not an exact science — consequently, how even less exact it must have been in Brunel's time.

The theoretical development of the strength of materials during the 17th and 18th centuries and, in particular, the testing of timber to establish its behaviour under load, has been outlined in some detail by Booth[1]. Therefore, it is possible to form a judgement of the extent of theoretical data, backed by practical test results, which were available to Brunel at the time he was preparing his designs for the Cornish viaducts. Through his French parentage and education, the extent of his knowledge on this subject should have been acquired from his studies of the works of such eminent scientists as Hooke, Parent, Euler, Young, Coulomb and, in particular, the theory of the bending strength of beams as finally established by Navier (1785–1836).

However, even in the late 1840s, in this country the majority of bridge design was evolved from empirical precedent; the considerable body of engineering theory that had been established was largely unused. Moseley had done much to develop the theory of strength of materials and structural design, based on Navier's original work. His book, *The Mechanical Principles of Engineering and Architecture*, published in 1843, presented an extensive theoretical analysis of these subjects but their practical application, however, was another matter. Nevertheless, there is evidence from Brunel's instructions to Bell in 1849, in connection with the testing of continuous beams, that he was anxious to apply the theories developed by Moseley. Generally speaking, however, there appeared to be a reluctance or lack of understanding of how theoretical knowledge could be applied and not until Rankine published his paper[2] on the subject in 1856, was a serious attempt made to bridge the gap between theory and practice.

However, the theory relating to frameworks or trusses and their solution by graphical methods, which brought their analysis within the competence of the engineering profession in general, did not become established until after Brunel had died[3]. In all these circumstances, his philosophy was to give absolute priority to practical considerations and apply the results of theoretical investigations only to the degree really necessary[4]. Hence, his enquiring mind doubtless pursued the solution of his design problems largely on the basis of practical investigation of the behaviour of sample frameworks or components under static test[5], coupled with the application of such theoretical knowledge as was appropriate and, for that matter, available.

Brunel's membership of the Institution of Civil Engineers led to his active participation in their meetings and discussions, while through the close relationship he enjoyed with other eminent civil engineers of his time, he was able to keep abreast of technical development in this subject. His contemporaries in this country made extensive use of cast iron in railway bridge construction, but Brunel firmly rejected using it as a structural material. He favoured the employment of timber and wrought iron for the main structural members of his designs, and restricted the application of cast iron to that of providing special seatings to locate the timber struts and beams within the structure. This arrangement was directed towards the more efficient use of these well established materials rather than research into new and untried concepts of bridge design. However, he was concerned to incorporate within his designs, the facility for easy replacement of any timber member which showed distress in service, due to decay etc — a feature which was later to lead to a general weakening of the structures involved and, hence, their early demise.

This feature also lent emphasis to the considerable attention he paid to the development and application of bolted laminated beams, being aware that, theoretically, two pieces of timber completely fastened together throughout their length, will safely span twice the distance of each single member. Laminated beams had already been applied to the construction of arched viaducts; indeed Brunel had himself followed the work of Green and Nicholson[6] when in 1840 he used this form of member for the skew bridge across the Avon at Bath, on the GWR. However, these comprised relatively light sections, laminated together to form the curved members of an arch. For his Cornish viaducts, Brunel now sought to incorporate heavier sections, used as straight members to form a beam of deeper section, laminated by mechanical means, so as to permit easy replacement of a decayed component.

During 1841 he had conducted experiments to establish a satisfactory method of preventing the two component parts of a laminated beam from sliding past each other under deflection, which involved testing a number of different methods of fastening the two members together. Booth[7] describes the results of these tests, leading to the conclusion that inclined cast iron plugs at the interface were the most successful in reducing deflection. However, in practice it would appear that both hardwood and cast iron keys were used as joggles, as these inserts were called. Examination of the working drawings for the Cornwall viaducts show that Brunel generally favoured hardwood keys, usually of oak, with the addition of wrought iron wedges to ensure a tight fit of these joggles in their notches; the two beams being clamped together by means of inclined bolts with special cast iron washers, nuts etc. This arrangement will be clear from a study of Fig.14, a detail taken from a drawing of a trussed beam, showing the joggles, inclined bolts and cast iron location shoes.

In 1978, Mercer[8] carried out a series of tests at Surrey University, on replica laminated beams, to verify the results of Brunel's original work. These showed that the most satisfactory result was obtained with the inclusion of the joggles, complete with suitable wedges, and clamping bolts, immediately adjacent to the supports, as shown in this illustration. The result was a composite beam generally as strong as a single beam of twice the depth of each laminate.

During 1846 Brunel had arranged for his engineering assistant, Bell, to conduct large scale tests at Bristol on timber specimens, with a view to establishing fundamental data regarding the behaviour of the material under different loading conditions. This work was followed in 1849 with Bell's investigation of the behaviour of a continuous beam, which was intended to be part of the bridge he was building for the South Wales Railway at Chepstow.

While his thinking was thus in the forefront of applying newly established theories in the development of his designs, the emphasis was more in corroboration of his practical approach rather than

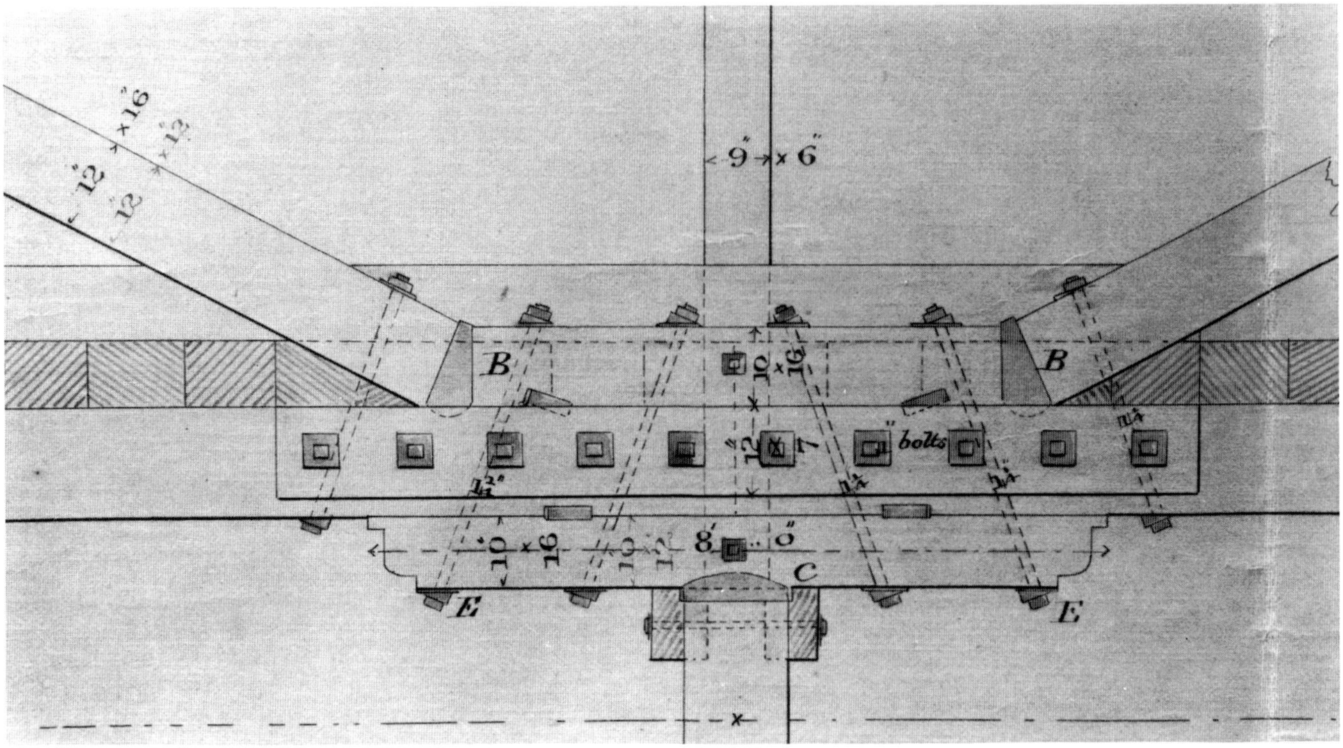

14. **An extract from an original drawing of a typical laminated beam construction, as incorporated in Brunel's viaduct designs. This clearly shows the hardwood joggles and wrought iron wedges driven into the slots formed between each member which are secured together by the angled bolts, with their nuts at each end located on special formed cast iron seatings. The arrangement shown here applied to the trussed beams of the Class C and similar designs.** ***Author's Collection***

in original design analysis. It is reasonable to assume, therefore, that the theory relating to the analysis of continuous beams, which formed the key element of many of his inland viaduct designs, would certainly have been available to him at the time he was working on the Cornwall projects. However, where he resorted to the application of trussed beams, as in the case of the tidal structures and the landward spans of some of the inland viaducts, the design was dependent on a static test of a complete truss in order to establish its suitability.

This then was the background of the design technology available to Brunel as he prepared the designs for his Cornish viaducts. Apart from the crossing of the Tamar at Saltash (which is not part of this story) he was faced with the challenge of carrying his railway across a combination of inland river valleys, some of which were very deep, and several tidal creeks. In total, there was to be fifty one different locations to be considered, apart from lesser bridges. The inland sites were often difficult of access while the tidal creeks involved a depth of mud such as to preclude the use of masonry piers (on grounds of cost) and were, additionally, subject to the twice daily incursion of the tide.

We have already noted in Chapter 1 the chronological development of Brunel's West Country timber viaducts. Essential to all his designs was the use of accurately cut and drilled timbers, both for the initial construction and any later replacement. Ordinary commercial sections were, therefore, not acceptable and consequently the members had to be cut from logs, die square, in the Company's own saw mills[9]. The carrying beams required their sides to be true so as to rest squarely on the legs and support the decking while at the same time, allow a full bearing for the coffin pieces on the sides. Similar remarks applied to the legs themselves as they had to fit accurately into their top and bottom seatings while in order to be effective, the bracings had to have a true bearing in their respective notches.

Subsequently, when timbers were being replaced, a new carrying beam needed to have bolt holes and joggle grooves prepared to the exact measurement of the original; legs had to be correctly formed and fitted so that the weight was evenly distributed over the whole span. It was particularly important for bolt holes to be true and symmetrical, since elongated holes would reduce the effective section and strength of the timber and the stiffness of the laminated beam. In practice, it was virtually impossible to achieve this overall standard of accuracy, so that as more members were replaced, there was a general loss of stiffness of the whole structure. From a study of the photographs of some of the viaducts in their later years, it can be seen that the decking and carrying beams were anything but true and level; an overall situation which served to compound a general deterioration in service.

Many of the viaducts were built on a curve, which poses the question of how the small differences in the lengths of the component parts were accommodated, not only of the horizontal carrying beams, but also of the legs, in order to produce a structure having the smooth curve which is apparent from a study of many of the relevant photographs. None of the original drawings, even of those viaducts known to have been built on a curve, give any indication of how these detail differences were achieved — unless, of course, the members were cut on site to suit. This then poses a further question, namely what steps were taken to protect the newly cut faces? One answer would have been to treat the ends with creosote, and while Margary had stated that this method of protection was never used as a general protection, it might well have been applied locally.

However, in adopting a curved formation for some of his longer viaducts, it is apparent that in his initial design consideration, Brunel failed to take due account of the lateral thrust[10] of a passing train. This tended to push the structure over sideways. With increasing levels of traffic the problem became more evident and was countered by the use of shores, introduced within the timber superstructure. However, according to Margary, there were some locations where the foundations of the masonry piers were not satisfactory and the piers themselves tended to tilt and had to be shored.

This problem was further accentuated in the case of the viaducts at Fal and Coombe St Stephens, which were built to incorporate a reverse curve within the structure — a configuration which became the subject of much criticism[11] at the Arbitration Hearing. The proposed rebuilding of the latter viaduct, with Largin, led to the setting up of that Hearing, which subject is covered in more detail in a later chapter.

There is the apocryphal story[12] of why Brunel chose to build many of his viaducts on a curve. When so questioned by a friend, his reply was characteristic — he merely drew a visiting card form his pocket and tried to balance it on its edge. The card refused to stand in this position but when Brunel bent it into a slight curve it stood easily on its edge, inferring that for such slender structures, a curved design would be preferable. While true insofar as static loading was concerned, it failed to take due account of the affect a passing train would have on the overall structure.

In their respective papers on bridge design in the early 19th century, both Booth[13] and James[14] comment on the lack of evidence of any calculations relating to either laminated timber arch or cast iron arch designs — such structures apparently being the result of a combination of empirical design backed by static tests of key component parts. Brunel was working on the designs of his timber viaducts in the 1850s and while the Brunel Archive at Bristol University contains a wealth of information regarding many of the other projects on which he was engaged at that time, there are few references to the Cornwall railways. His sketch books do include several sketches of viaducts supported by different formations of radial legs, but show little of real substance regarding the in depth design of the structures which were eventually to span the valleys of Cornwall. His Letter Books from 1849 through to 1860 record many instructions to Bell in particular, to carry out various calculations in connection with his other contracts, but no record has come to light of any calculations in support of the scantlings which Brunel chose for his timber viaducts. However, in the light of earlier comments, it would be reasonable to assume, having regard to the test work which had been carried out, that either Brunel or one of his young engineers, should have been capable of carrying out an approximate analysis in order to verify that the main beams and struts proposed for the inland structures were of adequate section. In this respect, it is perhaps significant that there is no record of a major collapse of any of the 51 viaducts on the Cornwall lines, although in his evidence to the Arbitration hearing[15], Gibbons recalled the sudden failure of a beam at Gover in 1876, a leg at Pascoe in 1882 and a beam at Tregagle. In each case, however, trains were allowed to cross the viaduct at reduced speed before repairs were completed, and none of these failures made the line unsafe. Presumably, repair gangs were brought in promptly to replace the faulty members.

Summarising this overall position, therefore, we can say that at the time Brunel was working on the design of his Cornwall timber viaducts it would have been possible to determine the sections necessary for the decking, main beams and legs of the fan type structures. However, no evidence has emerged to show that such calculations were, in fact, carried out. That beams of similar section were used for spans of different lengths, under similar loading conditions, would lend support to this conclusion. Furthermore, it would seem unlikely that he could have analysed with any degree of accuracy, the loads in the component members of the trussed beams which he used; their suitability would have been determined from a static test of a complete framework before installation, as described for the South Devon viaducts in his biography. However, such tests would have been limited to the framework of a single bay, subjected to a uniformly distributed load, which would have failed to reveal any inadequacy under the influence of rolling loads. In this respect we should note the inclusion of substantial tie beams incorporated in the fan type designs of the West Cornwall structures, indicating Brunel's awareness of the inter relation of the loading between the spans. This factor, as we shall see, was given greater consideration when he came to the building of the Moorswater viaduct. Finally, the affect of windloading appears to have been ignored — the significance of which was only to receive proper consideration in bridge design, following the Tay Bridge disaster of 1879.

At around this same time, he had prepared designs for the Landore viaduct on the South Wales Railway, to be brought into use in 1850. It was a striking example of his ingenuity in the application of timber and wrought iron in a single structure, which was both effective in use and graceful in appearance. We are indebted to Fletcher[16] for a detailed report of its design and construction; of particular significance to the subject of this investigation is the loading which the viaduct was calculated to carry, identified as:

'Ballast — 1ft. thick, 7ft. wide; per ft. run of each rail	7 cwt
Permanent Way — per ft. run of each rail	$\frac{3}{4}$ cwt
Load of Locomotive Engine — per ft. run	12 cwt
Total load per ft. run to each rail	$19\frac{3}{4}$ cwt
	Say 1 Ton.

The wrought iron in extension, was calculated to resist 5 tons per inch; the pine timber in compression was calculated to bear $\frac{1}{6}$th of a ton per inch.'

These latter remarks are or particular significance, since notwithstanding the absence of calculations relating to the Cornwall viaducts, they do furnish evidence of the probable level of static loading which the structures were required to withstand and the stress levels which were considered acceptable at that time. As part of this investigation, the author carried out a simple analysis of the various inland viaduct designs with a view to establishing their relative strengths, based on the above static loading used by Fletcher. These results are discussed in more detail in Chapter 5.

At around the time he was working on the Cornish viaducts, Brunel had already designed and probably built the light, framed beam structures, supported on twin masonry piers, for the South Devon Railway — albeit that they were not suitable for locomotive working. Each span incorporated a framework on each side, below rail level, to carry the decking, the feet of the main timbers being tied together by wrought iron rods. When the atmospheric system was abandoned, a strongly trussed timber parapet was added above these frameworks in order to provide additional strength. As an illustration of the state of the art of design at that time, and in support of the previous comments on the subject,

15. One of the South Devon viaducts, illustrating Brunel's original timber viaduct design, comprising for each span a pair of trussed timber beams to support the decking, followed by the later addition of a trussed balustrade and finally, as traffic loads increased, the introduction of wrought iron girders. The twin masonry piers which Brunel originally intended to perpetuate in his Cornish designs are also clearly shown. The structure is believed to be Slade. ***Courtesy Trustees, Science Museum***

even before the strengthening was introduced, he arranged to test a complete span of the structure at Bristol, before starting erection[17]. Slade viaduct (Fig.15) illustrates not only the addition of the timber parapets but also the later strengthening by means of wrought iron girders.

Brunel was working on the designs for the Cornish viaducts in the early 1850s, the drawings (many identified '18 Duke St') and specifications being prepared under his instructions by one of the pupils on his staff, W B Lewis[18]. The prototype of the fan type structures can be traced to a viaduct at Sonning, built in 1840, to carry a by-road over the London to Bristol line. The details of construction as originally envisaged by Brunel in his GWR Sketchbook No. 9 are shown in Fig.16. Although the operating loads were much lighter than those imposed on the Cornish structures, the pattern of design is readily distinguishable. The length of the bridge was 240ft and he used timber beams supported on four timber piers — two at the bottom of the cutting and one on either slope. They comprised large section members, on a wide rectangular base, that tapered to the apex which carried a corbel or bolster to support each of the three longitudinal beams. These were of square section, provided with additional support by four sets of raking timber struts, which fanned out from the pier at a distance of about 12ft below the roadway, to butt against filler pieces on the underside of the horizontal beams. Cross members located at the points of support, carried the planks of the roadway. In view of the relatively light loading, no horizontal ties were necessary between the piers.

While acknowledging Brunel's remarkable ability to involve himself with much of the detail of his designs, having regard to the wide range of his activities during those years, sheer lack of time must surely have forced him to delegate some of this work to his assistants, probably at site. There would appear to be no other explanation to account for the differences in detail between similar structures, or to explain the fundamental errors in the line of the viaducts at Largin, Coombe St Stephens and Fal.

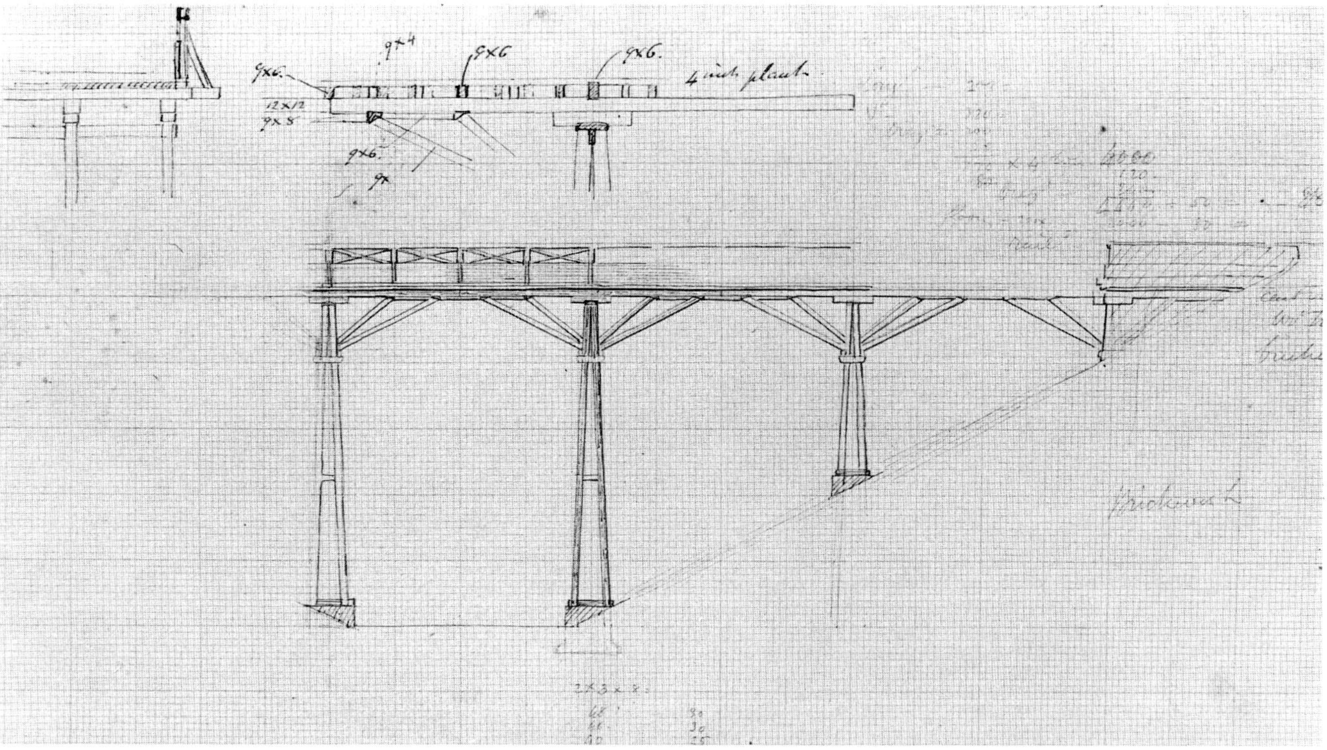

16. Taken from one of Brunel's original sketch books, this extract shows his design for the road viaduct across the Great Western Railway at Sonning. From this concept of supporting the three main horizontal beams of the structure by radial struts, evolved the eventual idea of the Cornish fan designs. ***University of Bristol***

We turn now, to a broad consideration of some of the design features of the viaducts. Common to them all was the decking, comprising lateral timbers, varying in thickness depending on the viaduct type, with a ballast board each side topped by a fender, to form a trough to carry the ballast. This was of sufficient depth:

> '...to enable the track to be kept in repair in the same manner as the other parts of the line. As there was no change in the nature of the support given to the rails, no concussion was caused on a train entering or leaving a bridge. The ballast took off from the structure the vibration of the train; and, in the event of carriages or even engines getting off the line, it helped in a great measure to prevent their ploughing through the flooring.'[19]

Although the ballast added to the weight to be supported, it protected the timber decking from fire and, the same source goes on to say that, in the case of long viaducts, there was no need to make allowance for the affect on the structure of changes in temperature. However, this statement needs to be qualified by Brunel's own comments, regarding the problem he encountered with the timber viaducts on the Dare branch in South Wales. These two structures were completed in 1854, just after the opening of the West Cornwall Railway, and from an examination of Fig.17, of the viaduct at Gamlyn, it will be seen that they were similar to the early fan type structures in Cornwall. In 1857, during an exceptionally hot summer, the expansion of the rails on a curved structure[20], forced the 'viaduct sideways a few inches and disturbed the Line, so as to render it impassable'. He went on to say, that any recurrence of the this problem, however improbable, was guarded against upon this and other viaducts under similar circumstances by the introduction of expanding joints in the rails. We do not have any details of this feature, but in all probability, he was referring to the principle of track 'fish-plates'.

The presence of ballast effectively distributed the load of a passing train over the structure. Furthermore, it enabled the trackwork to be set up true and level to accommodate the inevitable variations in the heights of the decking across the length of a viaduct, notwithstanding the paramount requirement for the supports of a continuous beam to be true and level. While these early drawings make no particular reference to drainage from the floor of the decking (the deck timbers are shown butting together), surprisingly, there appeared to be little evidence in service of decay on those members; presumably, water drained away through the joints between the decking timbers. However, a GWR drawing[21], dated 1932, referring to the Falmouth Branch viaducts, specifically calls for a $\frac{1}{2}$in drainage gap between the decking timbers, from which it is to be inferred that a problem had arisen at some time with regard to deck drainage from the original design. Interestingly, an examination at site, in 1990, of the deck timbers of the existing Hayle viaduct, showed that they butted, with no gap.

It was in the method of supporting the troughed decking that variations occurred between the different types of viaduct. On the majority of the inland structures it was carried by three horizontal beams which ran the length of the viaduct, each comprising a lamination of two members, one above the other, secured together with joggles, wedges and inclined bolts. In turn, these beams were supported by a series of radial legs, springing from the top of either masonry piers or timber supports, according to the location and date a particular viaduct was constructed. Single whole timbers were used for the legs and as these supported the horizontal beams at intervals no greater than 20ft, no intermediate trussing was required[22].

17. Although not a Cornish viaduct, this photograph of the structure on the Dare branch in South Wales, built within a year or so of those on the West Cornwall Railway, gives a clear impression of Brunel's first fan type design, which we identify as Class Y. The later addition of masonry piers in place of the original timber ones, the pair of horizontal tie beams and the overall frailty of the design are well illustrated in this 1920s view. ***L T George Collection***

This same source went on to say that, as these raking legs were only of moderate inclination, the outward thrust caused by unequal loading of the horizontal beams was not great, and was easily counteracted by light wrought iron ties. However, from an examination of available photographs, it would appear that over the years these ties, while probably satisfactory in a single bay subject to a uniform loading, failed to act adequately when adjacent bays were subject to the affects of rolling loads. In many instances they can be seen to be sagging while at one stage, Margary reported the total absence of diagonal ties at St Austell and Gover. To some extent, this situation could have been ameliorated by the provision of means to tighten the ties, such as the inclusion of turnbuckles. While one of the earlier drawings does show a double nut, there does not appear to be any evidence of this component in any of the photographs. Even if they had been provided, there was always the problem of access in order to carry out the necessary adjustment.

Summing up, therefore, we can see that the inland or fan type viaducts were built up from timbers of moderate size and weight (the heaviest pieces were probably no more than 17cwt). These were fitted together as shown in Fig.18, (taken from an original drawing) to form a simple design so as to allow speedy and easy

18. An extract from an original drawing, showing how the component parts of the Class A1 design fitted together. The laminated horizontal carrying beams were generally supported by the raking legs at 15ft centres, although on some viaducts this dimension was increased to 15ft 4in. The hand rail posts were spaced a nominal 7ft 9¾in apart across the structure, but even this dimension varied between viaducts. Note the location of the pairs of joggles and their associated clamping bolts at each support, the heavier section centre carrying beam and the overall viaduct width of 15ft. ***British Rail***

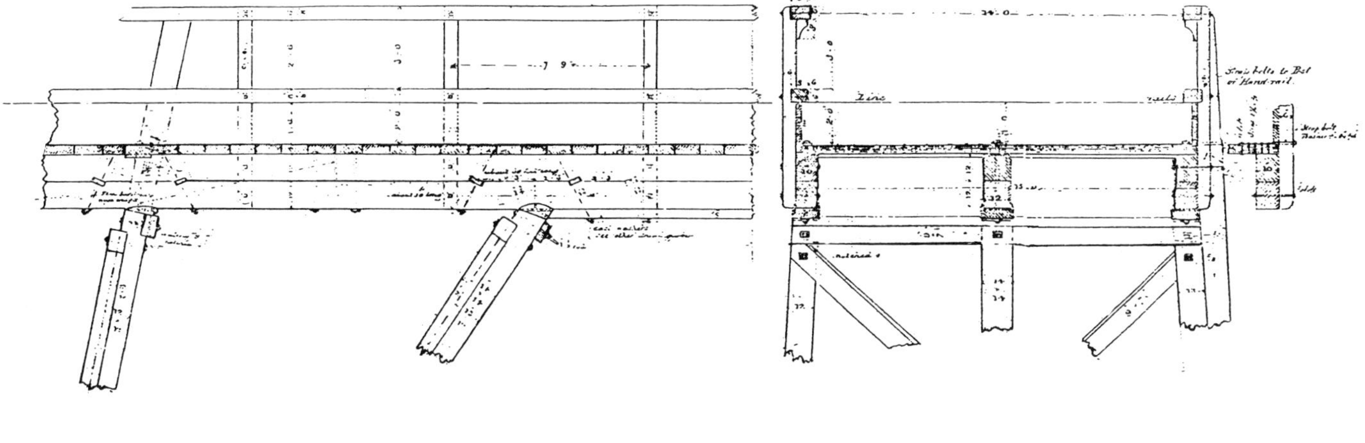

19. A detail of the trestles of a typical Class C viaduct, taken from a photograph of Forder. This shows the formation of the intermediate trestles, with their pair of double beamed legs and the triangulation of a main trestle to provide longitudinal stiffness within the overall structure. The legs of these trestles were each seated on clusters of four piles driven into the mud.
B Ward Collection

replacement in service of any defective member. For the tidal viaducts, the deck and associated ballast boards etc, was supported by means of two trussed beams, located one on either side of the structure. Each incorporated a heavier section parapet rail, complete with queen posts, principal struts and straining pieces and vertical through bolting. These beams were themselves carried on timber trestles or piles, according to location. However, in their case, the changing of the timbers in any part of the main trusses involved the breaking up of that truss; consequently, temporary support had to be provided to carry the decking on one side and involved lengthy occupation of the line for this purpose. The main trussed beams were carried on simple cross braced timber piles, or trestles, with little longitudinal bracing, which gave the appearance of a very frail structure. Nevertheless, the tidal viaducts west of Saltash, of which Forder was a typical example (Fig.19 shows a detail of its trestle supports and trussed beam construction), gave service until 1908, when they were finally taken out of use following rerouting of the line inland from the Lynher estuary.

Thus, in his initial conception, Brunel envisaged a range of standard structures, designed with ease of maintenance in mind. Yet it will be apparent from a study of the viaducts as finally built that, as the construction of the route progressed, he was forced to make several departures from this principle. In particular, this is borne out by there being three different forms of wooden structure on the four tallest viaducts on the line, at Liskeard, Moorswater, St Pinnock and Largin; all within a distance of under five miles.

As a measure of economy, Brunel generally omitted large abutments or wing walls from these designs, the adjacent embankment being graded with a slope of $1\frac{1}{2}$ to 1. Where it was then necessary for the landward span to be of a length greater than the link between adjacent sets of fans, it was formed from two trussed beams each with a queen truss in the parapet, the outer ends of which rested on a platform at the top of the embankment. In his early designs for the West Cornwall viaducts, these trussed beams supported the decking with no centre carrying beam. On later designs, a centre carrying beam was introduced, supported at mid-span by two lateral timbers underslung from the trussed beams. The platform on the embankment incorporated hardwood wedges under the main horizontal beams, which enabled the span to be adjusted for level, in the event of embankment settlement. This arrangement applied to some 60 cases on the Cornwall Railway[23].

From the chronological development of Brunel's designs, it will be recalled that in Cornwall the first line to be completed under his direction was the West Cornwall link between Hayle and Penzance, involving the viaducts at those locations. They were of modest heights and, according to MacDermot, were of similar construction to that of Penponds (Fig.6). The decking, as described above, was supported by three laminated carrying beams, each incorporating a corbel resting on a cill timber, seated on vertical timber struts or legs.

The other viaducts on this line were higher and while retaining an all timber construction, Brunel introduced his first concept of the fan type arrangement (Fig.7) thereby being able to increase the span between piers to 50ft. In appearance, they were not dissimilar to the viaduct built in 1849 to carry Treffry's Newquay Tramway across the Trenance Valley near Newquay, which, according to Crispin, owed its design to Captain Moorsom. Although the all timber construction must have added to their frailty (especially in the case of Angarrack), the subsequent introduction of masonry piers (from 1865) would have gone some way to mitigating that problem, and allowed service into the late 1880s — a period longer than that of some of the later Cornwall Railway viaducts.

All these structures were in service from 1852 and furnished Brunel with practical experience of his designs. He was then working on the drawings for the Cornwall Railway viaducts, which were to be completed in the late 1850s. The frailty of the timber supports of his original West Cornwall designs prompted the introduction of masonry piers for this new construction, and by increasing the number of legs to four in each fan, while still retaining the distance between supports at 15ft, together with a 20ft linking span, he was able to extend the span between piers to 65ft. Later, by spreading the supports to 15ft 4in, the maximum of 66ft between piers was achieved. Gover (Fig.4), Liskeard (Fig.10) and Milltown (Fig.20), are typical of the viaducts in this group.

On viaducts up to a maximum height of 115ft, the masonry piers were of simple rectangular form, built from locally quarried stone. Depending on location, either alternate or every third pier was buttressed but the resulting appearance was one of frailty, as will be apparent from the plain and buttressed piers of St Austell viaduct (Fig.21). For the higher structures the piers became massive fully buttressed masonry constructions in their own right, incorporating gothic arched openings, which are still in use today on some of the replacement viaducts. Although now a redundant pier, Moorswater (Fig.22) is typical of this type.

In an endeavour to keep down costs, an even lighter all timber fan design was resorted to for the viaducts at Probus, Draw Wood and Penadlake (all of which required a maximum height of 42/43ft), by replacing the vertical strut arrangement of Penponds with a Vee formation of the legs, springing from stone plinths spaced at 39ft 6in centres. This arrangement supported the carrying beams at 19ft 9in intervals, and presumably Brunel considered

20. Milltown viaduct, buried deep in a valley above Lostwithiel, was typical of the Class A1 structures. This 1893 view shows the masonry piers, with every other one buttressed, the curved formation and the inclusion of additional shores in the fan in the foreground and in the third, fourth, and fifth fans from the camera; and the man refuges built out from the side of the structure. ***British Rail***

21. A close up view of the piers in the 109ft high viaduct at St Austell illustrating the plain and buttressed types. The slender construction of the former is most apparent and being built on a curve it was a marvel that this structure lasted in service until 1898. *Royal Cornwall Polytechnic Society*

22. A 1989 view of one of the six complete masonry piers which remains standing at Moorswater. Towering over 100ft high, these piers represented architectural achievements in their own right, whatever may have been the criticism of contemporary travellers. Even at this distance in time, the massive buttresses at each side, into which were located the 2ft square clusters of vertical timbers that reached up from ground-level to support the feet of the legs of the timber fans, and the gothic openings in the pier wall, lend an air of truly Brunellian majesty to each pier. What a pity such a magnificent overall structure did not enjoy a happier and longer life — just 22 years after completion it had been replaced by its masonry successor. Nevertheless, the piers at St Pinnock and Largin of similar form, support the replacement structures which remain in use today. *Author*

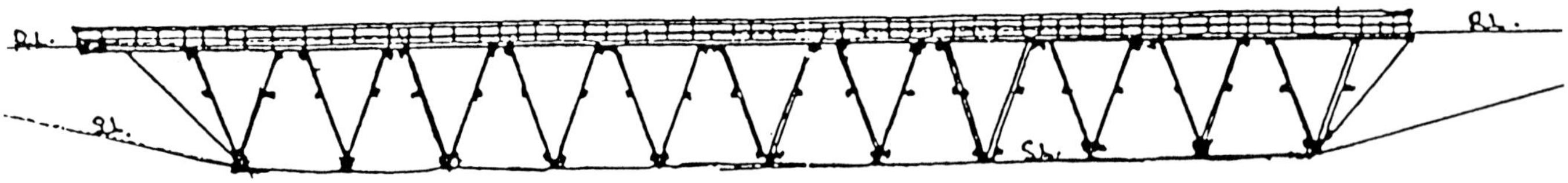

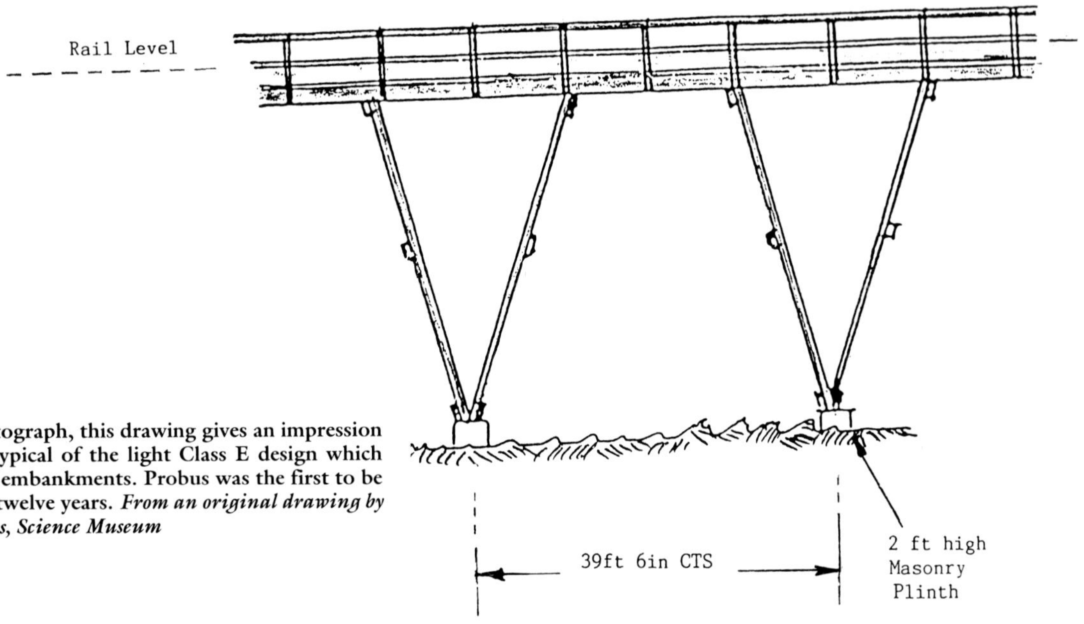

23. In the absence of a photograph, this drawing gives an impression of the viaduct at Probus, typical of the light Class E design which Brunel used in place of low embankments. Probus was the first to be replaced after a life of only twelve years. ***From an original drawing by S J Crispin. Courtesy Trustees, Science Museum***

that the Vee formation would provide greater stability than that achieved at Penponds. However, as all three had been replaced by 1877 it would appear that this hope was not realised in practice. Regrettably, no photograph of this design appears to exist (other than the variant at Grove, Fig.66), but the sketch (Fig.23) illustrates the construction. It is perhaps ironic to realise that the original 1852 design of Penponds, which apart from the introduction of a laminated beam construction, followed the simple arrangement of supporting the beams on vertical struts, saw service into the year 1900, whereas many of the later structures with masonry piers had been replaced by the 1880s.

For the crossing of the tidal creeks, the paramount need of economy determined the use of all timber constructions, particularly as some of the piles had to extend to depths of 74ft[24]. Each pile would have been built up from at least two lengths of timber, doubtless scarfed and jointed together, in a manner as we shall see, similar to that used for the trestles. The structures all incorporated trussed timber beams, and Forder (Fig.19) is representative of the class. However, for the tidal viaducts at Coombe by Saltash and St Germans, Brunel made exceptions. For the former, being built on a curve, he chose to support the trussed beams on a fan type superstructure, carried on timber trestles. For St Germans, he could have adopted a similar construction, in order to achieve maximum spans of 66ft. Instead he chose to introduce a unique composite construction incorporating timber trussed beams with wrought iron ties carried on timber trestles, doubtless evolved from his experience at Landore. While we may question the reasons which prompted this departure from the range of designs already established in Cornwall, no explanation has emerged from the available records.

At the same time as the Cornwall Railway was being completed, the South Devon branch to Tavistock was also under construction. Brunel was only appointed as engineer in 1857, following the death of its original engineer, A H Bampton, and for the six major viaducts on the line he adopted the Cornwall Railway type of fan superstructure. It would appear that the masonry piers on these structures were fully buttressed, a factor which probably contributed to three of them continuing in service until the early 1900s. Brereton adopted a similar construction for the piers of the two viaducts on the Falmouth branch where no earlier works had been prepared, which were completed in 1863.

Thus, while it is not possible to chart the development of his viaduct designs with certainty, there is sufficient evidence to enable a fair assessment to be made of how Brunel evolved solutions to the different obstructions and problems which he had to overcome, in taking the railway down through Cornwall. In a later chapter we will examine the constructional features of his designs in meeting this objective.

Chapter 4

THE TIMBER OF CONSTRUCTION

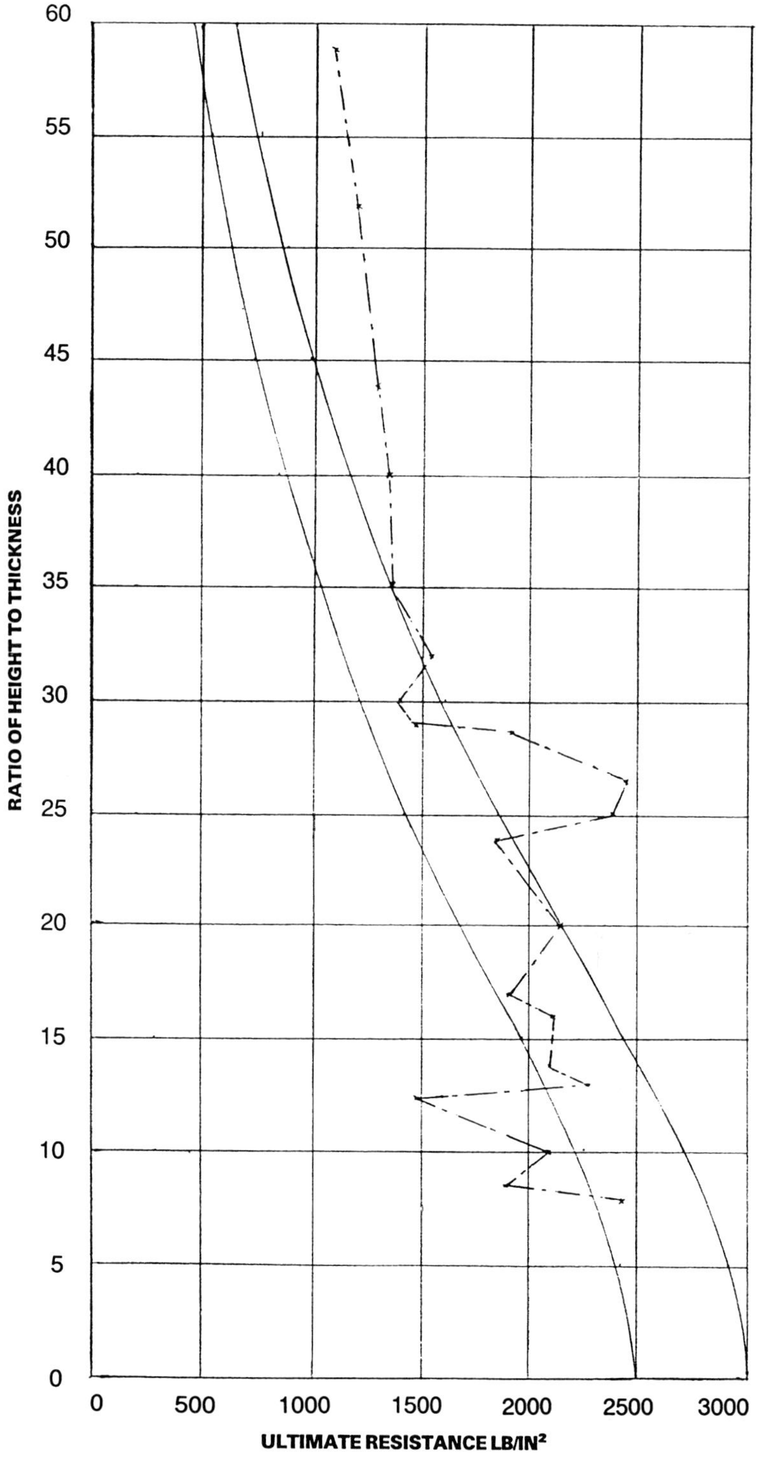

24. A graph showing the results of the compression tests carried out in 1846 for Brunel, on American 'White Pine'. The full lines indicate for comparison the theoretical strength as calculated from Lister Sutcliffe's own formula. ***Lister Sutcliffe***

Among a wealth of statistics quoted in a Supplement published with the 6th May 1859 issue of *The West Briton & Cornwall Advertiser*, to commemorate the opening of the Cornwall Railway, are details of the large quantities of masonry, cast iron and wrought iron used in the viaducts. Our principal interest, however, is concerned with the timber — its type, quantity and protection. Through his love of that material, Brunel would have investigated the types which were readily available and suitable for his various projects. In order to furnish fundamental data he had, during 1846, arranged for his engineering assistant, Bell, to conduct large scale tests at Bristol on American White Pine — *pinus strobus*. This material was then in plentiful supply, cheap and, because of its matured growth, of durable quality. When used in this country[1], it became described as 'Yellow Pine'.

This testwork was carried out on specimens from 10 to 40ft in length and of section between 6in and 15in square, using equipment which had been developed for this purpose. It is described in detail in his biography[2], whereby struts of different length and section could be subjected to end loading until they collapsed. A typical result of such a series of tests is shown in Fig.24, which is reproduced from Seddon's *Builder's Work and Builder's Trades*. Unfortunately, the precise arrangement of these tests is not known while the record does not detail the quality of timber nor moisture content.

The transverse stiffness of long specimens was also determined, by supporting them at each end and imposing a load in the centre of the span. Tests were also conducted to verify the safe bearing pressure which could be applied to these beams on their sides, so as to establish the area required for the cast iron washers that formed the seatings for the wrought iron tension members incorporated in the final structures. Sadly, the records of all this testwork do not appear to have been preserved.

As mentioned in the last chapter, in 1849 he arranged for a further series of tests to be carried out by Bell[3], in order to investigate the behaviour of a continuous beam extending over five spans when subjected to various loading conditions . This work led to the establishment of a number of formulae, their reliability being verified by this experimental work. Thus by 1850, Brunel had been able to amass a considerable amount of data regarding the properties of 'Yellow Pine' which he could use as a basis in his designs.

He was, of course, well aware of the need to protect timber against the affects of biodeterioration and any tendency to ignite easily from sparks emitted by a passing locomotive. His biographer reports that:

> '...as early as 1835 he had been in communication with Mr [Michael] Faraday as to the best method of testing the extent to which the Kyanising solution penetrated into the wood'.

Having conducted trials on the various methods of preserving timber, he adopted the Kyanising process, applied to the baulks under the direct supervision of Company personnel. Even so, he was not firmly convinced of the efficacy of that method since he stated[4] that:

> '...little was positively known of the relative value of the various preparations, or of the mode of using any of them'.

Mention should be made of the alternatives: in a report[5] dated 1865 by J Grierson and M Lane, they refer to the timbers of the mainline viaducts as having been Burnettized, and those of the Falmouth branch as being Kyanised. The use of the former means of protection is also recorded in Captain Laffen's Report[6], dated 10th March 1852, of his inspection of the West Cornwall Railway in which he refers to the viaducts as 'all formed of Burnettized timber' while the above supplement[7] also noted that: 'creosoted and Burnettized timber' was used in the viaducts. Surprisingly, in his evidence to the Arbitration Hearing[8], Margary stated that creosote was never used.

Kyanising not only acted as a preservative for the timber but also rendered it less inflammable and, compared with untreated material, made it less slippery, an important consideration since each piece of timber had to be manhandled into its final position within a structure. The process of Kyanising involved placing the well dried baulks in a large open tank filled with perchloride of mercury and leaving them submerged for a period of one day for each inch of the greater length of section. This gave a depth of penetration of about a quarter of an inch[9].

The quality of timber used in the original constructions gave exceptional life, particularly in the case of those viaducts built in West Cornwall and between Truro and Lostwithiel. In many instances a number of legs and beams were only removed after a service life of 45 years[10]. Even then, decay had only set in on the ends, and the remainder of the member was suitable for further use as another component. However, even by the early 1880s Margary was reporting the difficulty in obtaining supplies of material to the standard of quality of that used for the early viaducts. Furthermore, it should be remembered it was not until the later years of the 19th century, that experimental and theoretical work relating to the development of timber engineering had become established, to take account of the various physical factors which affect the life and strength properties of the material. Clearly, Brunel was using timber with only a limited knowledge of its technology.

Until the advent of the Great War of 1914, supplies of Yellow Pine timber were still available, albeit with some difficulty. Subsequently, the only species which could be obtained in any quantity was Oregon Pine and Pitch Pine; neither of which met the quality standards of the original specification[11]. They had a much shorter life, leading to more frequent replacement of component parts of the structure and hence, an increase in maintenance costs.

The question of timber specification and corresponding service life, was the subject of investigation by the Engineering Department of the GWR during the 1920s, insofar as it then affected the several timber viaducts still in use on the Falmouth branch. From those reports[12] it is possible to establish that the material used in the original construction, called by the older bridgemen 'old fashioned yellow pine', was cut from large trees of slow growth in a cold climate under the best conditions of light, soil and altitude. A close-grained structure was desirable and it was thought that the most suitable material was obtained from the American continent. It has been suggested that supplies could also have come from the Baltic countries, although there appears to be no documentary evidence to support this contention.

None of the later alternatives proved really suitable, since there was an early onset of decay, resulting in the replacement of timbers after a service life of less than five years. This led to a sharp rise in maintenance costs and hence, the decision to complete the replacement of the remaining timber viaducts as soon as possible. Throughout their life, as a matter of routine, each piece of new timber when fitted to a viaduct, had the date painted on it and a record kept of its complete history; whether it remained in its original location or was taken out and moved to a different position. Close study of some of the illustrations will reveal these date references.

The onset of decay[13] first became apparent in legs at their ends where they fitted in the special cast iron seatings; followed by the area around bolt holes. Decay of the laminated carrying beams first appeared under the decking and also on the upper surface of the lower beam where it was in contact with the top beam.

As a concluding comment on the aspect of materials, it would be apposite to note the information available on the relative cost of the structures. At the Arbitration Hearing[14], evidence was submitted of the (then) estimated costs of construction, from which the following analysis can be established:

Timber, including Kyanising,	3/6d per ft^3
Labour	1/6d perft^3
Ironwork	7½d per ft^3
Total	5/7½d per ft^3

It is interesting to compare these figures with those which were included in the subsequent reports[15] prepared in the 1920s, to note that maintenance costs as established in 1928 were calculated as follows:

Timber	6/- per ft^3
Kyanising	1/7½*d* per ft^3
Labour	5/- per ft^3
Total	12/7½d per ft^3

Thus, over a period of some 40 years, the cost per cubic foot of viaduct timber more than doubled, with the most significant increase being in that of labour — from 1/6 to 5/-. The 1928 analysis was carried out with a view of omitting the Kyanising process, since it was suggested that the additional cost involved did not result in a proportionate increase in the effective life of the timber. However, in view of the marginal affect of such a change and the other benefits of the process, no alteration was introduced[16].

Chapter 5

THE VIADUCT CLASSES AND THEIR CONSTRUCTIONAL FEATURES

FOLLOWING THE OPENING OF the Cornwall Railway in 1859, a reporter wrote[1] in glowing terms of the engineering achievement of the line of which, of course, the Royal Albert Bridge was the centrepiece — 'this gigantic, magnificent and highly scientific work'. Nevertheless, the number and extent of the numerous earthworks drew favourable comment while the following remarks regarding the timber viaducts form an appropriate introduction to this chapter:

> 'The number and length of these are enormous, amounting to no less than [34] between Plymouth and Truro having an aggregate length of three miles and [1,605] yards. Owing to the great height of many of these viaducts their appearance from a distance is light and graceful and this has the effect of causing some parties to entertain doubt as to their stability. A closer inspection must, however, dispel such fears and show that they are not only of immense strength, being constructed on the best engineering principles, but that they are calculated to bear a far greater weight than is ever likely to be placed upon them'.

However, in spite of these glowing comments, fears that their lightness of construction rendered them unsafe was to plague not only the Cornwall structures, but also the earlier designs in West Cornwall, for much of their life.

Having so far considered both the technical background of the period Brunel was working on his designs, and their broad design conception, it is now appropriate to examine in detail the various designs which he evolved over a period of some ten years, to suit the different local conditions at the viaduct sites. Previous descriptions of these structures have placed them under one of three headings: the lighter West Cornwall types and the Cornwall 'Fan' and 'Tidal' viaducts. This arrangement, while presenting a convenient division, does not take due account of the variants within each group, particularly in the case of the fan type structures.

As has already been noted, from a chronological aspect, Brunel followed on from the South Devon viaducts with the early West Cornwall types and then evolved the Cornwall Railway designs. As a basis for our classification, therefore, we will take the system adopted by the (later) Engineer to the Associated Companies, P J Margary, in his comprehensive Report[2] on the Cornwall Railway viaducts. In order to accommodate all the variations in Brunel's designs, it will be necessary to add to Margary's five classifications — A, B, C, D and E — and these will be introduced as appropriate; see Fig.2.

In order to complement this investigation it would be helpful to assess the comparative stress levels in the Classes of Inland viaduct under a standard loading condition. Accordingly, a simple structural analysis has been carried out, based on the Landore loading of 1 ton/ft/rail. The method and results are summarised in Appendix 5 and, apart from establishing the resultant stress levels in the deck and carrying beams of the inland viaducts, the loading of representative raking legs and their corresponding strength are also calculated.

The West Cornwall Structures

Class Z

For the West Cornwall Railway, in rerouting the original Hayle Railway, one of Brunel's first tasks was to design a viaduct suitable for bridging the valley at Penponds, requiring a height no greater than 45ft. Figure 25 is a general view of this structure, taken in 1898, during its final days when the replacement masonry viaduct was under construction alongside. For convenience, we will identify the design as 'Class Z'. Brunel also adapted this design to carry the railway across the town of Hayle, with its associated foundry and engineering works, as well as the low structure required on the approach to Penzance.

Although dating from the 1850s, the Penponds structure has been well documented; to include an original design drawing[3] titled 'Penpons', and endorsed 'for Self & Partner Mr Ritson, [sic] signed and dated 15th April 1851'; from which Figs.26 and 27 show detail extracts. A further drawing[4] records the subsequent modifications, which were introduced at the time the broad gauge was laid on the West Cornwall line and included the introduction of three leg supports for all piers.

From the details of Fig.27, it will be seen that the decking in 4in thick timbers, together with the associated ballast 'trough', was carried on three laminated horizontal beams. The outer sets each comprised two 10in × 12in members and the central one of two 12in × 12in. The timbers of each laminated beam were secured together with inclined bolts and incorporated hardwood joggles and wrought iron wedges, all located adjacent to the points of support. The beams were arranged so that the lower one was jointed over the viaduct supports and the upper at the mid point of each span; thin hardwood wedges being driven in between these joints so as, in effect, to form a continuous beam. Under each carrying beam at the point of support and through bolted to it (complete with a pair of horizontal hardwood joggles) was a 12in × 9in deep corbel or bolster, 6ft in length, which rested on a 12in × 7in cross member. In turn, this latter member was seated in special castings which fitted to the top of each of the upright struts at the points of support. This arrangement of the corbel and laminated beam, complete with hardwood joggles and inclined bolts, embodied the results of Brunel's testwork carried out on this form of construction in 1841.

25. A fine view of Penponds taken at the time work had started on building the replacement viaduct in 1898, which gives an excellent appreciation of its 739ft length, the simple three leg timber supports at each pier and the formation of the original Hayle Railway embankment. Note the longitudinal diagonal bracing at two locations and the 'propping' of one of the piers in the foreground. Apart from Penzance, this was the last of the West Cornwall viaducts to be replaced, following a life of 47 years.
P Laws Collection

The sets of vertical supports, initially 34 in all, were spaced at 21ft intervals across the structure, and with a landward span of 25ft at the Penzance end, made up the total straight length of 739ft. This landward span rested on a timber platform seated on top of the embankment, with timber wedges to provide height adjustment. The adjacent twenty sets of pier supports (Fig.26) each comprised two outer legs of section 14in × 14in, with a batter of 1/20, seated at their bottom end in a casting which was strapped to a 15in × 8in cross timber, set in the ground. Towards their upper ends the two legs were tied together by a pair of 6½in × 9in walings, each leg above this level being shaped to accommodate a pair of 12in × 9in diagonal struts which at their apex seated in a special casting to support the centre of the 12in × 7in cross timber, under the centre laminated carrying beam.

At the Truro end, the viaduct terminated in a substantial masonry abutment, while over the immediately adjacent spans, the supports, in place of the two leg construction, each comprised three legs, the outer ones having a batter of 1 in 20, while the centre was vertical (Figs.27, 28 and 29). In general, these members were of section 14in × 14in, although, for no apparent reason, some were shown as 13in × 13in. The bottom end of each leg fitted into a cast iron seating located on a 13in × 6in timber, grouted on to a masonry footing, of size 6ft 6in × 22ft 6in. Each set of supports included 9in × 6in walings and 8in × 5in diagonal cross bracing, slotted into the legs and secured with ⅝in dia through bolts and nuts.

In the case of both forms of support, there did not appear to be any means of fixing the corbels, with their associated horizontal carrying beams, to the cross member at the top of the legs; the design apparently relying on friction in order to keep the superstructure in place, in the face of the West Cornwall gales. The line of rails, set 1ft 6in above deck level, was carried on the ballast enclosed between the 2½in × 1ft 6in deep ballast boards, complete with their 8in × 5in fenders. These were located on each side of the structure and secured to the handrail posts, which were of section 9in × 4in at the viaduct supports and 5in × 4in for the in between posts. The 6in × 5in parapet rail seated on top of the posts and all these members were secured together by ⅝in dia bolts. The parapet rails were spaced 13ft 6in apart, a dimension well below the 15ft later considered desirable by Margary. At three locations across the structure longitudinal diagonal bracing was included, formed from 9in × 8in timbers while on the north side six man refuges were built into the handrailing.

The construction of this particular viaduct has been described in some detail, since many of its features were incorporated in Brunel's other designs. The structural analysis, based on the Landore loading, indicates a maximum bending stress in the centre horizontal carrying beam of 1,325lb/in^2 or almost at the limit of the Permissible Stress level; yet remarkably, this viaduct was in service until 1900, carrying far greater loads than those originally envisaged by Brunel. The compressive stress imposed in the struts of the three leg supports, at 27% of the calculated Permissible Stress appears to come within the figure considered acceptable by Fletcher, viz '⅙th of a ton per inch'.

As already mentioned, this basic form of construction of the Class Z design was also adapted for the viaducts at Hayle and Penzance and their respective differences, together with the later changes to Penponds, will be considered when describing the individual viaducts in a later chapter.

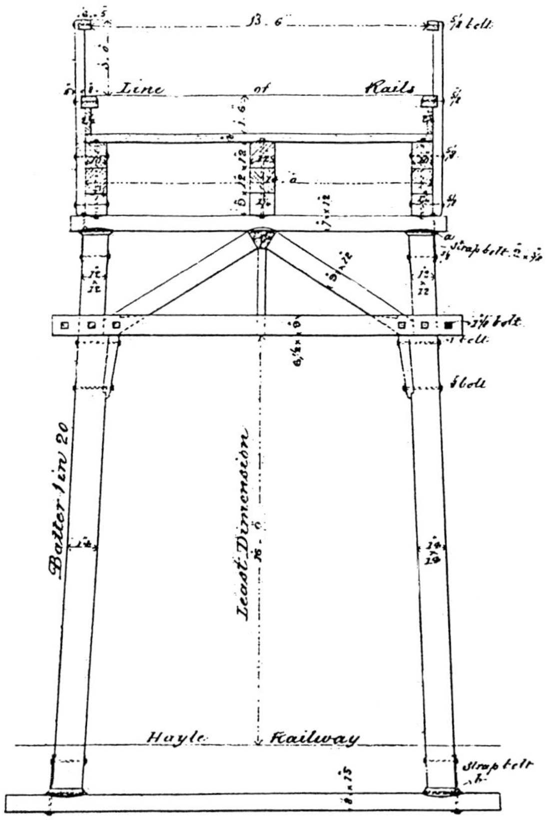

26. An extract from the original 1851 drawing of Penpons, (as it was originally spelt) showing the two leg type pier, of which there was a total of 21 in the viaduct as first constructed. When the West Cornwall line was converted to mixed gauge in 1866 these two leg piers were strengthened by the addition of a centre vertical leg together with diagonal bracing etc. It is believed that this same type of two leg support was used for some of the piers on the Hayle viaduct. *British Rail*

27. Another extract from the same drawing, showing the construction of the three legged trestle, with its associated bracing, together with details of the main viaduct timbers, including handrailing, corbels and location castings. *British Rail*

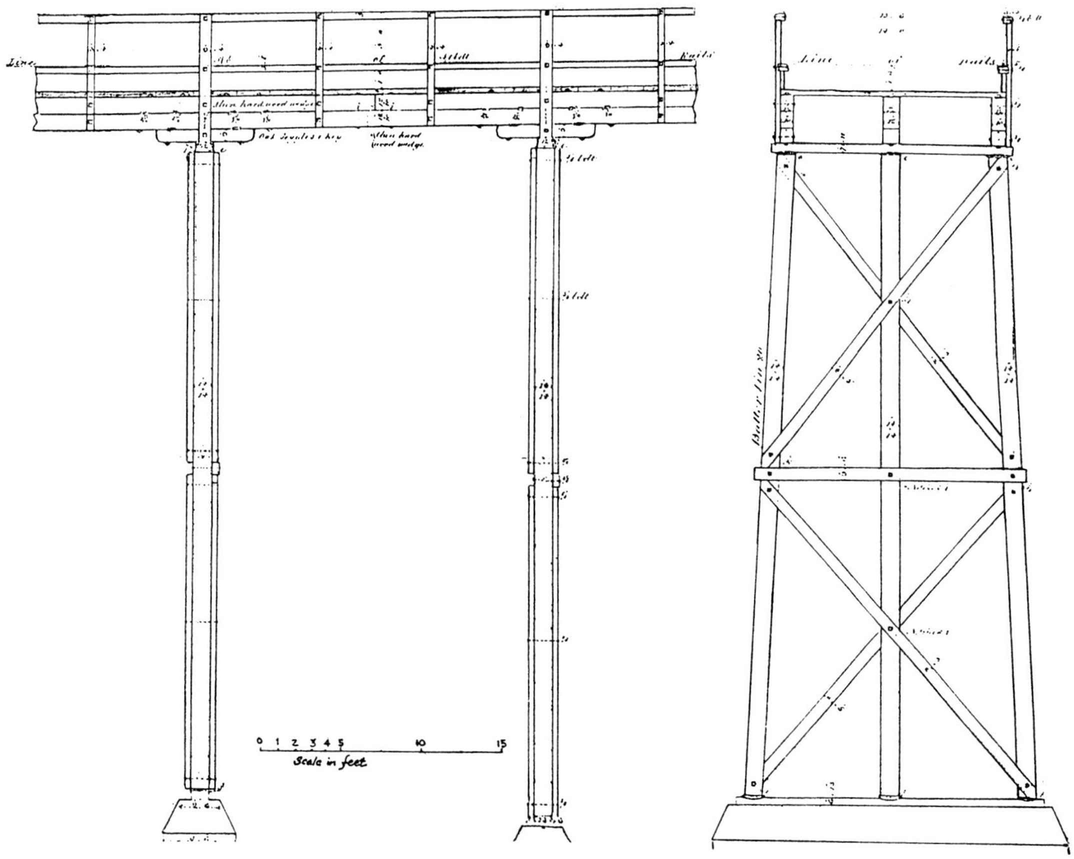

28. A close up view of the three legged trestles at Penponds, showing the corbels, laminated carrying beams, decking, handrailing and man refuge. *P Laws Collection*

29. Another close up view of the timber legs at Penponds, showing the detail at ground level, including the bottom cross timber resting on a masonry plinth. The standard gauge trackwork in the foreground was used for the conveyance of materials during the construction of the replacement masonry viaduct. *P Laws Collection*

The First of the Fans

In order to cross the deeper valleys between Truro and Penzance Brunel evolved the first of his fan type structures, which were eventually to develop into a total of six variants. This initial design dates from 1850, which for ease of reference, we identify as Class 'Y'. As first built, it was an all timber formation and while no final working drawing has been located, there is a record of Brunel's original conception in his General Calculation Book of 1850–1858. Figure 30 is a reproduction of that entry from which the general configuration involved can be deduced, while Whitley[5] included in his paper of 1931 an outline drawing of Angarrack viaduct (Fig.31). Photographs of the structures in this Class are scarce, but we do have Figs.7 and 117 of Redruth while Fig.32 gives a close-up of the timbers at Guildford, taken during the construction of the replacement masonry viaduct c1884/5.

However, as good an illustration as any of this form of construction, is that of one of the viaducts on the Dare branch in South Wales (Fig.17) taken in the 1920s, which were similar to the Class Y design and, having been completed in 1854, were contemporaneous with the West Cornwall structures. In 1941 both of these viaducts, at Dare and Gamlyn, were surveyed and drawings[6] produced which reveal the details of construction and thus provide a valuable illustration of the design. From the limited knowledge we have of Brunel's original conception, they do not appear to have been greatly changed over the years. They were not dismantled until 1947 and hence became the last of his timber structures to remain standing.

Thus, from a consideration of all the available Class Y information, we can conjecture a description of their construction. It would appear that initially, the supports, spaced at 50ft centres, comprised timber struts, generally similar to the arrangement of those originally intended for Keyham viaduct and shown in Fig.33. Each was formed from three sets of three vertical timbers, bolted together with their feet bearing in cast iron seatings which in turn fitted memel cills, resting on either a timber platform or on a shallow masonry plinth. These centre vertical struts were 13in square and the outer ones 12in square and were braced by 9in × 7in diagonals, linked by horizontal timbers of similar section, to form a trestle.

In turn, at its top, each trestle carried the special castings from which sprang three sets of fans, each comprising one vertical and two raking legs. These supported the horizontal carrying beams at 15ft centres. According to Whitley, they were initially all of section 12in × 12in, later increased to 14in square for the legs of the centre fan. This is confirmed from the Dare drawings.

At cill level, a nominal 41ft below rail level, horizontal tie beams, of section 9in × 12in, linked by wrought iron straps, joined the tops of each set of trestles. According to the Dare drawings, the laminated carrying beams comprised two 12in square timbers for both the centre and outer beams, but it is probable that the West Cornwall structures used 10in × 12in members for the outside beams, while retaining the double 12in square sections for the more heavily loaded centre beam. This arrangement would conform to the Class Z design and thus have achieved a measure of standardisation.

The lower member of each laminate was located in a special casting which fitted the top of each raking leg, while a cast iron cap fitted on the top of the vertical leg, provided intermediate support. The upper member of the laminated beam was jointed at the mid point of each span. Pairs of hardwood joggles with wrought iron wedges, complete with 1¼in dia inclined bolts, located on either side of the leg supports, secured the component parts of each laminate. This was, of course, similar to the arrangement used on the later Cornwall Railway viaducts.

Although the Welsh viaduct drawings showed slightly heavier sections for the handrailing, it is assumed that the construction was similar to Class Z, the 6in × 5in parapet rail on each side being supported by sets of 9in × 4in and 5in × 4in vertical posts, with the distance between parapet rails 13ft 6in. These posts in turn, located the ballast boards and their fender capping pieces, which thus formed the ballast trough, with the rail height a nominal 1ft 6in above deck level.

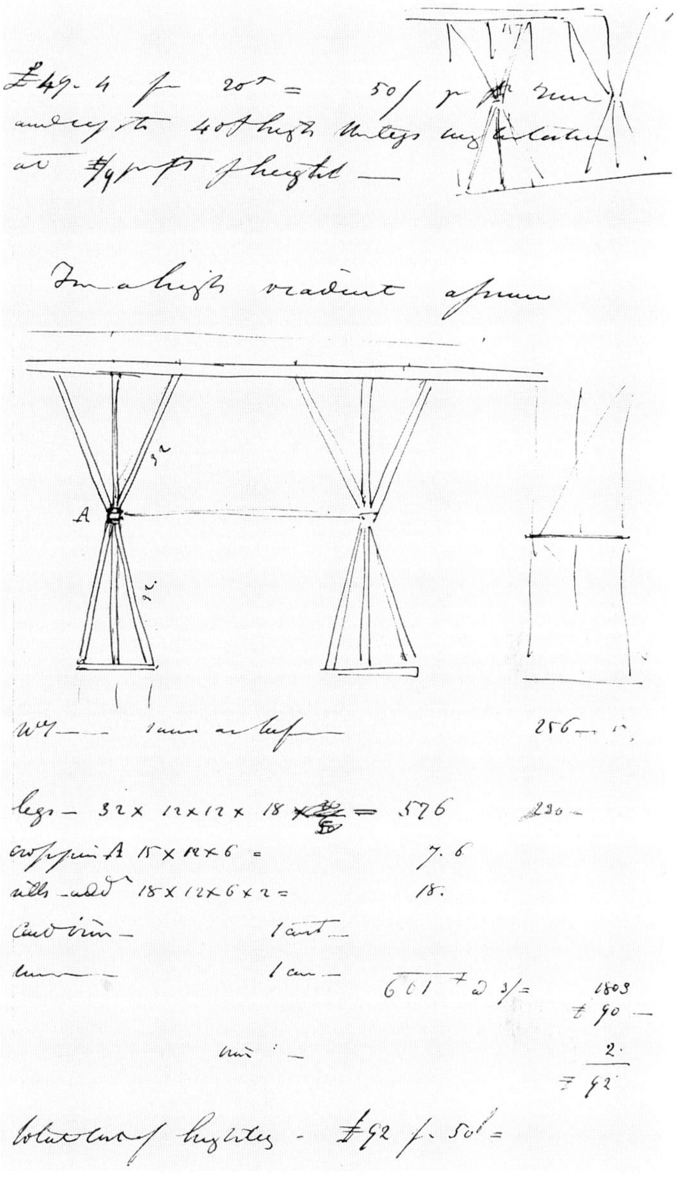

30. One of the few sketches in Brunel's notebooks relating to the Cornish viaducts is this early concept of the Class Y design, intended for the West Cornwall line. Included in his General Calculation Book 1850–58, the accompanying notes relate to cost rather than design. ***University of Bristol***

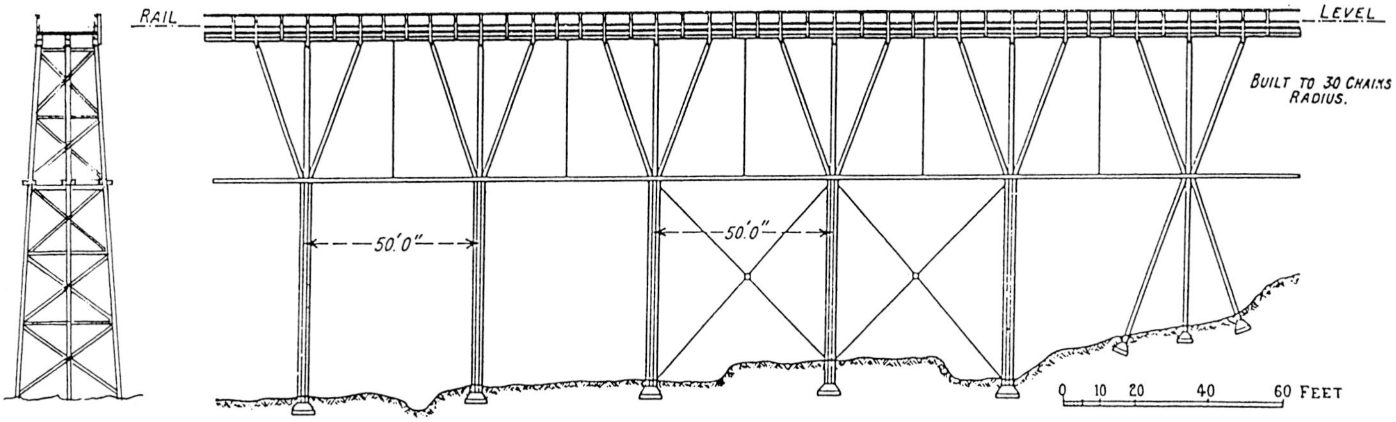

31. A sketch of the viaduct at Angarrack. Despite its massive proportions, its remarkable construction and the criticism which it attracted throughout a life of 33 years, no photograph of this impressive structure has been discovered. This drawing shows the design as it was believed to be in its early years, before the lower timber supports were replaced with masonry piers in 1864–5. The anxiety that attended its crossing can well be appreciated from this illustration. ***Whitley***

As in the case of Penponds, the deck timbers were probably of 4in planks, although it is interesting to note the Dare drawings show, in their case, that they were of 9in × 3in Jarrah. This was probably a later modification. At the mid point of each of the spans linking adjacent sets of fans, a vertical wrought iron stay, 1in dia, connected each horizontal carrying beam to its appropriate tie beam while, according to the Dare drawings, horizontal bracing of 9in × 7in section, could have been incorporated between the tie beams.

There are two significant pieces of information on the Dare drawings, which merit comment. The first concerns the accuracy of the positioning of the raking leg supports across the viaduct, the 15ft nominal dimension as surveyed varying between 14ft 9in and 15ft 3in. Based on the quoted 20 chain radius of the structure, this variation is greater than that necessary to accommodate the differences due to the curvature of the viaduct and could, therefore, have reflected on the accuracy of the levels of the supports of the continuous beams, to the detriment of their load carrying ability. The second refers to a note which, while commenting on the generally unsatisfactory state of the structure, adds 'there has always been movement of the piers, sideways and vertically up and down, necessitating adjustment to trestles and alignment of track'. If this condition was endemic to the design, it is no wonder that the nineteenth century traveller expressed alarm for his safety.

From the extracts of contemporary comment which have been included so far it is very apparent that there was indeed real concern regarding the stability and safety of these viaducts, despite the reassuring remarks of Mr Pendarves MP quoted in Chapter 1. Brunel's early designs were light and lacked stiffness, doubtless the result of financial necessity and his natural tendency to adopt bold and imaginative concepts, not always supported by adequate design analysis. Inevitably, these shortcomings manifested themselves with the travelling public through the alarming instability of the viaducts as trains crossed them and, probably, from gossip among the viaduct maintenance teams. Brunel apparently appeared indifferent to this concern for he did little to improve matters with the later Cornwall Railway structures. The harsh discipline of cash shortage meant that the Companies had to put a brave face on a difficult situation and it was indeed fortunate that no fatality occurred during their lifetime.

Insofar as the Cornish Class Y structures were concerned, according to Whitley, the timber trestles were replaced in 1869 by masonry piers at which time, as mentioned above, the section of the centre fan legs was probably increased to 14in × 14in. However, these changes may have dated from the mid 1860s when the route was being upgraded to broad gauge, under the recommendations of Col. Yolland of the BoT. Whitley also mentions the introduction of a centre beam into each of the end spans which, rather surprisingly, had been constructed with only outside beams. This would point to those spans being comprised of two queen post trussed beams, with their landward ends seated on the wedge type platform mentioned earlier. The construction of this 30ft span shown in Fig.33 is described later in this chapter. The deck timbers on these spans would also have been thicker, probably 6in. The Dare drawings show that these Welsh viaducts incorporated this type of landward span, of length 33ft, with 8in thick decking and a pair of 12in × 13in cross members to support the centre laminated beam.

With the piers set at 50ft centres, the span joining each set of fans would have been 20ft. Based on the Landore loading and the structural sections as described, the bending stress in this centre horizontal beam would have been just over the Permissible Stress level. This 20ft linking span was a common feature in a number of the viaducts and in later years was to prove to be one of their weaknesses. However, the centre beam bending stress over the fan span of 15ft, at 768 lb/in^2, was 57% of the Permissible Stress level, while the compressive stress in the 14in square raking strut would have been 19% of the Permissible Stress, and the critical ratio of the strut, P_c/P_m, 3.06.

32. A photograph of Guildford, c1884, showing the construction of the replacement masonry viaduct alongside, with a broad gauge wagon in the background and the team of workmen involved. Close study of the original structure on the left enables the formation of the timbers of the Class Y design to be understood; the horizontal tie beams between the piers at cill level can be seen in the bottom left hand corner. ***R.I.C.***

Although the overall construction of this Y class was lighter than that of the later Cornwall Railway fan viaducts, they remained in service until the late 1880s — there did not seem to be the same emphasis on their replacement, albeit, at the cost of some anxiety to the travelling public. None of these viaducts apparently formed part of Margary's reports, the West Cornwall being a direct Great Western responsibility while the Cornwall Railway was, of course, subject to the control of the Joint Committee. No records concerning their condition or cost of maintenance have been discovered, from which to make comparison with the information we have on the viaducts of the Cornwall Railway.

The Cornwall Railway Viaducts

Turning now to the next stage of his developments, as already noted, for the Cornwall Railway Brunel had most ambitious plans for a double track broad gauge line down through the County. These would have involved viaducts to suit and he had prepared drawings of the type of structure he had in mind, those for Fal and Carvedras[7] surviving in the BR Records Office at Swindon. They show a development of the South Devon type of construction (Fig.15) but with the opening between piers reduced from 61ft to 40ft and the cross timber decking supported by five sets of massive timber frameworks, the width between parapets being 28ft. Sadly, these grandiose plans foundered through lack of adequate finance and in the face of ever pressing financial constraints, Brunel was forced to adopt the cheapest yet most effective designs for the large number of inland viaducts which lay on the route between St Germans and Truro.

With his first fan type (Class Y) in service in West Cornwall and, presumably, satisfactorily carrying the then current loads despite public anxiety regarding their safety, he adapted its basic formation to evolve a series of designs capable of spanning a greater distance between piers. In the first of these developments, which Margary was later to identify in a general description as Class A, he increased the number of raking legs or struts in each fan from three to four. This arrangement of supporting the troughed timber decking, carrying beams and parapets became the most widely applied type of superstructure in Cornwall.

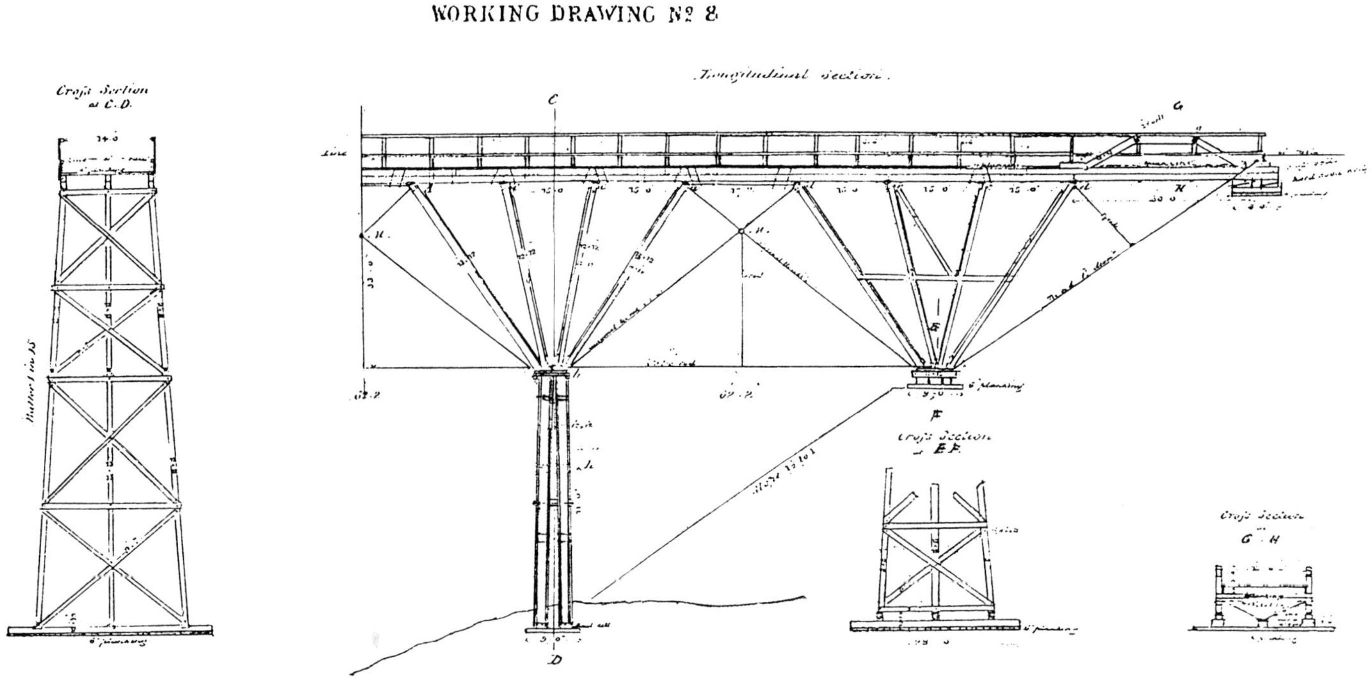

33. This extract from an original drawing of Keyham shows the detail of an all timber Class A1 Fan type structure, based on pier centres of 62ft 2in, with the horizontal carrying beams being supported by the radial legs at 15ft centres. So far as can be established, no viaduct was built to this design but the formation of the timber piers probably represents the construction previously used for the early Class Y West Cornwall designs, as does the formation of the 30ft landward span, and for these reasons, the drawing forms an important link in our story. *British Rail*

However, from a study of available records, it is apparent that this Class A comprised two types of structure: an earlier design applied to those viaducts between Truro and the Glynn Valley, which it is convenient to identify as 'A1', and a heavier construction, which was used for the inland structures East of Liskeard, identified as 'A2'. This design was also later applied to all but one of the viaducts on the Falmouth branch.

There was an interim stage in the development of these designs, apparent from the details shown on a drawing of Keyham viaduct[8] which give an excellent appreciation of how Brunel evolved a construction from the Class Y (all timber three leg fan) design to the first four leg fan superstructure supported on masonry piers (Class A1). This is shown in Fig.33 from which it will be seen it was intended that the supports for each of the three sets of four leg fans would have been similar to those used for the Class Y viaducts. Yet, in this case, they comprised a cluster of two pairs of timber struts, instead of the three struts of Class Y. The bottom of these legs fitted in castings located on Memel baulks, which in turn were seated on a 6in thick timber platform, 33ft × 9ft, resting on the ground. However, there does not appear to be any evidence that a viaduct was ever constructed to this design, some of the dimensions of which appear peculiar to this drawing. Nevertheless, its existence could have prompted MacDermot to refer to Keyham as being of all timber construction.

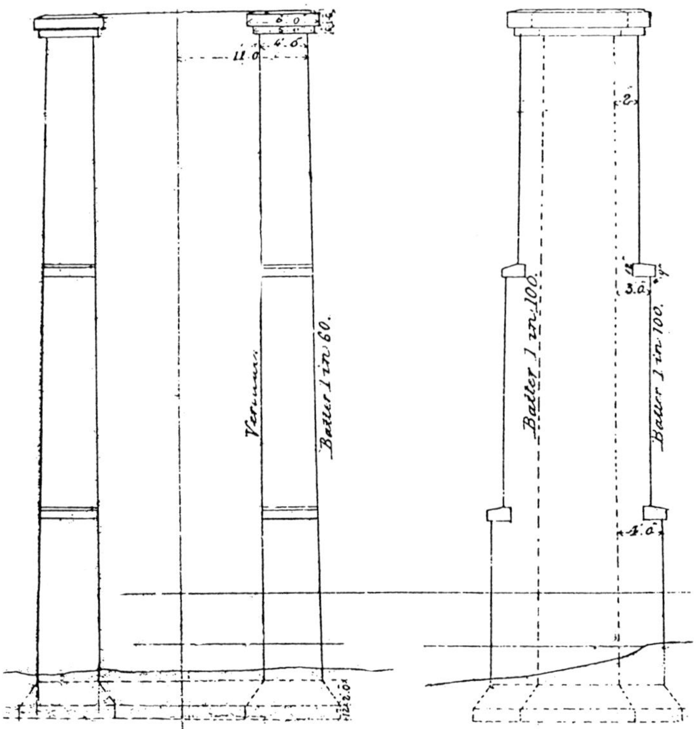

34. From a drawing of Keyham viaduct, these extracts show the construction of a typical buttressed masonry pier, as used on the inland viaducts having a maximum height no greater than 115ft. The plain piers were formed as a masonry slab set on a foundation approximately 7ft thick and 23ft wide, having a similar top plinth. *British Rail*

Class A1

For Class A1 as finally built, the superstructure followed the construction shown in Fig.18, an extract from the same drawing as Fig.33. This retained the Y Class distance of 15ft between each of the four points of support of the horizontal carrying beams, but with the fans carried on masonry piers. While retaining the 20ft length of linking span, Brunel was able to increase the distance between adjacent piers from the 50ft of Class Y to 65ft for Class A1. However, in some instances, as in the case of both of the viaducts at Truro, by increasing the support centres to the 15ft 4in of Class A2 described below, the pier centres were extended to 66ft; an inexplicable departure from what little standardisation he had achieved.

The construction of the masonry piers is shown in Fig.34, one of the original Keyham Creek drawings[9], and followed two patterns; a light, slab formation set on a foundation approximately 7ft thick and 23ft wide, the sides incorporating a batter of 1/100, and a heavier type in which the same slab section was reinforced at each corner by a 4ft wide abutment. Depending on the pier height, these buttresses were often stepped in order to provide greater stability. There did not seem to be any set pattern of how these two types were built to suit a given location, in some instances being arranged as alternate piers while in others, there were two light piers to each buttressed pier. No doubt the local ground formation influenced the arrangement for each site as to the extent of buttressing considered necessary.

The tops of the masonry piers were designed to provide a section 22ft × 6ft, to carry a plinth 23ft × 8ft, which formed the cill, at a level approximately 34ft 6in below rail height. Mounted thereon by means of five short lengths of 12in × 6in timbers, grouted onto the plinth, were the special cast iron seatings which provided the location for the raking timber struts — a pair of castings bolted back to back for each fan. Figure 35A shows a detail of this feature from a typical Class A1 drawing[10]. In addition, there were two wrought iron tie rods of $1\frac{7}{8}$in dia which spanned the width of the pier at cill level to link the outside pair of legs of each outer fan, while the fans of adjacent piers were joined by $1\frac{5}{8}$in dia horizontal tie rods, together with $1\frac{1}{8}$in dia diagonal links. A detail of these arrangements is shown for Carvedras viaduct (Fig.36).

Thus, each pier carried three fans, with each fan formed from four raking struts, their section varying according to position. However, as the centre horizontal beam was the more heavily loaded, the legs tended to follow a pattern of the outer ones of the outside fans being of section 13in × 12in, and those of the centre fan 14in × 14in; the inner legs of all three fans being 12in × 12in. Horizontal walings and two sets of diagonal bracing, all of 9in × 7in timbers, notched to a depth of 2in in the main members, and through bolted, tied together the corresponding legs of adjacent fans. The outside legs of this overall framework included a batter of 1/15.

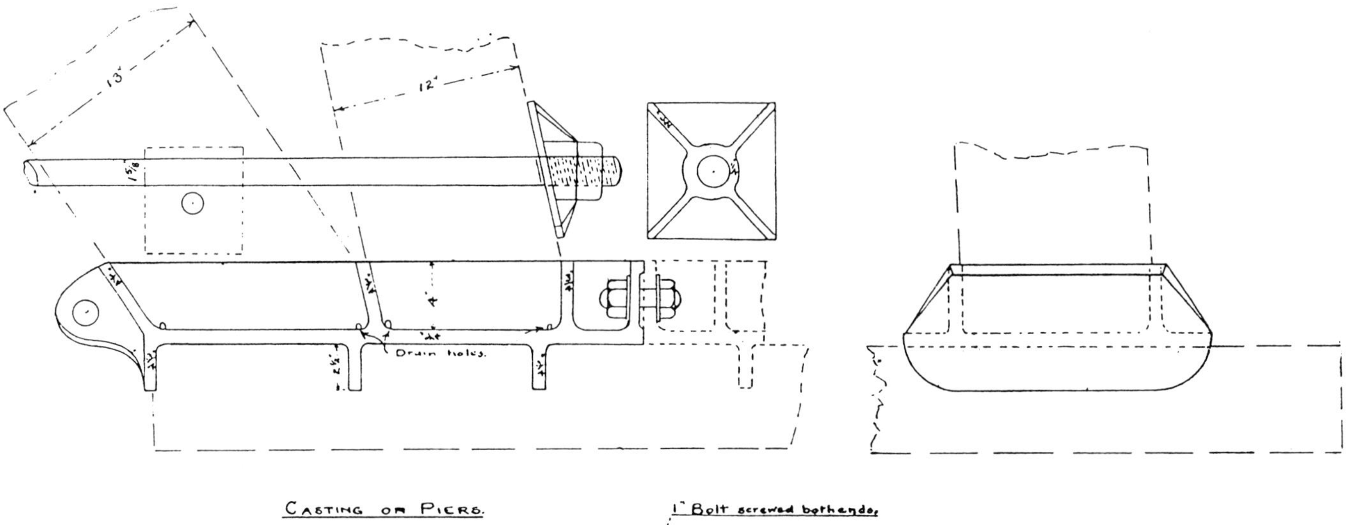

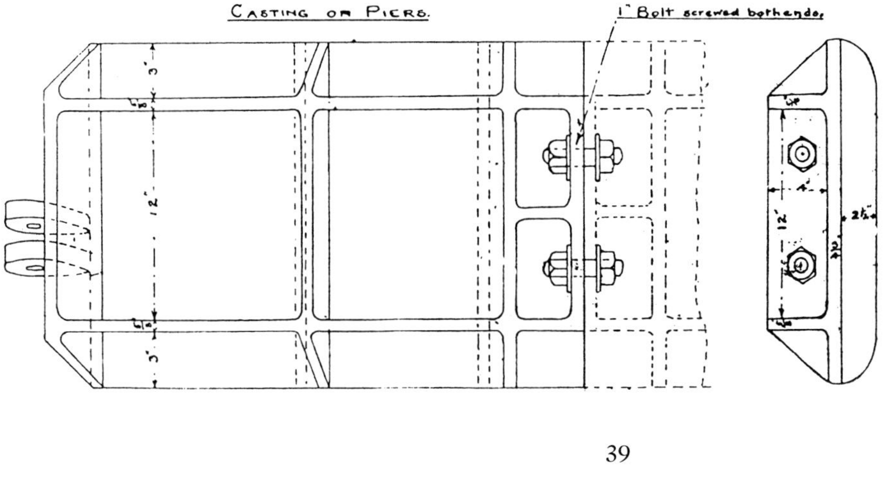

35A. A further extract from an original drawing showing the detail of the seating casting, from which sprang a pair of radial legs, their bottom ends being shaped to fit the casting, as shown. For each fan, a pair of these castings was bolted back to back, and were mounted on sets of lateral cill timbers, seated on top of the pier plinth.

The upper end of each strut fitted a second cast iron seating, Fig.35B, into which slotted the lower members of the laminated longitudinal carrying beams, their ends located by a ½in thick rib. As will be seen from Fig.18, these laminations comprised two timbers, one above the other, bolted together so as to form a composite member; similar to the Class Z design. The outside beams were each of two 10in × 12in and the central beam, of two 12in × 12in timbers. In general, the lower timber of each laminate was in a series of lengths which closely fitted into the upper seatings carried by each leg and located therein against the ½in thick rib, thus positioning the upper ends of the legs. The upper beam, 'about 30ft long', spanned these joints and was itself jointed at the adjoining mid position. Thin hardwood wedges were driven into the gaps between the ends of these timbers in order to complete what was, in effect, a continuous beam, the two members being bolted together with 1¼in dia diagonal bolts, with hardwood joggles and wrought iron wedges on either side of these bolts. In addition, a 12in × 4in crown piece bolted to the underside of each laminated beam between adjacent fans, formed an abutment for the upper castings of each outer leg.

These three horizontal laminated beams extended over the length of the viaduct and carried the decking, formed from 12in × 4in thick cross timbers, with a 6in thick cross member notched into the carrying beams at each inner strut location. The original contract drawings show all these planks butting but, as previously mentioned, a later GWR drawing calls for ½in gaps, presumably in order to assist drainage. Vertical ballast boards, 2½in × 1ft 6in deep, capped by a 8in × 6in fender, provided the walling of the ballast trough, which carried the permanent way. Whitley[11] reported this to comprise 14in × 7in baulk timbers, transoms and 72 lb/yd bridge rail, compared with the sections quoted in Chapter 2. The rail height retained the 1ft 6in dimension above the deck level.

The parapet rails were 8in × 6in timbers, spaced 14ft apart, and supported 3ft 6in above rail level by vertical posts, of section 6in × 6in, bolted to the outer horizontal beams and spaced, according to drawing, at intervals of 7ft 9¾in across the viaduct. These posts also located the ballast board and fender and the detail of these arrangements will be seen from the previous illustrations. This spacing of the vertical posts, at a nominal 7ft 9¾in, could provide a convenient means of assessing approximate viaduct length from available photographs, but as their location followed a positional pattern across the structure rather than a dimensional one, due to variations in pier centres, it is not a reliable method of measurement.

On the A1 design as finally built, the two inner raking legs of each outer fan included additional timber braces linking the legs to the parapet rail. Because of their particular shape to suit the 1/15 batter of the fans, these braces were called 'Coffin Pieces'. In general, on the longer viaducts, a man refuge was incorporated on the outside of the structure, on one side of every other span, so as to provide a safety refuge for personnel working on the line, during the passage of a train.

Based on the Landore loading, the maximum bending stress incurred in the centre horizontal beam over a 15ft span was calculated to be 627 lb/in^2, or just under 50% of the Permissible Stress value of 1,340 lb/in^2; the compressive stress in the more heavily loaded 14in square outer strut under the worst loading condition being 283 lb/in^2, well within both the Permissible Stress and the Fletcher permissible figure. The critical ratio of the strut, P_c/P_m, is calculated to be 3.28.

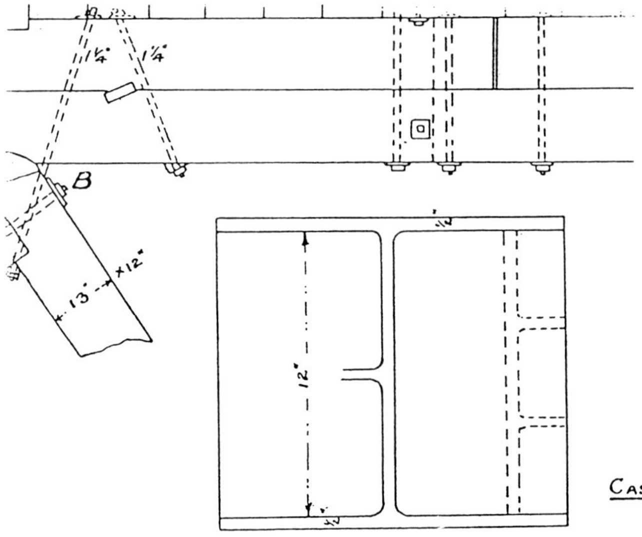

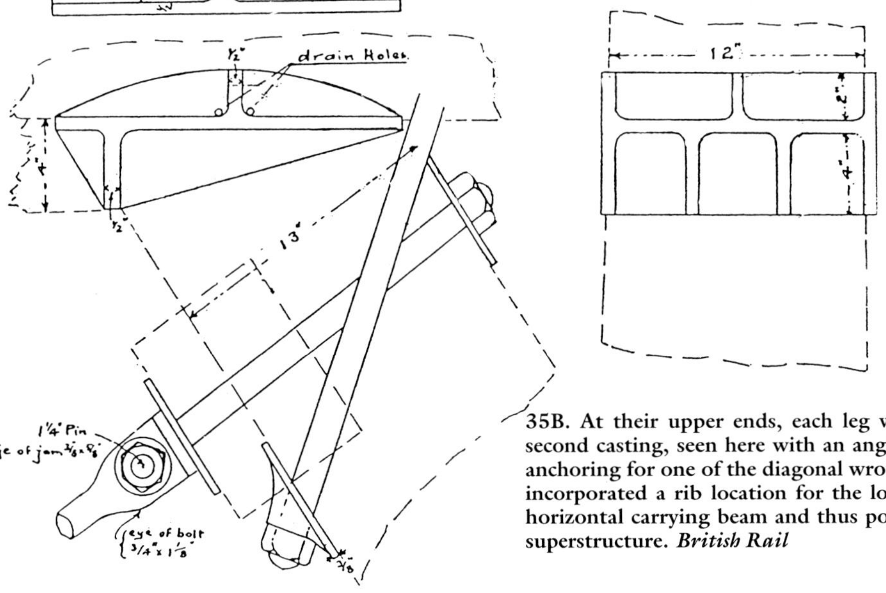

35B. At their upper ends, each leg was again shaped to fit into a second casting, seen here with an angled clamping bolt and the end anchoring for one of the diagonal wrought iron ties. The casting also incorporated a rib location for the lower member of the laminated horizontal carrying beam and thus positioned the framework of the superstructure. ***British Rail***

36. A close up view of the plinth at the top of one of the piers of Carvedras viaduct, showing the lower cast iron seatings, timber legs, bracing etc and wrought iron tie rods referred to in Fig.35A. ***R.I.C.***

Class A2

This later design of superstructure retained a similar arrangement of carrying beams, decking and ballast trough as that of Class A1 but the distance between the points of the raking leg support of the horizontal beams was increased from 15ft to 15ft 4in. This had the affect of increasing the centre beam bending stress to 693 lb/in^2 — or just over 50% of the permissible figure. However, by retaining the length of the linking span between adjacent sets of fans at 20ft, the distance between piers was extended to a maximum of 66ft, while the decking also incorporated a 6in cross member at each support location.

The details of this form of construction will be apparent from the extract shown in Fig.37, which is taken from a later drawing[12] of Keyham viaduct. The distance from the top of the piers to the rail height was increased to 35ft while, insofar as the handrailing was concerned, Brunel strengthened the simple construction of Class A1 by adding a heavy balustrade. This comprised a parapet rail of section 12in × 10in, supported at a height of 4ft 6in above rail level by 12in × 6in vertical posts, in addition to the 6in × 6in handrail posts. While, according to drawing, these were spaced at nominal intervals of 8ft 3in across the viaduct, they followed a

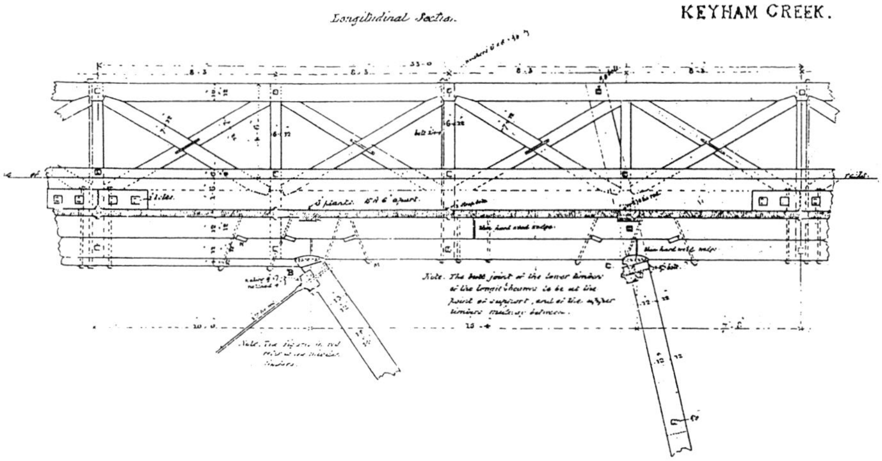

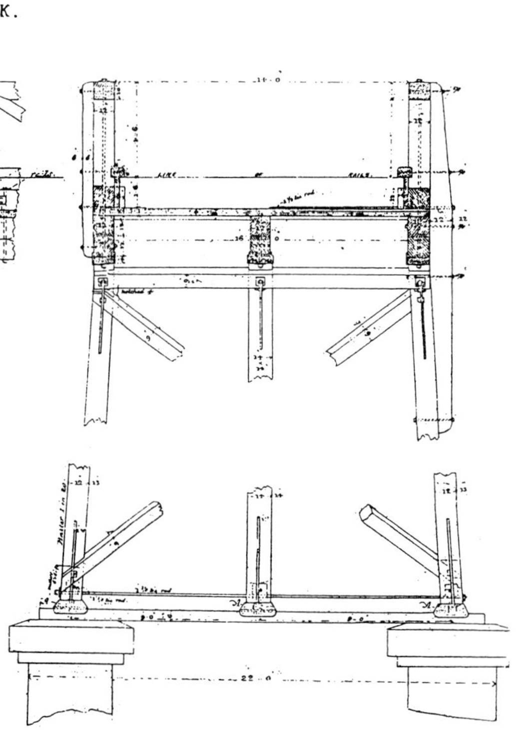

37. A detail of a Class A2 structure, showing how the various component timbers fitted together and were located in the special cast iron seatings which fitted under the laminated horizontal carrying beams. The balustrade type handrailing, with its vertical supports spaced at 8ft 3in centres , and the location of the joggles relative to the structure as a whole, together with their associated inclined clamping bolts and seatings, can be clearly seen. Note the 6in thick deck timbers located at 15ft 4in centres adjacent to each support. ***British Rail***

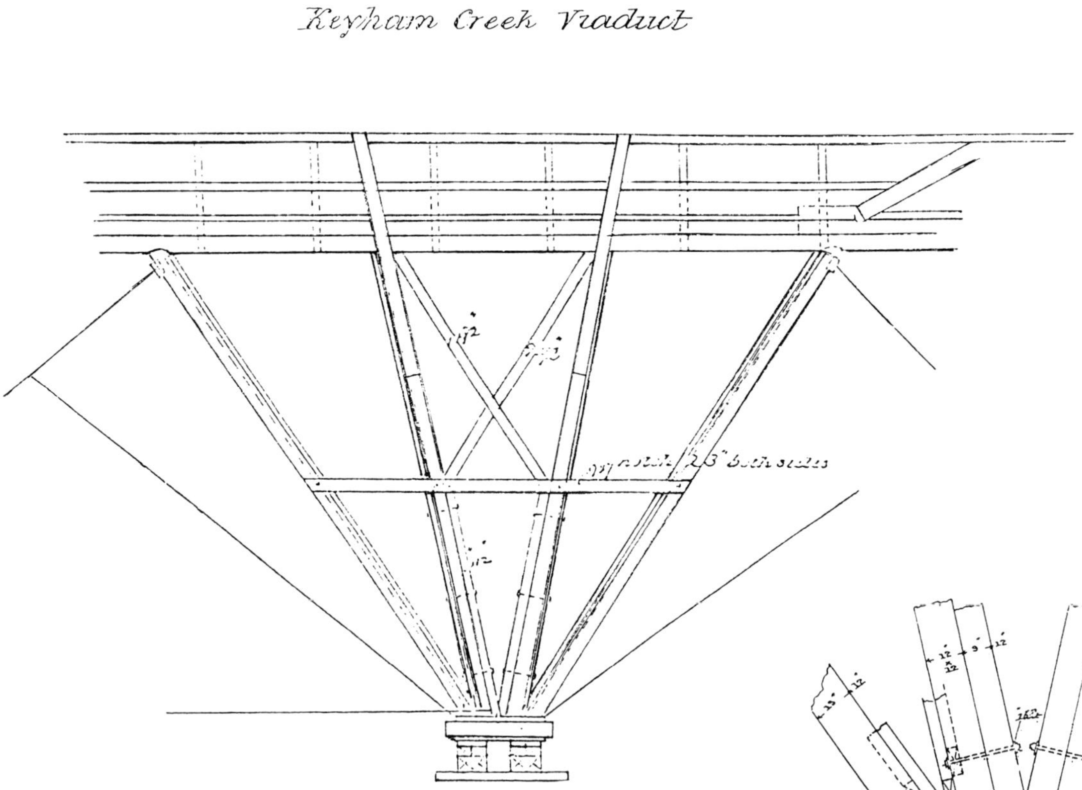

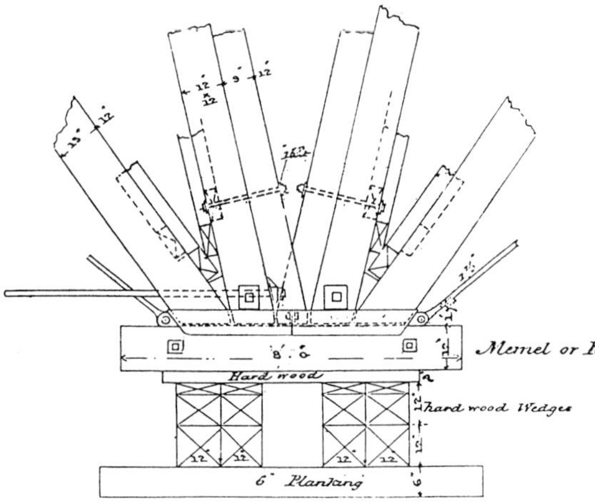

38. At several locations the landward fans, instead of being carried on a masonry plinth, were mounted on a timber platform which seated on a ledge formed in the embankment slope. The details of construction of this arrangement is shown here, being an extract from the Keyham viaduct drawing. It will be seen that the lower pairs of castings were mounted on a pair of Memel or Red Pine longitudinal timbers which in turn were supported by a pair of hardwood wedges, resting on the timber platform. By means of these timber wedges, the level of each fan could be adjusted to take up any settlement. Note also the additional diagonal braces and horizontal brace included in the fan construction which appeared to be unique to these locations. ***British Rail***

pattern of eight posts within the length of a fan support and the adjacent linking span. However, variations in pier centre distances at different sites again meant that this dimension varied between spans of the same viaduct, so that it was not a reliable measure of overall viaduct length.

This balustrade included 12in × 7in diagonal bracings, morticed at their upper ends into the parapet rail and at their lower ends into a 12in × 12in longitudinal timber seated on top of the decking, and forming part of the ballast trough. This whole structure was then tied together by means of $1\frac{1}{4}$in dia vertical bolts etc, passing through the parapet rail and the outer laminated horizontal beams. The latter were also increased in section to two 12in square timbers, complete with the usual inclined bolts, joggles etc, and this overall arrangement thus introduced a trussed parapet into the spans, to provide a stronger overall design.

From available photographs it is apparent that this design was incorporated in the viaducts built between Liskeard and St Germans, and at Keyham and Stonehouse Pool. They often included a landward span of about 30ft in conjunction with a timber platform seated on the embankment, as described later in this chapter.

This arrangement allowed the beams to be adjusted for any settlement in service.

At some sites the fans at the landward end of a viaduct, instead of seating on a masonry plinth, were often carried on a timber platform set in the embankment slope. A typical arrangement of this method of support is shown in Fig.38, an extract from an original drawing[13] of Keyham. The platform was formed from 6in thick planks, to provide an area 28ft × 9ft. Two pairs of 12in square baulks, either of Red Pine or Memel, seated laterally on this platform and in turn carried pairs of hardwood wedges under the two 12in square Memel or Red Pine cill timbers. These were bolted together with $\frac{3}{4}$in dia through bolts, to form the support for the pair of bottom leg castings for each fan. The sets of legs springing from these castings were, of course, linked laterally by the bottom horizontal waling as well as by a $1\frac{1}{8}$in dia lateral tie rod. Each fan built on these timber platforms also included pairs of 9in × 7in horizontal ties as well as additional diagonal members of similar section. The fan base was also linked to its neighbour by the usual horizontal and diagonal tie rods. Figure 39 shows a typical fan of this construction at Tregagle. Again, it will be seen that the wedges enabled each fan to be levelled and adjusted for any settlement in service.

39. This photograph, of one of the landward supports at Tregagle, shows a variation from the form of construction described in Fig.38; the fans are supported on a timber platform on the embankment, while the taper wedges, which enabled the level of the fan to be adjusted to take up any settlement, can be clearly seen. No additional bracing in this instance. ***L G Booth Collection***

40. A close up view of the timber work involved in the Class B type of superstructure, at Ponsanooth, showing a total of sixteen legs seated on the plinth of each pier. While this form of construction undoubtedly provided improved lateral strength, the fitting of replacement legs with their attendant bracing must have been quite a problem for the viaduct maintenance teams. ***L G Booth Collection***

From an examination of photographs of some of the Class A1 and A2 viaducts in their later days, it will be noticed that an additional cross member, probably of section 4in × 12in, was introduced at the mid point of each linking span. It was supported at each end by means of a wrought iron or steel stirrup, slung from the decking on the outside of each outer laminated beam. This was intended to provide additional mid span support to the centre laminated carrying beam which, as mentioned earlier, was likely to be showing signs of distress in the face of ever increasing traffic loading over its 20ft span. We have no date for the introduction of these additional timbers, but their absence from photographs of Truro viaduct in the late 1880s and their presence at the time the replacement was under construction in 1900, points to the change of gauge as probably being the determining factor. According to the photographs, these additional timbers were also introduced on the 20ft linking spans of the Falmouth branch structures.

Class B.

A further development of the Class A superstructure modified the formation of the central raking legs, to provide greater support to the central horizontal carrying beam, coupled with increased lateral strength. This construction was defined by Margary as Class B. It was generally similar to Class A1 but the central fan was replaced by two sets of legs, inclined to those of the outside fans, to form an inverted vee, thus making a total of sixteen legs on each pier compared with the normal twelve.

The raking leg supports of the carrying beams were at either 15ft or 15ft 4in centres, depending on viaduct location. At their lower ends these inside legs fitted into the special cill seatings of the outer fans while at their upper ends they were scarfed to support the underside of the central horizontal beam, located in a suitable cast iron support seating. A detail of Ponsanooth viaduct, Fig.40, illustrates the overall form of construction, from which it will be seen that the weight of the superstructure was concentrated on the outer buttresses of each pier.

According to details of St Pinnock viaduct[14] given by Margary in 1882, the carrying beams were supported at 15ft centres while, with the exception of the outside pairs of legs of the central fans, all the raking legs were of section 12in × 12in: those former members being 12in × 13in. The outside fans incorporated a batter of 1/15 and the legs of adjacent fans were tied together by the usual 9in × 7in walings and cross bracing, notched 2in into the main members; the decking was of 6in thick timbers.

The centre distance between piers of this class of viaduct varied up to a maximum of 66ft and, as this form of superstructure was used where the maximum height was in excess of 130ft, the piers themselves were of massive proportions. From current measurements at site, the centre section was a nominal 4ft 6in thick and, in addition, substantial buttresses were constructed at each side and at the ends, so as to provide a pier of double cruciform section. These buttresses, besides being stepped, incorporated a batter of 1/115 and 1/150.

Thus, the cast iron shoes supporting the fans were centred within the area of each cruciform, as mentioned above, to locate the load bearing at these two points on each pier. In some instances, the wall of each pier was pierced by openings of gothic design, presumably with the intention of saving weight. As will be seen from Fig.22, which illustrates a redundant Moorswater pier, they were impressive structures in their own right. On those viaducts where the original timber superstructure has been replaced by wrought iron or steel girders they continue to carry the heavier loads of today's traffic and stand as a tribute to their original designer and the craftsmen who built them.

It was probably Brunel's original intention to establish a standard range of viaducts, with the facility for interchangability of the major components. However, in practice it was necessary to adapt each viaduct to its particular location. According to today's measurements, the pier centres vary from site to site to such an extent that each structure was in effect unique. Any benefit from such standardisation was thus lost.

Furthermore, in viewing these Class designs in relation to their respective locations, there did not appear to be any logical plan. For instance, St Pinnock, 633ft in length and 151ft high of straight formation was built to Class B and lasted 23 years while St Austell, 720ft long and 115ft high was built on a curve to Class A1 and lasted 39 years. The combination of the quality of original construction, the viaduct Class and its formation (straight or curved), train speed and the amount of timber replacement obviously had a bearing on the safe life of each viaduct and determined its replacement date.

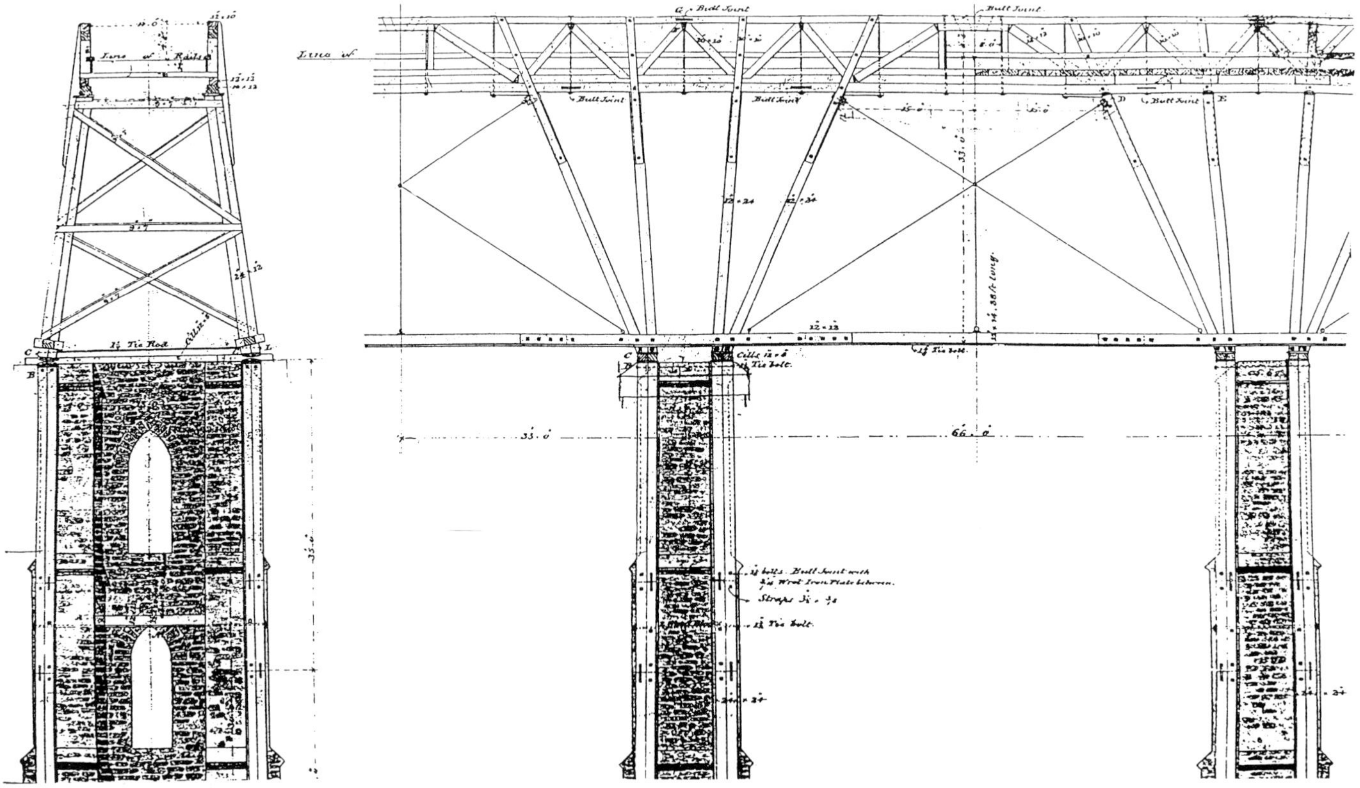

41. An extract from a drawing of Moorswater, showing the Class D formation of the superstructure with the raking legs springing from two separate locations, astride the four clusters of vertical timber supports set in the corners of the buttresses. Note the gothic openings in the massive masonry piers. ***PRO RAIL 134/47***

42. A close up view of two of the sets of timber fans at Moorswater. Some idea of their size can be appreciated when it is realised that each leg was of section 2ft × 1ft, that the horizontal linking tie beams fitted on to the fans at cill level each comprised a formation of timbers 3ft in width. The piers were at 66ft centres, while the track level was 147ft above the level of the valley below. *R.I.C.*

Class D

Although Brunel had thus developed a range of different superstructures for the crossing of the inland valleys, he evolved yet a further variation of his fan type configuration, which under the Margary notation became known as Class D. It incorporated only two fans each of four raking legs, each fan supporting a laminated horizontal beam in combination with a trussed balustrade for the parapet. As will be seen from the analysis of Appendix 1 within the superstructure and associated members, it comprised nearly 50% more timber per foot of span than Class A1. It was, therefore, a formidable design, applied with distinctive variation, to the viaducts at Coombe by Saltash, a tidal structure, and Moorswater, an inland viaduct.

The general form of construction is shown in Fig. 41, an extract from a drawing[15] of Moorswater viaduct, where the legs of the superstructure in that instance, included a batter of 1/5 compared with the usual 1/15 or 1/20. Each raking leg was formed from two 12in × 12in timbers bolted together to form a raking strut of section 12in thick and 24in lateral width, which seated at its lower end into a cast iron shoe. This, in turn, rested on the appropriate timbers of the cill. The upper end of each strut also carried a cast iron shoe that provided support, at 12ft centres, for the lower 14in × 12in member of the laminated horizontal beam. The upper member was of 12in square section and the two were secured together by means of the usual inclined bolts, hardwood joggles and wrought iron wedges adjacent to each fan support. The lower member was jointed between each pair of outer struts, so that it extended over the linking span between adjacent fans; each joint including a hardwood wedge and bolted wrought iron strap. The drawings do not indicate where the upper member was jointed and it can only be assumed that this was respectively at the centres of each pier and each linking span.

Horizontal walings and diagonal cross bracing, from 9in × 7in section timbers, linked the raking struts of each fan, while the bottoms of the struts were connected by a lateral $1\frac{1}{4}$in dia wrought iron tie rod. The decking comprised 12in × 8in timbers, supported by the horizontal laminated beams; at the location of the raking struts a 6in × 12in side piece was through bolted to the beams to provide local support for the decking. The parapet rail, 12in × 10in, was supported 6ft above the decking by 12in × 10in diagonal struts, their ends seating in cast iron shoes. This framework was clamped between the top of the parapet rail and the bottom of the horizontal beam by a series of $1\frac{1}{2}$in dia vertical through bolts, complete with cast iron seatings and nuts, spaced at approximately 6ft intervals across each span.

The usual $2\frac{1}{2}$in thick ballast boards, topped by 8in × 6in fender rails, contained the ballast for the permanent way, to give a rail height of 1ft 6in above deck level. Coffin pieces, from 12in square timbers, linked all four raking legs to the parapets at each side (compared with only two on Class A and B structures) while $1\frac{1}{8}$in dia through bolts connected both trusses at deck level, adjacent to the raking struts. The parapets were spaced 14ft apart.

Between each set of fan supports, the linking span of the trussed beam incorporated a queen post construction within the parapet. This was formed by the addition of a 12in × 10in member to the underside of the parapet rail, over the centre 8ft of the span, to form a laminate, secured by raking $1\frac{1}{2}$in dia bolts, joggles and taper wedges. The parapet rail was jointed at this mid point, and also at each pier centre, each joint including a hardwood wedge and linking wrought iron straps. The principal struts and straining pieces, in 12in square timbers, formed the trussed beam, their ends seated in cast iron shoes.

At cill level, 33ft below rail level, a continuous tie beam formed a horizontal brace on each side of the structure. This was built up from two 12in × 12in timbers, each notched 6in deep to fit either side of each set of fan legs. A 14in × 12in linking timber was clamped between them, and extended to the adjacent set of fans. These members were secured together by $1\frac{1}{8}$in dia through bolts, nuts and 5in square × $\frac{3}{8}$in thick cast iron washers, together with vertical hardwood joggles and wrought iron wedges. Finally, the Class incorporated $1\frac{5}{8}$in dia horizontal tie rods between the piers at cill level, together with the normal diagonal and vertical linking wrought iron ties which, because of the double timber configuration of the legs, were in pairs. All these details will also be apparent from a study of the close-up view of the superstructure of Moorswater in Fig.42.

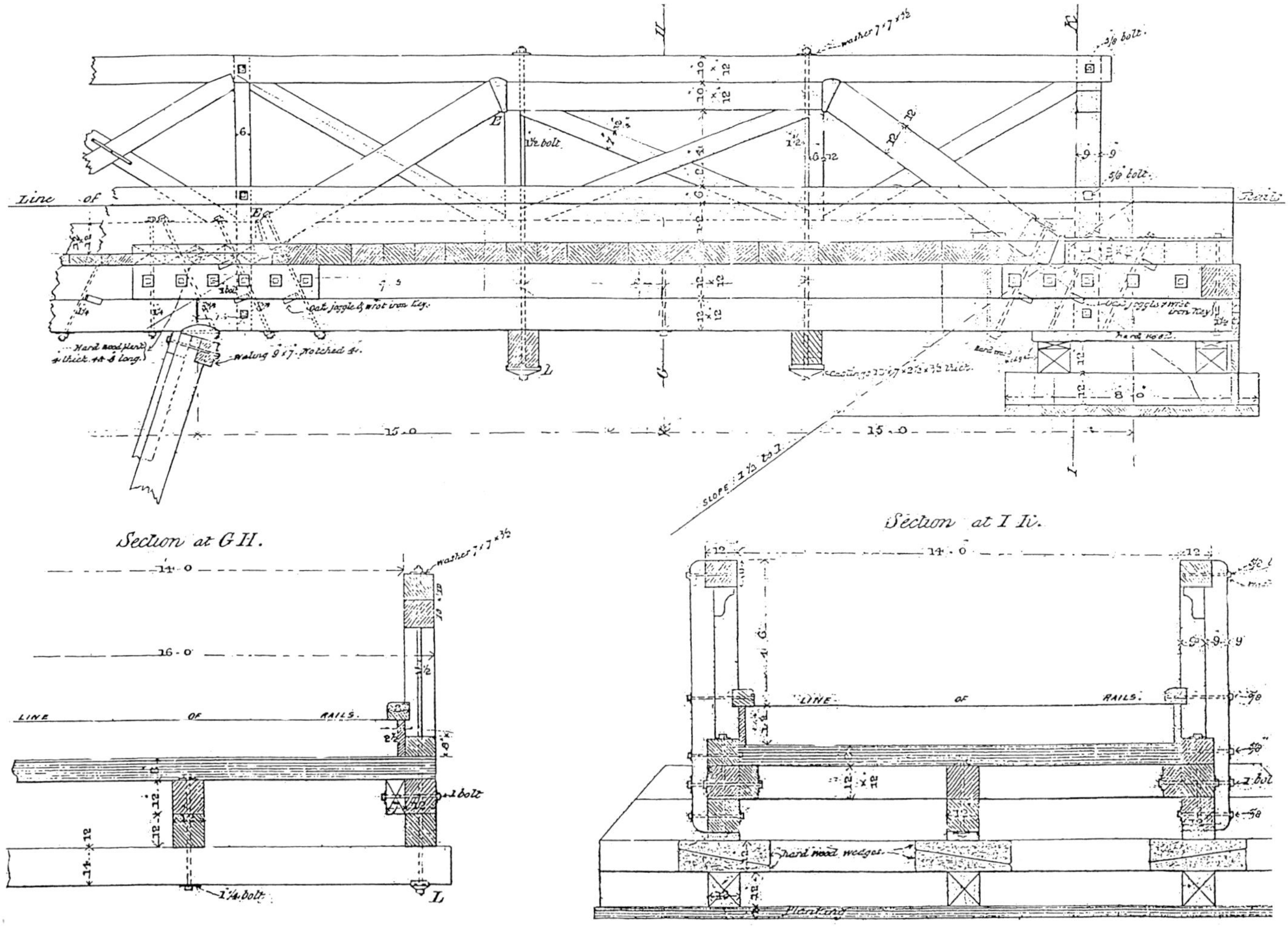

43. An extract from an original drawing showing the construction of a typical landward span of up to 30ft length. It incorporated a queen post truss in each parapet together with a pair of intermediate lateral cross timbers to support the centre horizontal carrying beam at 15ft centres, with the deck timbers increased from 4in thick to 8in. The landward end of the span seated on a special timber platform as shown and incorporated wedges to take up any settlement. *British Rail*

Class E

The sixth and final variation of the fan type designs, identified by Margary as Class E, was evolved by Brunel for use where the line crossed a shallow valley, as being a cheaper alternative to an embankment. It was of a much lighter construction than even his Class A1 design, incorporating only two raking struts in each of the three fans, which sprang from low masonry plinths set but 2ft above ground level. It has not been possible to trace any original drawings or photographs of these structures, although we do have a drawing illustration of Penadlake, taken from Whitley (Fig.95); and an outline diagram included in Margary's Report[16], from which Crispin was able to produce the drawing of Probus (Fig.23). There is also a photograph of Grove (Fig.66) which, although at a tidal crossing was of a modified Class E construction. Accordingly, the following description is largely conjecture.

It would appear that, overall, the design was similar to Class Z, the three laminated horizontal carrying beams, decking, ballast trough and handrail parapets comprising the sections and construction of that Class. However, in place of the vertical leg supports, the superstructure was carried by two sets of raking struts, which sprang from cast iron shoes, seated on shallow masonry plinths, spaced across the structure at 39ft 6in centres. At their upper ends, each strut fitted a further cast iron seating, which located and supported the lower member of each laminated longitudinal beam. Thus, support was provided to the carrying beams at 19ft 9in centres, these legs incorporating the usual horizontal walings and diagonal bracing similar to the raking legs of the other Classes. A crown piece fitted to the underside of the carrying beams between adjacent fans, also served to locate the upper ends of the legs.

Whitley refers to the horizontal beams as sections of two 24in × 10in timbers but nowhere has it been possible to find this section recorded in original drawings or records. It must be concluded therefore, that he meant the outer horizontal carrying beams to be of section 10in × 24in deep, so that the design and timber sections would then be in line with those of the other viaduct classes.

The sections and scantlings assumed in the foregoing description have been used in carrying out the investigation of the comparative stress levels in the timber viaducts under the imposition of the Landore loading. The centre horizontal beam would have been subject to a stress level well above that of the other fan types, at 1,202 lb/in^2, some 90% of the Permissible Stress. The compressive stress in the legs at 462 lb/in^2, or 37% of the Permissible Value, coupled with the P_c/P_m ratio of 1.61, represented the most highly loaded condition for these members. These factors, in conjunction with the relatively low timber content of the supporting structure (see Appendix 1) resulted in an exceptionally frail overall design. As all these Class E structures were sited at locations where traffic would have been crossing at speed, it is not surprising that they enjoyed only a relatively short life and were soon replaced.

Landward Spans

It has already been mentioned in Chapter 3 that, as a measure of economy, Brunel generally omitted large abutments or wing walls at the ends of his viaducts, the adjacent embankments being graded with a slope of 1½ to 1. Where it was then necessary for the landward span to be of a length greater than the 20ft link between adjacent sets of fans, it was formed from two trussed beams each with a queen post truss in the parapet. The outer ends of these frameworks rested on a timber platform seated at the top of the embankment.

Reference to these arrangements has been made earlier in this chapter and the relevant details of construction can be seen from Fig.43, an extract from an original drawing[17]. Each trussed beam, usually of 30ft length, was formed from a laminated horizontal carrying beam comprising two 12in square timbers with the usual joggles, wedges and inclined bolts, and a parapet of section 12in × 10in, supported at a height of 4ft 6in above rail level, by 6in × 12in vertical posts. This framework incorporated 12in square diagonal straining pieces with an additional central horizontal member of the same section, bolted under the parapet. The ends of all these members were located in cast iron shoes, and thus formed a trussed beam on each side.

The lower laminated beams of each truss carried the decking, increased to a thickness of 8in, complete with the usual ballast trough and permanent way. In addition, the decking was supported by a central laminated carrying beam formed from a pair of 12in square timbers, which was carried by two underslung 12in × 14in cross timbers, situated at 15ft centres across the span. These cross timbers were secured by a pair of 1½in dia through vertical bolts, nuts and 7in square washers, extending from their underside to the top of the parapet rail; thus clamping the whole framework together.

The landward ends of the trussed beams and the central carrying beam each seated on a pair of hardwood wedges which in turn were mounted on 12in square baulks located on a timber platform. This was formed from 4in thick planks, to provide a support area of 22ft × 8ft, packed and levelled on top of the embankment. Thus any settlement of the ends of the structure could be adjusted by means of the wedges, so as to maintain the track true and level.

The outer ends of the trussed beams and central carrying beam were, of course, supported by the outer legs of the adjacent fan of the appropriate Class structure involved, the deck thickness across the viaduct thereafter being reduced to the usual 4in or 6in.

44. No drawing having come to light showing the details of the Class C trussed timber beam construction, this illustration has been composed from available records, study of photographs and related to similar structural details. While not necessarily authentic, it shows the form of construction believed to have been adopted by Brunel for the tidal viaducts, evolved from his earlier work on his South Devon designs, the structures on the Swindon and Gloucester line and in South Wales. *Author*

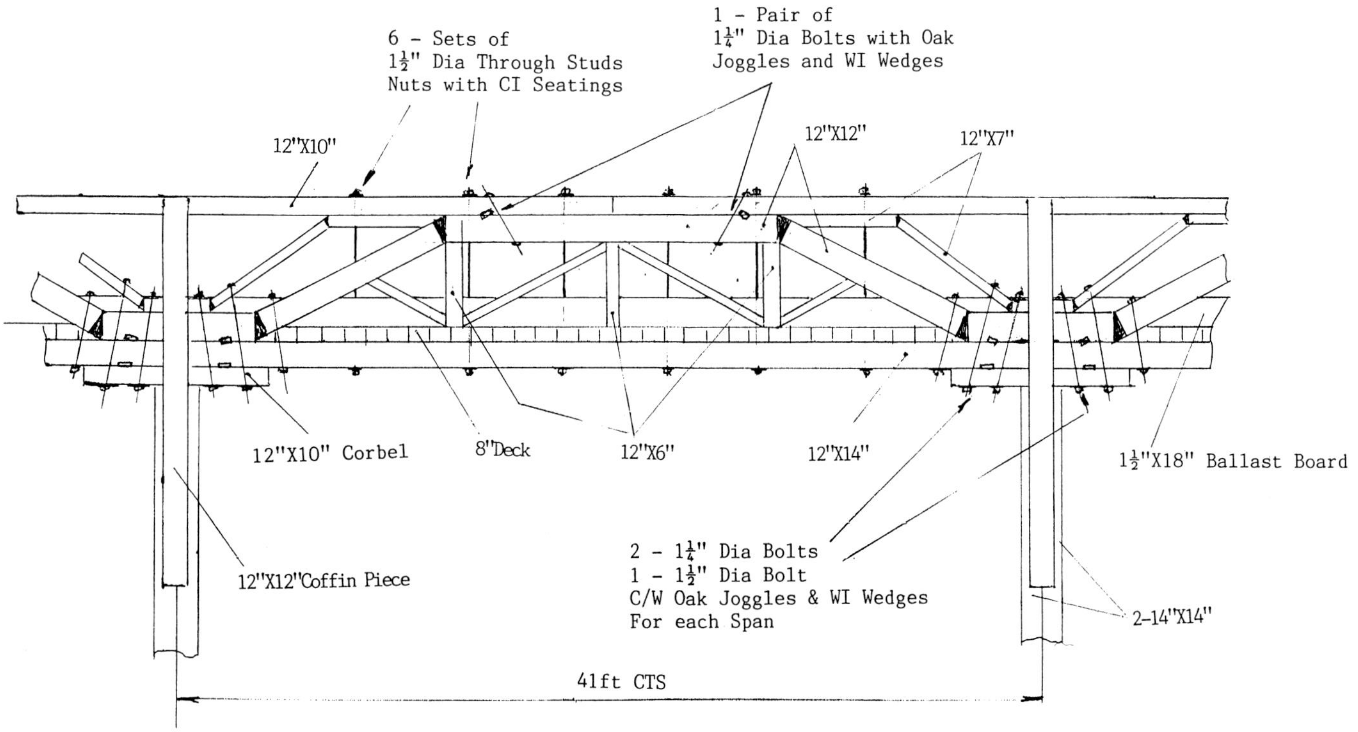

Class C (or Tidal Viaducts)

Where the railway crossed the tidal creeks between Devonport and St Germans the mud extended in places to a depth of some 70 feet. Accordingly, Brunel resorted to the use of wood piles for the foundation of the timber trestles, which supported the superstructure of what became known as his 'Tidal' viaducts, or under the Margary notation, Class C design. Each pile was built up from four baulks[18] below the mud line and then two sets of timbers extended upwards to form the trestle.

In the case of the Weston Mill, Forder and Nottar viaducts, the trestles were nominally spaced 41ft apart. They consisted of a pair of legs each formed[19] from two timbers of section 14in × 13in, bolted together to form the vertical posts, erected with a batter of 1/10. These were linked together by means of horizontal walings and cross bracing in 9in × 7in timbers, while a long raking strut, probably of 12in square section, extended from mud level to the trestle top, so as to provide transverse rigidity. Generally, every sixth support was strengthened by providing this raking member on both sides of the trestle, with the addition of a pair of inclined struts, probably from 12in square timbers, to each leg and stiffened by two pairs of longitudinal timber ties; this overall arrangement assisting in the longitudinal stability of the structure. The trestles shown in Fig.19, from Forder viaduct, illustrate the general form of construction. Where they adjoined the navigable channel, timber fenders were provided for their protection.

In the absence of an original drawing from which to establish the details of the superstructure of the 41ft span design, we can only surmise that in general it followed the construction shown in Fig.44. This drawing was prepared by the author from a study of available reports and photographs and, in particular, a drawing[20] of the shorter span viaduct at Wivelscombe (Fig.64). We can deduce that at their top, the vertical timbers on each side of a trestle fitted into a casting which, in turn, accommodated a corbel, of section 12in × 10in. This member supported the lower horizontal beam of each adjacent timber truss, secured by two 1¼in dia and one 1½in dia inclined bolts, complete with hardwood joggles and a thin timber wedge at the interface between the horizontal beams. Each truss was built up from this lower horizontal beam, of section 12in × 14in, which carried the 8in thick timber decking, and a series of principal struts and straining pieces in 12in × 12in timbers, with their ends seated in special castings. The resulting framework, together with the 12in × 6in posts and intermediate braces, supported the 12in × 10in parapet rail at a height 4ft 6in above rail level. This parapet was jointed at the centre of each span and 1¼in dia bolts secured the sections to the 12in × 12in horizontal straining piece, on the underside of the parapet rail. The inclusion of a pair of oak joggles and wrought iron wedges, thus formed a short lamination at the centre of each span. Vertical through bolts, 1½in dia, immediately adjacent to each post, with their nuts seating on special square section cast iron washers located respectively on top of the parapet and the underside of the main horizontal beam, clamped this whole framework together, to form each truss.

For each span, these trussed beams were spaced 14ft apart and the decking carried the usual 2½in thick ballast boards and 8in × 6in fender rails, to enclose the ballast and baulk timbers for the permanent way, with the rail height 1ft 6in above deck level. Timber straps from 12in × 12in section, shaped to accommodate the batter of the trestle legs, were through bolted to the trestle legs and the truss on either side at each support.

45. The 1,134ft length of Nottar Viaduct, viewed from Grove Turf, the saltings to the south east of this crossing of the Lynher River, taken in 1899. Again, the inordinate length of the structure combined with the slender piers emphasises the frailty of the Class C design. The fenders built around the piers in the navigable waterway, can be seen on the left while flying scaffolding around two mid-length piers would indicate maintenance work in hand. ***L G Booth Collection***

Having regard to their considerable length, as will be seen from the photograph of Nottar (Fig.45), we can understand how these structures gave the impression of a frailty and inadequacy for their task. Nevertheless, some remained in service until 1908, carrying the ever increasing traffic loads; indeed, viaducts of similar construction on the Kingswear branch in Devon were in service until the early 1920s. Their strength may be judged from the fact, that on one occasion two goods trains met head-on on Nottar viaduct and, although derailed, were prevented from falling into the estuary below by the parapets.

In this type of construction, the changing of the timbers in any part involved the breaking up of that truss[21]. This meant that it had to be cast adrift from the viaduct span while the work was carried out, temporary support being provided to carry the decking on one side. Consequently, the fact that their design did not permit piecemeal replacement of faulty timbers, did mean that the framework of the trusses was not weakened by intermittent repair work; a factor which could well have contributed to their longevity.

No design calculations having been traced relating to this Class of structure and, in the light of the 'state of the art' examined in Chapter 3, it must be assumed that it was evolved from practical experience and, in particular, backed by the development of the South Devon structures. Summarising this chapter we can say that, with the exception of St Germans, the construction of which stood on its own and is described under its heading in Chapter 8, the Cornish timber viaducts fall into one or other of the foregoing eight classes, albeit with some detail modifications at different locations. These are examined in the later description of each viaduct.

We know from contemporary reports that Brunel often immersed himself in the minutiae of his designs. However, having regard to the period of time taken for the construction of the railway, coupled with the other major projects in which he was involved at the time, it seems apparent that either under his direction or at the initiative of the resident engineer, his original broad design conception was often modified to suit local conditions. These changes were made without due account necessarily being taken of their affect on design performance.

Simple stress analysis appears to indicate that all these structures (with the possible exception of Class E) were adequate for the Landore level of static loading. However, the imposition of rolling and braking loads on the relatively flimsy frameworks, together with increasing levels of traffic, meant that, based on today's design criteria, they were all initially under designed. Furthermore, the continuing replacement in service of individual timbers of the inland viaducts (a cornerstone of Brunel's original design philosophy), led to the onset of further deterioration. That this point was well understood by Margary is apparent from his report[22] of 1883, wherein he refers to viaducts being either on a curve or having an:

> '...inherent weakness in the original construction, and in these there has been some distortion in the shape of the timber superstructure, necessitating the introduction of numerous shores, which formed no part of the original design, in order to check the lateral movement. And this becomes increasingly the case as the original timbers are removed, and others substituted; for these renewals are made piece by piece under circumstances of considerable difficulty, with the traffic going over the viaducts while the renewals are taking place; and the frames are necessarily weaker than when put together at one time and under very different circumstances at the original construction of the viaducts'.

As a general rule, the introduction of additional shores involved inserting within the superstructure an extra leg at each pier. This raked from the top of a pier at the outside radius of the curve, to the underside of the main outer horizontal carrying beam on the inner radius of the curve. A typical example of this additional support, showing the members involved, can be seen in the illustration of Milltown viaduct, Fig.20.

Chapter 6

A CRITICAL ANALYSIS

WHILE WE MAY NOT have the original structural calculations relating to Brunel's different designs, we can investigate them from a consideration of their respective timber content. From the drawings which are available, together with photographs, we can with some degree of certainty, establish their scantlings. The result of this approximate analysis of the eight Classes involved is summarised in Appendix 1. From this it will be seen that, in considering the fan type structures, the decking, carrying beams and parapet for Classes A1, E, and Y were the same, at 14ft^3 per ft of span, with Class Z slightly less at 13ft^3 per ft of each span, whereas for Classes A2 and D there was a significant increase to 20 and 26ft^3 per ft of span respectively; Class B coming out at an intermediate figure of 16ft^3 per ft.

However, the most significant variation relates to the timber content of the fan supports, which over the 66ft span of Classes A2, B and D were respectively 792, 924 and 1,254ft^3, representing 38%, 47% and 49% of the total timber content of each span. In the case of Class E (39ft 6in span), although the support timbers represented 39% of the total, they only amounted to 9ft^3/ft of span, compared with the comparable figure of 46% of the total, or 12ft^3/ft, for Class A1. It should also be noted that in the case of Class Y, the supporting structure (50ft span) accounted for 52% of the total timber content of each span, at 15ft^3/ft. In considering this aspect, it is significant that some of the Class A1 viaducts saw service for 45 years, whereas all the Class E structures (with the exception of Grove) had been replaced after only 18 years.

Analysis of the data of Appendix 1 in conjunction with the author's simple stress analysis shows that, in considering the centre horizontal carrying beam, Brunel adopted a section 12 × 24in for spans varying between 15ft (Class Y and A1) and 21ft (Class Z), leading almost to a doubling of the maximum stress for the longer span. Bearing in mind the comments of Chapter 3, referring to the extent of the design calculations which could have been carried out on these structures, this evidence does lend weight to the conclusion that they were indeed minimal.

Accordingly, in order to reduce the maximum stress to a figure comparable with that of Class A1, the centre beam for both Class E and Class Z should have been of section 14in × 28in. Likewise, if we compare the ratio of the timber content of the deck, beams and parapet to that of the supporting structure, these data show a figure of 1.05 for Class D compared with 1.55 for Class E. This would indicate that the timber content of the Class E supporting structure should have been about 550ft^3/span compared with the actual figure of 356ft^3/span. The inclusion of heavier legs (say 14in square in place of 12in square), with two additional centre legs to form an inverted vee support for the centre beam, similar to Class B, would have gone some way towards meeting this figure. (In the case of Grove, these additional supports were, in fact, introduced at some time in its history, which probably contributed to its longevity). The resulting structure would thus have been stronger, with improved lateral strength, a combination of factors which could perhaps have enabled this Class of viaduct to remain in service for a longer period. It would certainly have resulted in a design more comparable with the other inland structures.

It is also interesting to compare the total timber content involved in similar length spans for the different classes, varying from 1,980ft^3 for Class B up to 2,574ft^3 for Class D. We may well question how effectively these amounts of timber were applied to the different designs, bearing in mind that the Class D types had been replaced by the 1890s, whereas some of the Class A1 viaducts, containing 1,690ft^3 per span, admittedly for a slightly shorter span, lasted into the early 1900s.

Having recorded the range of designs which Brunel developed for the Cornish railways, to meet the traffic conditions of the mid nineteenth century, examination of their performance in service is relevant, bearing in mind that in several instances, some designs remained in service well into the 1900s. At the time of the Arbitration Hearing (reported in more detail in Chapter 9) Margary had accumulated records regarding the cost of maintenance of the main line viaducts between Plymouth and Truro, in support of his plea for their early replacement. These data are summarised in Appendix 2. With the relevant details from the Table in Chapter 1, together with those of Appendix 1, they have enabled the establishment of the tabulation shown in Appendix 3. This gives an estimate of the timber content (above ground level) of each structure, based on the author's assessment of viaduct dimensions to take account of variations in published records. These figures together with Margary's data, enable a yardstick to be established of the annual maintenance cost per 1,000ft^3 of timber content for each viaduct. The results cover two periods: the first, in the main, over some 20 years for all the viaducts where records are available and the second, for a selected few, the cost over the latter ten years or so of that same period.

This analysis calls for some comment. Firstly, dealing with the viaducts in Classes A1, A2, B, C, and D, other than those structures between Cartuther and Clinnick, inclusive, the annual maintenance cost for each viaduct over a period of 22 years compares closely to an average figure of £7.50/1,000ft^3 of timber content. The corresponding figure for the Cartuther to Clinnick viaducts is less, at £5.29. However, for the period from 1869 to the date of replacement, this cost had risen to an average of £8.33, showing an increase of nearly 60% over the later years of their life, and indicating a deteriorating position. Nevertheless, there does not appear to be an immediate explanation as to why, despite their initially lower maintenance costs, these structures were among the first to be replaced. The answer may lie in Margary's comment to the Arbitration Hearing, that the speed at which trains travelled down the Glynn Valley was cause for concern, and was of far more significance in prompting their replacement than the level of their maintenance costs. There was also the suspected weakness in the masonry piers at Cartuther, Bolitho and Moorswater which was probably a contributory factor. However, the exceptionally low figures for West Largin (£2.63) and Clinnick (£2.67) defy explanation. Although over the later years these figures had nearly doubled, they were still less than the overall long term average.

Doubtless due to their exceptional frailty, and varying service life, the Class E structures, with the exception of Grove, show comparative figures well below the above average at £3.54/1,000ft^3 pa. The Grove figure could have been distorted by virtue of its small size. Again, factors other than maintenance, played their part in determining replacement. Apart from Wivelscombe, the Class C designs compare closely at £7.42/1,000ft^3, the higher figure for that structure reflecting the cost of its partial rebuilding with a wrought iron span.

All these results lend weight to the conclusion that Brunel's approach to the design of all these viaducts was very much influenced by practical considerations, based on earlier practice. Theoretical analysis, which was well within his capability, did not appear to have played any significant part.

Ringwell Viaduct in the 1920s with a 45XX class Prairie tank heading a goods train. ***RIC***

Chapter 7

THE BUILDING, TESTING & MAINTENANCE OF THE VIADUCTS

IT IS NOW APPROPRIATE that consideration should be given to the work actually involved in the building of these timber viaducts, viewed against the background of living conditions in the rural communities of Cornwall in the mid nineteenth century. Then, travel was slow and uncertain, either on rough farm tracks or by sea; the only communication was by messenger or indifferent post. The majority of Cornishmen had never travelled outside the county, or for that matter, far from their immediate neighbourhood. Hence, the arrival of firstly, the railway surveyor with his impedimenta, followed by the contractor, with his equipment and the railway navvies with their families, must have been a great shock to the tranquil village life along the route.

Contemporary accounts concerning the methods of construction of these fascinating structures do not appear to exist, so that we can only conjecture the scope of the work involved. Many of the inland sites were deep in the countryside, difficult of access, with steep valley sides, often wooded, making the initial survey and preparation for construction extremely difficult. Mechanical aids were few, generally limited to simple steam operated cranes and hand winched jibs to lift and position the stonework of the piers. Unskilled manpower there was, of course, in plenty. The skilled timber men, granite cutters and trowel masons (to use the vernacular) were sometimes in short supply (see Chapter 2). They had, of necessity, to work in exposed and, judged by today's standards, unsafe locations; surprisingly, there is no evidence of extensive scaffolding being used. Indeed, photographs taken during the building of the piers for the replacement viaducts, dating from 1879, show personnel working on top of the piers, hoisted there with their materials by the several derrick cranes shown at site. Not until the building of the new viaducts on the Falmouth branch in the 1920s, do the relevant photographs show scaffolding around the piers; this change reflecting the greater awareness of safety in the twentieth century.

Significantly, photographs taken at those locations where the existing piers were being raised to accommodate wrought iron girders, do not show any scaffolding either. Margary, in his report, comments on materials being lowered to the men working below, but makes no mention of their protection or safety. On the basis of this evidence, which presumably perpetuated earlier custom and practice, it could be assumed that Brunel's piers were built in the same way, despite the inherent difficulties and dangers involved in this method. That said, we can but marvel at the general quality of workmanship which was achieved: examples are a uniform batter, neatly trimmed corners and well pointed stonework, with a perfect match between adjacent piers.

Each site would have employed a labour force probably in excess of 150 men to cover all the constructional trades required. Wherever possible, stone for the piers was taken from local quarries — the remains of several can still be seen alongside the route — but transport of the substantially sized blocks must have posed difficulties, particularly in the wet Cornish winters. Then during the dry summers, water supplies for the steam cranes could often have been a problem. Inevitably, the billeting and feeding of such a large labour force, often with their families, usually over periods of two or more years, strained local resources of food and accommodation. In the face of all these difficulties, it speaks highly of the skill and determination of the contractors and their men, firstly to prepare the foundations, then to build the masonry piers, many of them standing to this day, despite criticism during their lifetime regarding the quality of some of the workmanship. In this respect, for instance, the difference between the stonework of the piers at St Austell and Moorswater should be noted from their respective illustrations. Then the timber superstructure had to be prepared and erected. This work involved the accurate cutting and shaping of the legs to fit the cast iron seatings, the preparation of the horizontal carrying beams and their associated fittings, the fabrication of the laminated construction, whilst at the same time making due allowance for any curvature of the viaduct. These various members were then lifted into position, with the legs being set up and fixed, the decking and ballast boards added and the handrailing

46. A distant view of Weston Mill Lake, taken from the south east c1860, showing the bridge carrying the road from St Budeaux in the foreground, behind which can be seen the 1,200ft length of Brunel's timber railway viaduct. Today the greater part of this area has been infilled, but from this photograph, it is possible to appreciate the vast area of mud exposed at low water, across which Brunel had to construct this viaduct. *Devon CRO*

secured. Finally, the cill timbers were packed and grouted to secure the bottom leg seatings, and thus set the level of the timber decking, prior to receiving the ballast and permanent way.

According to J P Elms[1], it had been estimated that the content of all the timber in the structures of the Cornwall Railway as first designed, was in excess of 800,000ft^3, exclusive of the deep piling in the tidal creeks. The analysis detailed in Appendix 3, which is based on the author's estimates of the net timber contents, closely accords with this figure, although the estimate for the timber content of Moorswater appears to be on the low side compared with Elm's quoted figure for this viaduct. The content for the West Cornwall line probably amounted to a further 145,600ft^3. Thus over the period between 1850 and 1863, a total in excess of 950,000ft^3 of 'yellow pine' was imported into Cornwall, probably through the ports of Penzance, Par and Fowey. It then had to be cut and prepared, before being further transported to the various viaduct sites. This would have been by road to the inland locations, and by water to the several quays that were prepared adjacent to the sites of the tidal viaducts. These operations were only the start since after the first few years, following the opening of the lines, there was an ongoing maintenance programme. This required a steady supply of replacement material, including the provision of the additional shores, which from experience, had been proved to be necessary on some of the inland structures. Based on the eventual annual maintenance cost of £8–£10,000, this would probably have required timber supplies of around 30,000ft^3 per annum.

The absence (in the case of the majority of the viaducts) of masonry abutments would have allowed settlement of many of the high embankments; this factor which Brunel referred to in one of his reports, would have added to the problem of maintaining true levels. As previously described, in such instances, the landward span was seated on a timber platform set on the embankment while often the landward fan, instead of being carried on a masonry pier, was itself seated on a timber sub structure which incorporated timber wedges to give the final adjustment of levels.

Notwithstanding previous comments, the situation of different teams working on different viaducts, over a considerable period of time, inevitably brought about differences in the quality of the final structures. This factor needs to be taken into account when considering the subsequent pattern of replacement. There is evidence, both from copy reports in the Public Record Office, contemporary newspaper reporting and circumstantial comment to suggest that the piers of the viaducts at Moorswater, Bolitho and Cartuther were not built to the same standard as some of those on the Truro to St Austell section. Furthermore, from the evidence of the Arbitration Hearing[2], it would appear that the line of the viaducts at Largin, Coombe St Stephens and Fal was set out without due regard to the affect of curvature on their strength in service. While the ultimate responsibility for these shortcomings must have rested with Brunel, he would have relied upon his site engineers to ensure that the workmanship and route were satisfactory. It is to be regretted that, occasionally, they did not apply the same care and attention to detail which characterised Brunel's own site work, as given in a contemporary report by Conder of this aspect of his activities. He was renowned for his scrupulous attention to detail in approving work completed and acceptable for payment, often keeping retentions beyond the terms of contract.

The problems besetting the erection of the tidal viaducts were no less; Fig.46, which is a distant view of the structure at Weston Mill, gives some idea of the environment in which their construction was carried out. In the face of the twice daily incursion of the tide, clusters of piles had to be driven into the soft mud of the tidal creeks for the many trestles which formed the basic supports of these structures. Supplies and personnel had to be transported to remote locations and the remains of the several quays alongside the estuary indicate that water transport was often used. Once delivered, the timberwork had to be cut and formed for the trussed beams, with their final building and installation at site. It is a matter of conjecture as to whether the massive composite timber frameworks for the spans of the St Germans viaduct were built complete on the shore, and then floated out and hoisted into position, or whether they were erected piecemeal on the trestle supports. Sadly, no records of what must have been a challenging operation, have come to light. Doubtless, the building of the Saltash bridge drew all the attention, and these lesser operations on the timber viaducts, significant as they were, went unnoticed.

All these factors presented an ongoing challenge to the many contractors involved in the building of the railway through Cornwall. Because of the scope of work involved, Brunel and his assistants had to maintain a close and rigorous inspection at all times. This was particularly so insofar as the measurement against contract was concerned, and to counter the practice, detailed in his letter[3] of 7th June 1855, to W H Bond, Secretary of the Company, in which he complained of contractors being paid calls over and above his recommendations.

Turning now to the testing of the viaducts, as noted in Chapter 2, Captain K M Laffens carried out an inspection of the Penzance to Camborne section of the West Cornwall Railway on 8th and 9th of March 1852 and issued his Report[4] on 10th March. While this does not include details of any testing of the viaducts, a contemporary newspaper account[5] relates how:

> '...the Penpons [sic] viaduct was subjected to the severe test of having a train weighing about 130 tons passed over it, being about three times as much [sic] as will be required under the ordinary traffic'.

He commented on the six viaducts involved to the effect that he believed 'these structures to be sufficiently strong'. Later in the same year, Captain G Wynne inspected the Redruth to Truro section and in his Report[6] dated 18th August made no mention at all of the three viaducts on that line. Accordingly, the above is the only record we have of what may have been considered an acceptable level of loading for the West Cornwall structures.

However, on the completion the Cornwall Railway it was subjected to a much more rigorous inspection by Col. Yolland, which he carried out over the period 18th to 20th April 1859. His report to the BoT[7], among the many other relevant matters, commented that good foundations had been found for the masonry piers, while:

> '...the timber piers have the legs on good piles driven down to the rock or to good foundations, extending in one case (Weston Mill) through to a depth of 74ft of mud to the rock'.

He tested the viaducts 'with a load averaging about one ton per foot lineal' and reported that the greatest deflection observed was in the middle of a 65ft [sic] opening at St Germans, where it amounted to 0.6in. As this viaduct was the last to have been constructed it had scarcely had time to be thoroughly consolidated which could account for this figure. In no other instance did he record a deflection exceeding 0.4in and in general they did not exceed ¼in. In the light of the contemporary 'state of the art', this level of deflection would appear to be very satisfactory.

He went on to say:

> 'The viaducts are however very large structures, containing very large quantities of timber, and they will require to be carefully looked after especially with reference to the subsidence of the platforms, the state of the foundations and possibly, as regards the higher viaducts, the effect of the passage of heavy trains on the tall piers and as a very large proportion of these viaducts are curved, and in some cases 'S' curves occur on them, great attention will have to be paid to the packing of the longitudinal sleepers and the maintenance of the proper Cant on the outer side of the curves'.

These comments are indeed prescient in the light of the problems which were to manifest themselves in later years. We can but wonder whether they would have been couched in such cautious terms had the designer not been Brunel. They should certainly be borne in mind when reading the later chapter on the Arbitration Hearing, and in particular, Col. Yolland's remarks to Counsel.

With the lines completed and open for traffic, there followed over the years a steady annual increase in the amount of maintenance called for on all the viaducts. According to the reports given at the Arbitration Hearing, the level was not significant during the early years. However, with the passage of time, the viaducts demanded more attention, with the annual cost steadily increasing, until it reached the generally quoted level of £10,000 per

47. The plates of viaduct No 16, Moorswater, and No 22, Derrycombe. They were large items, their number being clearly visible at some distance. ***Dane Garrod Collection***

48. A 1989 view of the western end of Liskeard viaduct, showing the bridge number identification plate on the down side. Originally, each viaduct had such a cast iron plate fixed at both ends but now most have disappeared. ***Author***

annum. This gave rise to concern, not only in its financial implication, but also in the resultant affect on the intrinsic safety of some of the structures — a problem which will be considered in more detail in a later chapter.

As noted in Chapter 1, at sometime the viaducts were all numbered sequentially from Plymouth westwards and each structure carried a large cast iron number plate set up at each end. Typical examples are shown in Fig.47 but with time they have disappeared from most of the viaduct locations. However, Liskeard still retains its cast iron plate, No 15, at its western end (Fig.48).

Some idea of the extent of the labour force subsequently involved in the routine maintenance and repair of these original timber viaducts, may be assessed from the fact that, before it became necessary to replace them, an Inspector and 54 men in nine gangs[8] were continuously employed in their inspection and replacement of defective members. Working at heights frequently in excess of 100ft above ground level, with the minimum of safety precautions, since they were often suspended at the end of a manila rope, the older hands became expert in their work. As a matter of routine they swung themselves sideways from one location to another, remaining there until a particular task had been completed. Accidents were rare and the teams enjoyed an exemplary record for safety, having regard to the dangerous nature of their work.

Renewal of legs and beams could only be carried out between booked trains, on a Sunday, with occupation of the line[9]. Preparatory work involved removal of all the ballast and placing the permanent way on packing and wedges, a 10mph speed limit being imposed across the structure. The replacement timber had been earlier marked out accurately for bolt holes, grooves etc and cut to length; ends tapered, notches for the bracings cut and holes bored so as to make, as closely as possible, an exact replica of the original.

When replacing a leg it was necessary to lift the carrying beams and decking directly over the work, so that the leg could clear the top casting. For this purpose a service girder, about 16ft long, was used which was sufficiently long to span the width of the structure involved; to this was attached iron stirrups made from 3in × $\frac{3}{4}$in material which was placed around the beams. The lifting gear consisted of two square cut, threaded bolts, $2\frac{1}{2}$in diameter attached to each end of the girder and worked by a ratchet spanner. Before lifting, the casting at the top of the leg was dog spiked to the carrying beam, to prevent it coming away with the old leg.

Meanwhile, men had first been lowered in bowlines from the top of the viaduct, and remained slung until they had unbolted and freed the cross bracings, thus releasing the old leg ready for removal. Having lifted the beam, they were then able to withdraw it from its seatings and, by means of rope and tackle and a hand winch, lower it to the ground under the viaduct. The replacement leg was then lowered into its place, assisted by a bridgeman standing on top of the pier. The ends were shaped and fitted by saw, adze and axe[10] and the new strut finally fixed in position and the cross bracings attached; the structure then being restored to normal use.

The renewal of the beams was a longer and more difficult task, but even this actual replacement could be carried out in two hours. The same attention to the accurate preparation of the new member was, of course, carried out during the days preceding the changeover. In this case the permanent way was removed and the deck timbers drawn back clear of the beam being dealt with; the timbers positioned by parbuckling, the ropes being passed from one parapet to the other. Renewal of parapets, decking, diagonal and cross bracings, together with the wrought iron tie rods were generally carried out on week-days.

Each piece of timber which was replaced was identified with the date and year of replacement and these identifications can be seen in several of the accompanying illustrations.

In their early life an annual inspection of each viaduct sufficed, but after the 1914–18 War, with the deterioration in the quality of available timber, examinations were increased to four times per year[11]. Inevitably, in the face of increasing traffic loads and ever rising cost of labour, action was taken in the early 1920s to start to phase out the remaining timber viaducts on the Falmouth branch, either by means of embankments or by building replacement masonry structures.

A concluding comment relevant to this chapter concerns the fire risk which attended these timber viaducts. According to the GWR site plans at Pascoe and Ponsanooth, water storage tanks were located at each end of the structures which provided a ready source of water in case of fire. This arrangement presumably perpetuated the practice which had hitherto existed at the mainline sites. The only record of a fire is that given by Margary in his report. to the Arbitration Hearing; he could not remember the viaduct concerned but the event was 'vividly impressed' upon his memory. However, the fire was not a large one; it had been 'discovered by a farm labourer and put out'.

Chapter 8
THE VIADUCTS AND THEIR INDIVIDUAL HISTORIES

HAVING EXAMINED THE DIFFERENT types of structure which Brunel built to carry his railway down through Cornwall, we are now in a position to investigate each viaduct, establish its classification and review its individual history. Their location is quoted in miles/chains measured from Paddington via Bristol and Millbay, together with details of their identification number and principal dimensions. These are also listed in the Table in Chapter 1 which has been compiled from the details recorded by MacDermot. However, in certain instances these vary from measurements given by Margary, or in various drawings or as checked at site. These inconsistencies are noted in the text. The viaduct Classification according to the analyses developed in Chapter 5, is also given, together with a note of the illustrations which refer, and where possible, a reference to the average annual cost of maintenance, as established in Appendix 3. Regrettably, records are not available for all the viaducts.

Although not in Cornwall, the three viaducts between Plymouth, Millbay and the Royal Albert Bridge, at Saltash, formed an essential link in the Cornwall Railway and their construction and replacement provide a fascinating start to our story.

The Plymouth Viaducts

At the time of Brunel's original survey, the countryside between Millbay and Saltash was vastly different from today's sprawling urban development. At high water, the sea extended through Stonehouse Pool inland to the Mill Bridge, above which was Stonehouse Mill Pond. The Cornwall Railway immediately on branching from the South Devon Railway at Cornwall Junction, crossed this inlet by means of the only double broad gauge timber viaduct constructed for the Cornwall Railway. After passing through Devonport, and its tunnel, a further tidal inlet, Keyham Creek, had to be crossed. In the intervening years, both of these waterways have been infilled and developed, but the viaducts, or rather, their successors remain.

Finally, Weston Mill Lake, or Camel's Head, an extensive area of water at high tide, presented yet another barrier which has since been greatly changed. The railway still crosses the area on a viaduct, but by a structure vastly different from the thirty span and almost quarter mile long timber creation of Brunel. The extent of all these changes will be apparent from the map (Fig.49) which shows the area in the late 1860s, while Fig.46, a view of Westonmill Lake, taken probably later in that decade, shows the timber road bridge in the foreground and Brunel's timber railway viaduct in the background.

Even as early as 1880, Margary was concerned to initiate the right steps in his viaduct rebuilding programme, having regard to the longer term phasing out of the broad gauge. One of his reports[1] points out that as the viaducts between Devonport and St Germans were, for the most part, built on piles each comprised of four baulks of timber below ground line and two above, with the depth of piling ranging from 20ft to 70ft, he did not foresee the line between these two locations being doubled for some considerable time. He therefore proposed that the viaducts as far as and including St Germans, should be rebuilt to accommodate a single line of broad gauge track while those beyond St Germans should be rebuilt to take a double line of rails, narrow gauge. Sadly, it was to be a further 28 years before his vision to replace all the timber viaducts between Plymouth and Truro was realised.

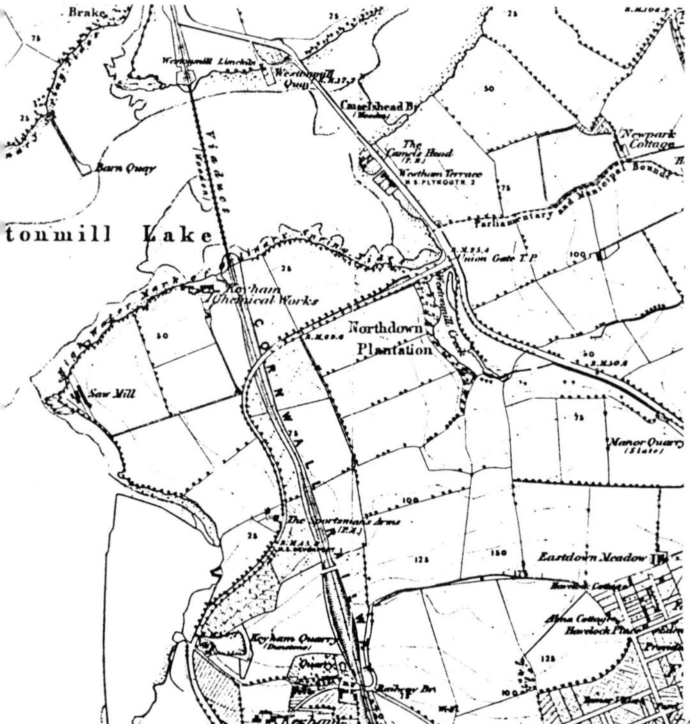
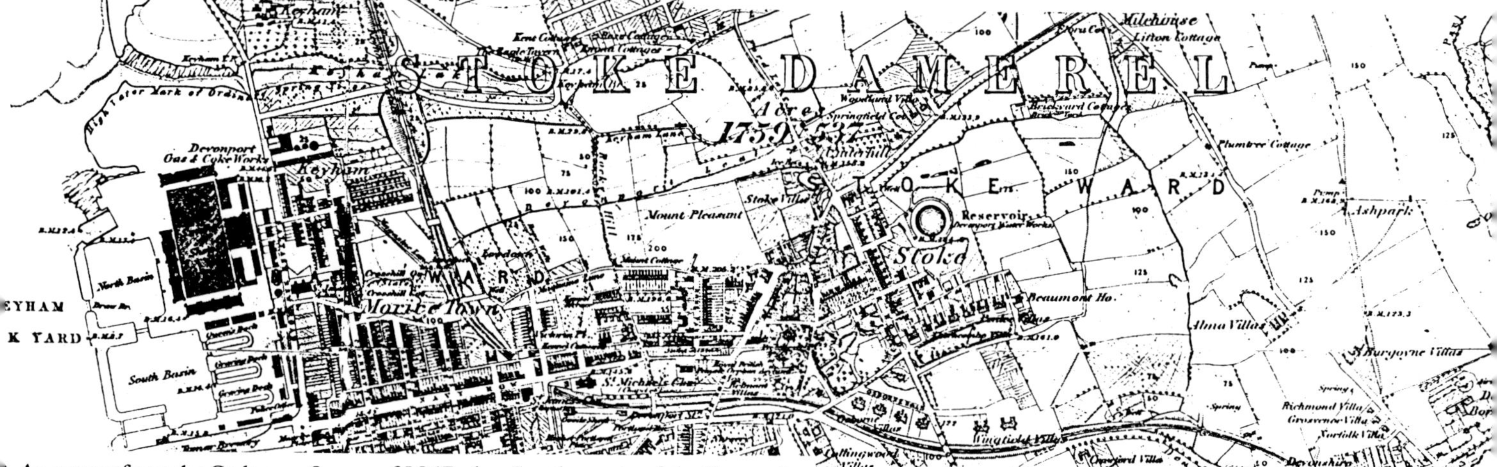

. An extract from the Ordnance Survey of 1867, showing the route of the Cornwall
ilway from Cornwall Junction, across Stonehouse Mill Pond, over Keyham Creek
d thence across Weston Mill Lake. The rural nature of the area will be very apparent,
mpared with today's urban sprawl, and in particular, how the fingers of the sea
iginally crept so far inland, requiring the construction of viaducts at these locations.
produced from the 1860 Ordnance Survey Maps courtesy of Devon CRO

50. A close up view of the supporting timberwork on the double track viaduct at Stonehouse Pool, showing the five sets of fans springing from each shallow pier, together with the wrought iron tie rods which stretched from fan to fan. The intricacy of the structure, with the horizontal walings and diagonal bracing, emphasise the magnitude of the task facing the maintenance teams over the years, in keeping the structure in good order. And remember, on this viaduct the piers stood but 5 or 6ft high, thus a relatively simple task compared with working at heights of over 100ft at St Pinnock, Liskeard and Moorswater. *Devon CRO*

1. Stonehouse Pool — Margary Class A — Figs.12, 50 and 51 Location 247/31 — Length 321ft — Maximum height 57ft

As already mentioned, this was built to take a double line of rails, broad gauge, and really comprised two Class A2 structures in parallel, set on shallow masonry piers, to provide a width between parapets, according to Crispin[2], of 27ft 1in. In place of the normal three sets of fans seated on each pier, there were five sets, each of four raking legs, erected at 7ft centres. The viaduct was built on a curve, and Margary reported that the piers were at 63ft centres, constructed of sound limestone, on a rock foundation. He quoted a length of 336ft and height of 56ft.

Figure 12 is a view taken during the early 1900s, with a steam rail motor and trailer crossing the structure; Victoria Park would appear to be under construction The close up view in Fig.50 does not indicate any additional shoring while, the fact that this was the last timber viaduct on the original main line from Millbay to be reconstructed (in 1908), would seem to indicate that the increased width gave added lateral strength to the whole structure.

From the details of Appendices 2 & 3, it will be seen that repairs over the period 1860 to 1882 amounted to £2,688, giving an average of just over £7 per 1,000ft^3 pa. This figure compares favourably with the values for the other viaducts between Plymouth and Truro. Margary recommended that 'to renew the present structure, the thickness of the piers be increased and arches turned; by closing one line of rails half the width of the arches could be built at a time.' However, no action was taken on this recommendation and he later reported[3] that the legs and beams were in good condition but that a number of the detail pieces of the parapets, including some planking, would need replacing at the next time of repair. However, it seems that the Joint Committee was prepared to allow this structure to remain in service, since it was not until 1908 that a replacement viaduct was brought into use.

Margary's original recommendation was not followed as, in the event, brick extensions were erected almost to rail height, on the original masonry stub piers, with slots to accommodate the three sets of inside timber legs, while intermediate brick piers were built at the mid points of the original spans. These new brick structures were to carry lattice steel girders as the replacement superstructure. The timber legs were then removed but the slots remain to this day, the original masonry piers being easily distinguished from the later intermediate additions, as will be seen from Fig.51.

The original route across this viaduct, from Plymouth Millbay to Cornwall, was closed on 16th January 1964, the mainline then running direct from Plymouth North Road. The tracks were removed by the following June, except for the retention of a short siding for the demolition of the superstructure. This completed, all that now remains of this unique structure are the red brick piers, visible on the downside when leaving Plymouth station en route to Cornwall.

51. A 1989 view of the remains of the piers at Stonehouse Pool. The pier in the foreground shows the original masonry plinth from which the radial legs of the fans sprang, while behind is one of the intermediate brick piers which were added when the structure was replaced, built up from ground level. It will be apparent that the new brickwork was built inside the line of the outside fans, with the inclusion of slots around the legs of the three inside fans, and taken up to the height necessary to support the wrought iron girders which replaced the timber superstructure. *Author*

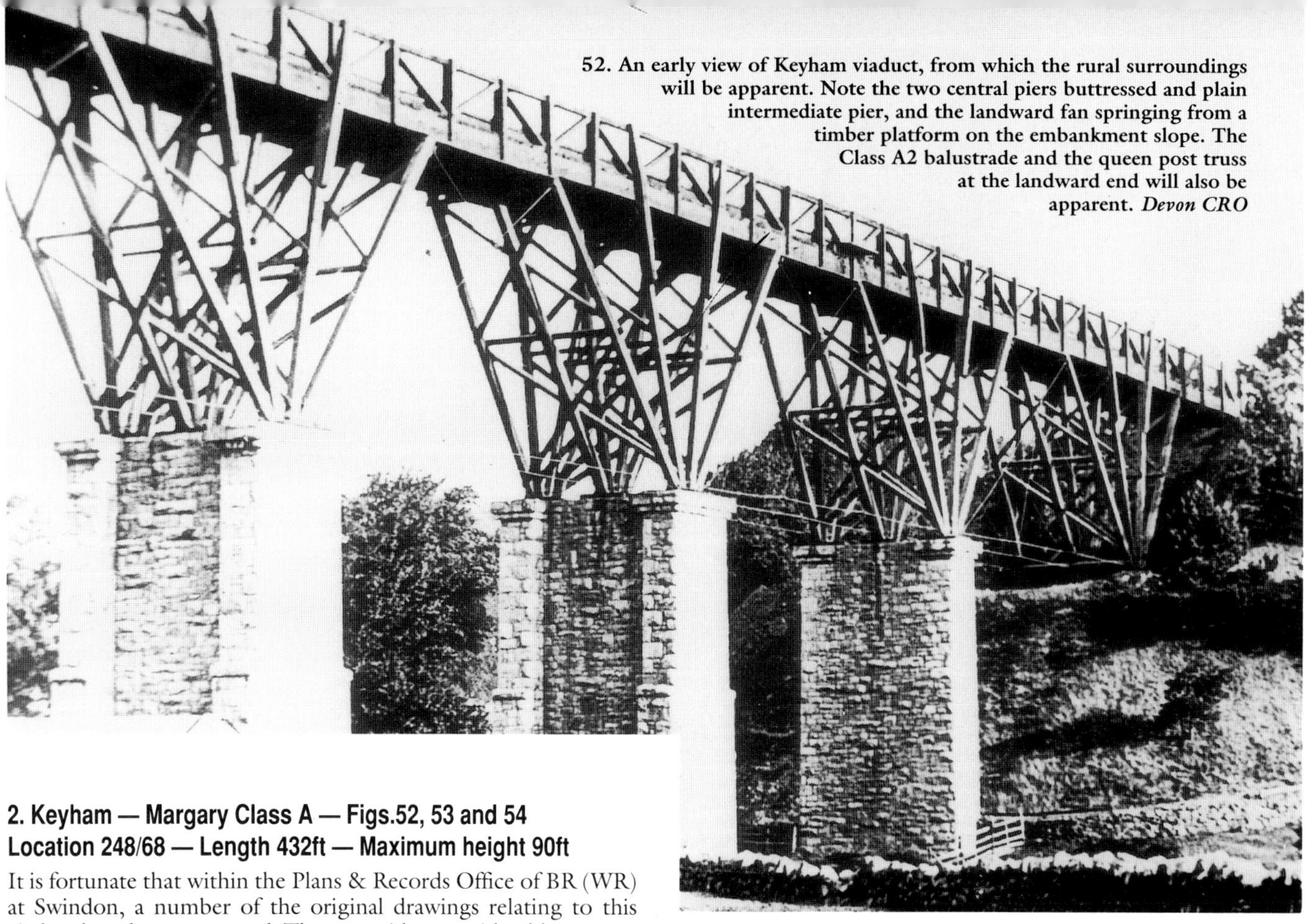

52. An early view of Keyham viaduct, from which the rural surroundings will be apparent. Note the two central piers buttressed and plain intermediate pier, and the landward fan springing from a timber platform on the embankment slope. The Class A2 balustrade and the queen post truss at the landward end will also be apparent. ***Devon CRO***

2. Keyham — Margary Class A — Figs.52, 53 and 54
Location 248/68 — Length 432ft — Maximum height 90ft

It is fortunate that within the Plans & Records Office of BR (WR) at Swindon, a number of the original drawings relating to this viaduct have been preserved. These provide a considerable amount of data regarding its details of construction, as well as information in general of the fan type designs. Among those drawings, is one showing an A1 Class superstructure supported on timber trestles (Fig.33) similar to those of the original Class Y viaducts in West Cornwall. MacDermot refers to Keyham viaduct as being of all timber construction, owing to the depth of mud in the creek, although there does not appear to be any supporting evidence to suggest that it was built with timber trestles. Other drawings and photographs show quite clearly that it was of Class A2 design, carried on the usual masonry piers, as confirmed in Margary's report that the piers 'seem to be of good lime stone masonry'. He recorded its length as 420ft and height 88ft.

The available drawings also indicate that the fans at both landward ends, instead of springing from masonry plinths set in the embankments, were supported from timber platforms (Fig.38) seated on the embankment slopes, as indicated in the illustration of Fig.52. Judging by the surroundings, this photograph was taken fairly early in its life, and also shows that the landward spans incorporated a queen post truss in the parapet (Fig.43) which rested on a timber platform on top of the embankment. Both these arrangements enabled the levels of the structure at each end, to be adjusted by means of the timber wedge construction.

53. A 1898 view of rebuilding Keyham viaduct, for the substitution of wrought iron girders in place of the timber superstructure. The piers are in the process of being built up in brickwork from the top of the masonry plinths to a height suitable for the girders which will be located outside the timber beams. It will be seen how slots have been left in the brickwork around the timber legs, to be infilled once they are removed; that the tie rods attaching to the outside fans have been removed and how all this work has apparently been carried out without any scaffolding around the piers, since the brickwork is only part completed. The cantilevered track along which trolleys carried the materials to be supplied to the pier locations is also clearly shown. ***L G Booth Collection***

Over the period to 1882, the maintenance cost totalled £2,242 to give an average of £7.37/1,000ft³/pa. In 1880 Margary suggested for the viaduct replacement 'that the present piers be raised, and wrought iron girders be erected upon them to carry the decking.' Again, in 1887, he advised that several beams, legs, planks and braces required renewal and that the viaduct was then under repair. However, it was to be a further twelve years before action was taken to replace the timber superstructure, with main outside girders, cross girders, rail bearers and pressed trough decking all in steel — estimated to weigh a total of 380 tons.[4] It was to be rebuilt suitable for double track, standard gauge. This involved building up the piers above their original cill height to the level necessary to accept this steelwork, together with the addition of new piers on the embankment slopes.

The preparatory work involved in this reconstruction may be understood from the state of the viaduct shown in Fig.53, probably taken in 1897, where the piers have been partly built up in brickwork around the raking legs, in preparation to receive the outer girders. It is interesting to note that there is no evidence of any scaffolding in use during the raising of these piers. Once the new girders were in place, with the associated decking, the timber legs would be withdrawn and the slots infilled. Close examination of the piers as shown in Fig.54, a photograph taken in 1989, reveals the evidence of this infilling. Gibbons[5] reported that it was necessary to widen some of the piers from their foundations, particularly as two were originally built of the simple slab type construction.

It should be noted that a further strengthening of this viaduct took place in 1937 when the 1899 steelwork was replaced by heavier construction, still carried on the original Brunel piers, but with extra brickwork added to some, and evidence of these additions will also be clearly seen in the illustrations.

54. A 1989 view of Keyham, from the south west, which clearly shows the brickwork additions to the original Brunel piers and the infilling from where the radial legs were removed. The landward pier was, of course, built on the site of the timber platform which formed the base for the original timber fan, while the adjacent pier started life as one of the plain, slab type but has had brickwork buttresses added. ***Author***

3. Weston Mill (or Camel's Head) — Margary Class C — Figs.46, 55, 56, 57 and 58
Location 249/45 — Length 1,200ft — Maximum height 46ft

Faced with the crossing of the extensive Weston Mill Lake, Brunel resorted to the all timber construction of a Class C viaduct, in this case supported on 29 trestles, of which three were carried on masonry plinths at the Penzance end, and the remainder on clusters of timber piles; these supports being similar to those shown in Fig.19. Margary quoted the length as 1,188ft. From Keyham, the line dropped on a gradient of 1 in 61 to cross this viaduct on the level, before climbing away on a similar incline to reach the Royal Albert Bridge.

Although this structure continued in service until 1903, and carried the growing level of traffic, it proved to be one of the more expensive viaducts to maintain in service — costing over £6,180 during the period 1860 to 1882. However, with in excess of 37,000ft³ of timber within its overall structure, including trestles, due to its length (it was the second longest on the line), the average maintenance cost, related to timber content, compared favourably with other viaducts, at £7.56/1,000ft³ pa. An appreciation of its length will be apparent from the view of Weston Mill Lake (Fig.46) with Brunel's railway viaduct in the background. Figure 55 is an 1895 view, with the LSWR bridge and embankment in the background, together with the bridge carrying the road from St Budeaux, while Fig.56 is a close-up view, showing the details of construction.

In his 1880 report Margary commented:

> 'It may be assumed from general knowledge of similar cases, that the piles below the surface of the mud are, and will remain sound for many years; but the timbers above will shortly come in for extensive renewals'.

55. A close up view of the timber trestles and trussed beams of the Class C viaduct at Weston Mill, taken in 1895, illustrating the expanse of water which existed at high tide at that time, before the site was infilled. In the middle background is the bridge carrying the road from St Budeaux, and behind it, the bow string girder bridge and embankment of the LSWR line into Devonport. ***L G Booth Collection***

56. A close-up view of one of the spans of Weston Mill, showing the details of construction. Note the straining pieces seated in their end castings, the vertical through bolts, the heavy deck timbers and the shaped coffin pieces linking the legs and top parapet rail. ***From the Clinker Collection, Brunel University Library***

In this respect, mud tended to act as a preservative and not cause rotting as may be commonly perceived, since the colder nature of their environment and the lack of oxygen combined to give longer life.

He went on to suggest in renewing the structure, that cast iron columns should be fixed upon the existing quadruple piles at a few feet below the level of the mud, and extending to about two feet above high water line. On these piles he proposed to construct piers of wrought iron, to carry wrought iron plate or lattice girders to support the decking, which would be in either iron or timber, of sufficient width for a single line of rails, broad gauge. However, no action was taken with regard to his suggestions since by 1887 nearly all the main tie beams had been renewed. By the latter date, he further reported on 'a great many of the strut and heel pieces of queen trusses, as well as planks that will require to be renewed before very long'.

57. The replacement Weston Mill viaduct viewed from the south west, taken in 1903, with Brunel's original structure in the background. This clearly shows how the level of the line was raised for the new alignment, to eliminate the 1 in 60 gradients which originally existed on either side of this location; it also dramatically illustrates the difference in proportions between the two designs and we can but marvel that Brunel's remained in service as long as it did . ***From the Clinker Collection, Brunel University Library***

58. A distant view towards Truro of the main line crossing the replacement Weston Mill viaduct, taken in 1989, which shows its four span steel girder construction and masonry approaches. On the right, at lower level, is the alignment of the original single track broad gauge route, while the line coming in from the left is the branch from Keyham Dockyard, opened in 1867; mixed gauge track was laid in for a distance of 10 chains beyond this junction so as to allow LSWR traffic to work into the Dockyard from North Road after 1878. ***Author***

Despite the obvious problems with this structure and ongoing repair cost, it was not until 1899 that work commenced on building a replacement. This project was let to J. Charles Lang, a Contractor of Liskeard, the plans being signed by G.L. Gibson, Resident Engineer, and by G. Inglis. They proposed a structure quite peculiar to the line, comprising four sets of steel bowstring girders, sitting on round caisson piers in mid span with elaborate masonry abutments at the ends, each incorporating three arched openings in brick. This new structure was sited just to the west of the original, and the opportunity was taken to raise the track level, as will be apparent from Fig.57, a photograph of the completed structure, taken in 1903. Brunel's original timber viaduct is visible in the background, modest in comparison with its substantial steel and brickwork replacement, its track level appearing to be some 15ft lower than that of its successor.

The illustration in Fig.58 shows that, today, apart from signs of the old alignment at either end and two stub masonry piers at its northern end, no trace remains of the original crossing. Furthermore, as Westonmill Lake has now been substantially infilled, with the creek culverted, it is difficult to appreciate the scenes depicted in the earlier photographs. It should be noted that by 1878 mixed gauge track had been laid from North Road to the throat of the viaduct so as to allow LSWR traffic to work to Keyham Junction, which was just short of the viaduct, and so into Devonport Dockyard.

Saltash to St Germans

4. Coombe by Saltash — Margary Class D — Figs.59, 60 and 61 Location 251/38 — Length 603ft — Maximum height 86ft

On leaving the Royal Albert Bridge at Saltash, the line curved through Saltash station and, continuing to curve, crossed Coombe Lake, a tidal inlet from the Hamoaze. Owing to the extensive depth of mud, Brunel was forced to use wooden piles for the pier foundations and therefore, constructed the viaduct on substantial timber trestles for the mid stream supports. They were in fact much heavier than the trestles used on the Class C design, which because of the curvature involved, would not have been a satisfactory design for this particular location.

Accordingly, the structure, completed in 1859 as part of the St Germans Contract, was built on 9 piers spaced at 64ft 6in centres — the two landward ones at each end being masonry and the remainder piled timber trestles, to support the Class D superstructure. From an original drawing[6], we know that the overall length was 609ft, as recorded by Margary, while each trestle was comprised of four raking legs, with each leg constructed from four 12in × 12in timbers, scarfed and bolted together. They were joined by horizontal walings spaced about 18ft apart, together with diagonal bracings; all from 9in × 7in timbers. The tops of the legs at the side of each trestle fitted into pairs of cast iron shoes, which incorporated the seatings for the five 12in × 8in cross timbers in Memel or American Red Pine that formed the cill.

A second pair of castings fitted on the cill timbers at the sides of each trestle, bolted back to back, provided the seatings for the two sets of four massive raking legs of the Class D superstructure. The feet of the raking legs on each trestle were linked by four $1\frac{1}{4}$in dia wrought iron cross ties while pairs of $1\frac{1}{8}$in dia diagonal ties linked adjacent fans. An appreciation of this overall construction can be obtained from Fig.59, a view dating from 1898, with the replacement masonry structure alongside in the background.

Being built on a curve, with the track inclination towards Penzance, inevitably, problems were experienced in service as it will be seen from the photograph in Fig.60, taken at the time the replacement masonry viaduct was under construction. Additional shoring by means of a series of diagonal transverse timbers, had been inserted between the cill of the outer radius of each fan and the underside of the opposite horizontal beam on the inner radius of the curve. In addition, a raking member had been incorporated in each trestle, which was not shown on the original contract drawing.

Over the period 1860 to 1882 repairs had cost £4,868, which based on a total timber content of the superstructure and trestles of nearly 29,000ft^2, gave an average annual cost of £7.65 per 1,000ft^3, which was in line with that of other structures. However, in the several reports prepared by Margary over the years 1880 to 1887 dealing with the viaducts as a whole, Coombe by Saltash received particular and repeated mention, so that undoubtedly it was subject to ongoing problems. Although built on a curve, trains would not be crossing at speed, since it was situated close to Saltash and the Royal Albert Bridge, where a speed limit applied. Furthermore, as it incorporated the higher timber content of the Class D design, it can only be concluded that the curvature imposed excessive lateral loads which the structure, as originally designed, could not accommodate. This situation would have prompted its replacement ahead of the other neighbouring tidal structures.

Margary in 1880 had recommended building a masonry viaduct as a replacement on the northern side. This would have allowed an improvement in the overall track alignment and, by extending the embankment at the western end, a shorter structure. However, no action was taken at that time since again in 1883 he was recommending that Coombe by Saltash, among others, should have precedence for replacement. There the matter

59. A general view of Coombe by Saltash, taken from the south east in 1898, some four years after the replacement masonry structure, seen in the background, had been opened. This clearly shows the five timber trestles supported on piles driven into the mud, together with the masonry pier at each end and the fan springing from the plinth in the embankment at the Truro end. This was the one tidal viaduct built with a Class D superstructure, doubtless because of its curvature, where the Class C construction of the other tidal structures would not have been suitable.
L G Booth Collection

60. A closer view of Coombe by Saltash, in which the additional shoring incorporated in the superstructure can be seen, together with the diagonal strutting added to the timber trestles, in order to combat the excessive lateral loading. ***British Rail***

appeared to rest until a further report in 1887 pointed out that parts of the superstructure renewed in 1873 and 1874 were showing evidence of decay, although he indicated that a further two years' delay in starting repairs could be accepted; provided by the end of that time a new viaduct had been built.

He went on to say that:

> '...should the present viaduct have to be maintained for a period of five years, then I consider that the renewal of the superstructure should be commenced in about a year from the present time, the cost of which I estimate at about £1,500. Referring to the other parts of the viaduct consisting of legs, tie beams and flooring I estimate the cost of maintenance for two years at about £100; for five years at about £700 in addition to the £1,500.'

Eventually, a replacement masonry viaduct was ordered by the Cornwall Railway, the contract being signed in 1889, after the GWR had taken over the line. It was built on the northern side of the original structure, and proved to be a costly project since the mud in the creek extended to a depth of some 45ft. Coffer dams were used in the building of the three central piers in order to reach rock foundations. The masonry used in its construction was Plymouth Limestone, from the quarries near Oreston, Devon, and it was the only viaduct in Cornwall to have been built with this particular stone. The completed structure is shown in Fig.61. Comprising seven arches, each of span 70ft, the single main line was diverted over it on 19 October 1894, while an up refuge siding was laid across in 1895, the main line being doubled to Wearde in 1906.

61. A view of the new Coombe by Saltash viaduct, taken from the north west in 1989. It was the only one built of Plymouth Limestone, quarried from Oreston in Devon, and comprised seven arches, each of 70ft span, with the foundations of the three central piers extending to a depth of about 45ft in order to reach rock. ***Author***

62. St Anthony Passage at low tide, showing a south easterly view of Forder viaduct, a Class C Tidal structure built on 16 trestle piers. The navigable channel is in the foreground and the two trestles outside the picture to the right incorporated fenders as protection. In the background can be seen the cottages and sheds on the quay, where it is believed that the materials for its construction were landed. *B Ward Collection*

5. Forder — Margary Class C — Figs.19, 62, 63 and 141
Location 252/54 — Length 606ft — Maximum height 67ft

Having crossed the Tamar at Saltash, followed by Coombe Lake, Brunel then chose the route for the Cornwall Railway close alongside the shore of the St Germans or Lynher River, to cross Forder Lake at Anthony Passage by means of a Class C viaduct. It was carried on 16 trestle piers (Fig.19) while Fig.62 gives a general view of the viaduct at half-tide. Based on the standard Class C design, the length as recorded by Margary, was 696ft.

The picturesque setting of this crossing will be appreciated from Fig.63, a view taken from the south east, which gives an excellent impression of the frailty of the overall construction of this Class. Forder viaduct was similar to Weston Mill, particularly insofar as the piling and pier supports were concerned, and Margary's report of 1880 recommended rebuilding in a similar way. However, as a rider he did suggest that the permission of the Admiralty should be sought to lower the decking since the sudden changes of gradient at these viaducts frequently caused the breaking of drawbars. An 1887 report noted that the piles were in good condition as also were the main trussed beams. However, several corbels, crown pieces, heel pieces, hand rails and some planking would need renewing at the next repair.

Over the period 1860 to 1882, this viaduct had cost £3,839 in repairs, a total which compared favourably with the other tidal viaducts at £7.38/1,000ft^3. Nevertheless, it continued in service, carrying increased traffic and, following the conversion from broad gauge, the heavier 4-4-0 locomotives that were then able to work into Cornwall. Whatever may have been Margary's earlier thoughts on replacement no action was taken to implement them, and it was not until the opening of the new line deviating inland between Saltash and St Germans, completed in 1908, that this structure ceased to be on the main line to Penzance. Its replacement masonry viaduct at the head of St Anthony Passage is shown under construction in Fig.141. At the site today, little remains to show Brunel's original route where his broad gauge trains crossed this waterway, other than the remains of the abutment on the Plymouth shore.

63. A delightful view of Forder, this time from the hillside overlooking St Anthony Passage, taken in 1899, showing the picturesque setting of this viaduct crossing Forder Lake, an inlet off the main St Germans or Lynher River. The masonry abutment at the Plymouth end can be seen on the right, together with the two trestles protected by fenders referred to in Fig.62. Nine years later the main line to Truro was to be diverted along the hillside seen in the background and this timber structure then taken out of service.
L G Booth Collection

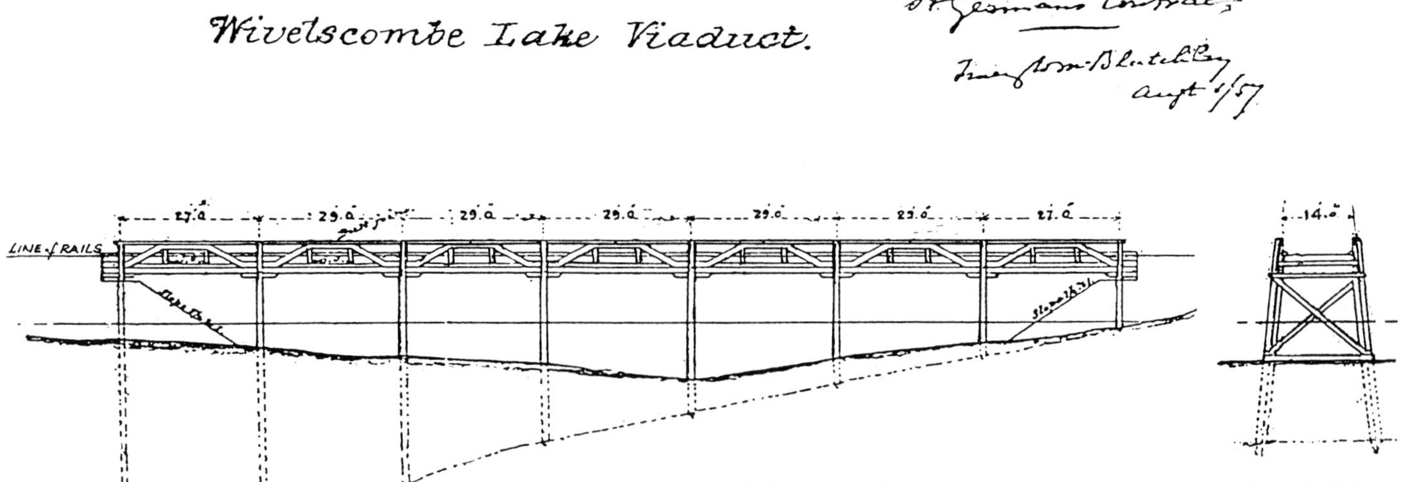

64. An extract of the original working drawing for Wivelscombe Lake Viaduct, dated 1857, showing a light Class C design comprising five spans of 29ft and two of 27ft, each formed from two trussed beams carried on simple piled legs. ***British Rail***

6. Wivelscombe — Margary Class C — Figs.64 and 65
Location 253/43 — Length 198ft — Maximum height 25ft

Although considered a tidal viaduct, this was a modest structure and differed in its main dimensions from others in its Class. According to a drawing[7] dated August 1857, of which Fig.64 is an extract, while following the Class C configuration, the spans were shorter and were to comprise two landward spans of 27ft and five intermediate spans each of 29ft, to make a total viaduct length of 199ft. A report[8] at the opening of the line confirmed this formation.

However, Fig.65 (taken in 1899) shows quite a different arrangement, comprising three Class C type spans presumably of 29ft each, a short timber span and a wrought iron girder span, giving an overall length of 129ft, as quoted by Margary.

Based on the original drawing, apart from the masonry one, the piers were formed from piles of two legs; each leg made up from two timbers 14in square, scarfed and bolted together, with a batter of 1/10. They incorporated the usual 9in × 7in walings and cross bracing to support the trussed beams of each of the three spans of the light Class C superstructure. There was a masonry abutment at the eastern end of the viaduct, where a pair of iron girders had replaced one of the timber spans at some stage in its history, the adjacent timber piles being superseded by the masonry pier. The date of this modification from the original drawing is not known, although in 1880 Margary refers to it as having been carried out 'some years ago'. At the western end, the structure terminated with a short timber span resting at its landward end on a timber framework, the embankment in general being graded to a slope of $1\frac{1}{2}$ to 1.

Margary recommended replacement of the timber bays by:

> '...erecting cast iron columns carrying braced struts of wrought iron in place of the present timber piles, with a superstructure of plate girders similar to those already fixed at the Eastern end of the viaduct'.

No action was taken in this respect. A later examination in January 1887 reported 'the timber piers are good; a couple of main beams and a few pieces of minor importance will soon require to be renewed.' In the event, apart from normal maintenance, this structure remained in mainline use until the deviation was introduced in 1908 and apparently carried the loads of the day without undue distress.

It is interesting to note, that the cost of repairs to this structure between 1860 and 1882 is quoted as £1,196, a figure which in relation to the total timber content gave an average annual maintenance charge of over £17 per 1,000ft³ — significantly higher than that of the other viaducts. This higher rate could have included the cost of replacing part of the timber work by the wrought iron span, as well as reflecting the modifying affect of the relatively small amount of timber in the viaduct on the way in which the average maintenance cost is calculated.

65. A photograph from the north of Wivelscombe Lake Viaduct, taken in 1899, after the modification to introduce a wrought iron span supported on a masonry pier and abutment had been incorporated, sometime before 1880. This would have shortened the structure to a length of 129ft. Again, access would have been extremely difficult by road and the materials were probably brought in by sea, although there does not appear to be the site of a quay immediately adjacent to the site. ***L G Booth Collection***

66. With a length of only 117ft, Grove was the shortest viaduct on the main line, built to cross yet another inlet from the St Germans or Lynher River. Although considered by many to be a tidal viaduct, it was built as a Class E structure, comprising three spans carried on two sets of fans. This illustration is the only photograph to come to light of the Class E design, but modified in this case from the original construction. The normal pairs of inclined legs, which sprang from shallow masonry plinths, were supplemented by the addition of an intermediate pair of legs in the form of an inverted vee, on the centreline of each plinth, which gave additional support to the centre horizontal carrying beam. This feature, together with a Class A2 balustrade doubtless contributed to it continuing in service until 1908. Note the trussed beam for each of the landward spans with additional shoring to support the centre carrying beam. *L G Booth Collection*

7. Grove — Margary Class E — Fig.66
Location 255/12 — Length 114ft — Maximum height 29ft

Strictly speaking, Grove was not a tidal viaduct in the context of our identification, since although it crossed a tidal inlet, it did not rest on timber piles. *The West Briton & Cornwall Advertiser* report of the opening of the Cornwall Railway describes it as 'resting on stone piers', while Margary considered it to be a Class E structure, of length 117ft and height 28ft. In effect, therefore, only the centre span and the two sets of raking legs which sprang from these shallow masonry plinths, conformed to the design of that class. Each of the landward spans comprised a queen post truss in the parapet, with their landward ends resting on the usual wedge type platform supports, seated on the top of the graded embankment slopes. At some stage in its history, an additional pair of legs was introduced to each plinth as an inverted vee to support the centre horizontal beam, while the normal Class E handrailing was strengthened by the addition of diagonal braces; these variations will be apparent from Fig.66. It is perhaps significant that this modification went some way towards incorporating the suggested strengthening of the Class E design discussed in Chapter 6 which in conjunction with its short length, probably contributed to it continuing in service until 1908. Even so, it will be noted from this illustration that additional shores had been inserted under the cross beams of both of the landward spans, to support the centre horizontal carrying beam, while an underslung cross beam had also been added to the centre Class E span.

Margary suggested that this viaduct should be replaced by means of a single 50ft span masonry arch, built on the north side of the line, with extensions of the embankment at either end. However, no action was taken on this recommendation and it was not finally taken out of service until the introduction of the 1908 deviation.

The structure gained notoriety very early in its history, as the location of the first accident on the Cornwall Railway. Within a few days of the opening, on 6th May, the 7.25pm down train from Plymouth, comprising the locomotive *Elk* with three carriages and a van, after descending the short 1 in 88 incline and reaching the level approach, was derailed 148ft short of the viaduct. Its momentum carried the engine onwards, to plunge off the structure and fall into the muddy creek finishing wheels uppermost, killing the driver Henry Biscombe, and fireman David Hannaford. The front coach was also derailed into the creek and the guard, William Hoskens, was killed. According to evidence given at the inquest[9] by the Cornwall Railway Engineer, Henry Bush, he estimated that the train was travelling at about 32 mph at the time it breached the parapet and fell into the creek. Close examination of the track approaching the scene of the accident did not reveal any apparent cause for the locomotive to be derailed, and the jury returned a verdict of 'Accidental Death'. The design and construction of the viaduct were in no way considered contributory to the accident.

Although the 1860–1882 maintenance cost was only a modest £633 having regard to its short length, this gave a significantly higher average annual cost, (£10.78/1,000ft^3) than that of the other Class E viaducts. It probably reflects the cost of the additional reinforcement which was incorporated during its life as well as a modifying factor, due to its small size, on the way the maintenance rate is calculated.

8. Nottar — Margary Class C — Figs.45, 67 and 144
Location 255/31 — Length 921ft — Maximum height 67ft

In general construction this viaduct was similar to those at Weston Mill and Forder, except that in crossing the River Lynher, the line was climbing towards St Germans and it was built on a slight curve. The superstructure was carried on 27 trestles, with their quadruple piles extending to a great depth in mud; those trestles adjacent to the navigable channel being protected by fenders. Based on this number of supports, the length of 1,134ft as reported by Margary was obviously the correct figure for this Class C structure.

According to his 1880 report, although only of a gradual nature, the curvature had introduced a tendency for trains to press the structure away from the centreline of the curve. This deflection was countered by the introduction of additional shoring, although details of their composition and form have not been traced. Indeed, Fig.45 taken in 1899, while an excellent illustration of the frailty of this design, shows no evidence of any additional shoring.

As a solution to the problem, he recommended replacement by construction similar to that of Weston Mill. Again, no action was taken, as by 1887 the viaduct was reported under repair with 'defective pieces being removed as discovered.' Over the period 1860 to 1882 the repair costs totalled £6,046. With a total timber content of nearly 39,000ft^3, the annual maintenance charge at £7.09/1,000ft^3 compared closely with the figures for those of the other Class C viaducts. Figure 67, believed taken soon after the opening of the line, is a view from close to the site of the quay used to bring in the materials of construction, illustrates its lonely and inaccessible location.

An interesting event concerning this viaduct was reported in the *Cornish Times* of 24th August 1872, relating to the problems sometimes associated with the replacement of the timbers. We must assume that, in this instance it was a timber not forming an integral part of one of the trussed beams, hence the action now reported. The viaduct was under repair and during the interval between the passage of trains of late afternoon, it was decided to take out:

> '...a large beam of wood and replace it with a new one, there being no other trains due for three hours. The beam was removed, and whilst the men were engaged in lifting the other to replace it, the gear gave way, the result being that the beam, as well as the gear, fell, carrying away the top braces, the falling mass of iron and wood being, however, stopped by the set of braces below. It was at once seen that this could not be repaired for sometime and a messenger was sent to St Germans to stop all traffic and to communicate with the officials at Plymouth.'

This soon brought a special train from Plymouth conveying Mr Margary, Engineer, with Mr Avery, Goods Manager, Mr Parr, Deputy Traffic Superintendent and a number of extra men to assist in carrying out emergency repairs. Meanwhile, the up mail was stopped at Liskeard and the 6.10pm down train from Plymouth ran as far as Saltash, before returning to Plymouth. It was not until late evening before the necessary repairs were completed and the line opened for traffic, 'the up mail train was at Liskeard detained for three hours and a quarter, and leaving there shortly before 10 o'clock passed over the viaduct quite safely, the beam having been properly replaced.'

Such were the trials of the viaduct repair gangs.

67. A view looking downstream of the Lynher River and out to the main estuary, with Nottar viaduct in the middle distance showing the fenders protecting the trestles on either side of the navigable channel. ***Courtesy Trustees, Science Museum***

Despite its fragile appearance, an accident on this viaduct in October 1891 demonstrated the inherent strength of the Class C design. An early morning up goods train should have stopped at St Germans, to allow a down luggage train to pass, but 'owing to the slippery state of the line' it dashed through the station and was only brought to a stand a mile beyond, on Nottar viaduct. Attempts to reverse the train back up the incline to St Germans met with no success, and the crew set off towards the oncoming down train to warn of the obstruction. Although that driver attempted an emergency stop, there was insufficient distance for this purpose and the locomotive crashed into the stationary goods engine on the viaduct. Fortunately, nobody was injured and, apart from damage to both locomotives and the derailment of a number of wagons, there was no major disturbance to the line. *The West Briton & Cornwall Advertiser* of 12th October 1891 commented:

> '...it is somewhat extraordinary that this viaduct, which has been condemned in connection with others on the line, should have withstood the great strain of a collision and that no serious accident followed'.

In spite of all the criticism over the years, this surely was a vindication of Brunel's original design.

Nottar was, of course, taken out of service with the opening of the inland deviation, which involved the construction of a fine new masonry viaduct to cross the River Lynher, located some 900 yards upstream from the original site, shown under construction in Fig.142. Figure 144 is a photograph taken during the demolition of Brunel's viaduct, which followed soon after the new route was brought into use. Today, little remains to mark the site of this original crossing except the earthworks of the old alignment.

9. St Germans — Figs.11A, 11B, 68, 69A and 69B — No Class Location 255/74 — Length 945ft — Maximum height 106ft

From a low level between Wivelscombe and Grove viaducts, the line climbed steadily to cross firstly, as we have seen, the Nottar viaduct, and then the River Tiddy, a tributary of the River Lynher, by means of this splendid 106ft high structure, which was unique in concept. It fell into none of the eight Classes which we have established, and was the last link to be completed in the construction of the railway between Plymouth and Truro. Because of its location, the materials of construction would have been delivered by water to the adjacent quay, where there was sufficient space for the component parts to be prepared and assembled before erection. As previously noted, we have no details of this work but having regard to the length of the longest spans (66ft) and the high tide twice each day, the trussed beams may well have been built up on the quayside and floated out on barges to their respective trestles, to be lifted into position by crane or sheer legs.

It is of interest to note that according to the 25 inch Ordnance Survey of 1857, a narrow gauge tramway existed at that time which extended from the quay to connect with the site of the proposed station at St Germans. It was probably used for the conveyance of materials from the quayside for the construction of the railway[10]; the extensive trackwork layout on the quay included an extension to an adjacent lime-kiln. There does not appear to be any other explanation for its existence, and by the date of the publication of the Second edition O.S. of 1908, the line had disappeared.

From the details shown in original drawings[11] the supports for the viaduct comprised timber trestles, framed at the corners by four raking legs, having a longitudinal batter of 1/12 and a transverse batter of 1/15. Each leg was formed from a cluster of four 12in square baulks, 35ft in length, scarfed and bolted together and linked by 9in × 7in walings notched 3in, with the addition of 7in × 12in diagonal bracing, half jointed. The general construction was similar to the trestles at Coombe by Saltash, the legs terminating at their upper ends in pairs of castings, shaped to suit the legs and accommodate the five 12in × 8in transverse cill timbers. The upper ends of the legs were bolted together through 12in × 7in filler pieces, incorporating four cast iron joggles, using pairs of $1\frac{1}{8}$in and $1\frac{1}{4}$in dia through bolts etc. This is the only application to come to light where cast iron joggles were used.

The trestles were spaced to provide, from the Truro side, seven spans of 66ft, then a further six of 64ft, with a 48ft span at each end. They rested on timber piles in the waterway, protected by fenders in the channel, and on masonry plinths built on the saltings above high water mark; those supports adjacent to the ends of the viaduct were buttressed masonry piers. A substantial masonry abutment was built into the hillside near St Germans station while at the Plymouth end, the embankment slope was graded $1\frac{1}{2}$ to 1, as at other locations, the landward span seating on a shallow masonry abutment set therein.

This close similarity to the supports of Coombe by Saltash, also in a tidal location, again poses the question as to why Brunel did not adopt the similar Class D construction for the superstructure of this viaduct. It would have been straight, a distinct advantage compared with Saltash, while the trestles could have been some 20ft lower in height. No evidence has come to light which would explain his decision to build a non standard design in place of two fans each of four raking legs springing from the top of each trestle, to support a trussed beam superstructure. Instead, he chose to incorporate for each span two massive trussed timber girders with wrought iron ties and bracings. And remember, it was unlikely that many calculations could have been involved in its design.

69A. A splendid view of St Germans, looking downstream at low water, taken in 1899. The all timber trestles carry the composite timber and wrought iron trussed beams for each span at a height of 106ft above low water, with the landward spans being supported by masonry piers. Although this was the last link to be completed between Plymouth and Truro (the Saltash Bridge had been finished several weeks earlier) little is known about how it was built. Materials had to be brought by water to the quay seen in the background but the erection of each trussed girder in the face of the twice daily incursion of the tide, must have presented a formidable problem to the contractor. No wonder he was late but there is no record of any penalty. *L G Booth Collection*

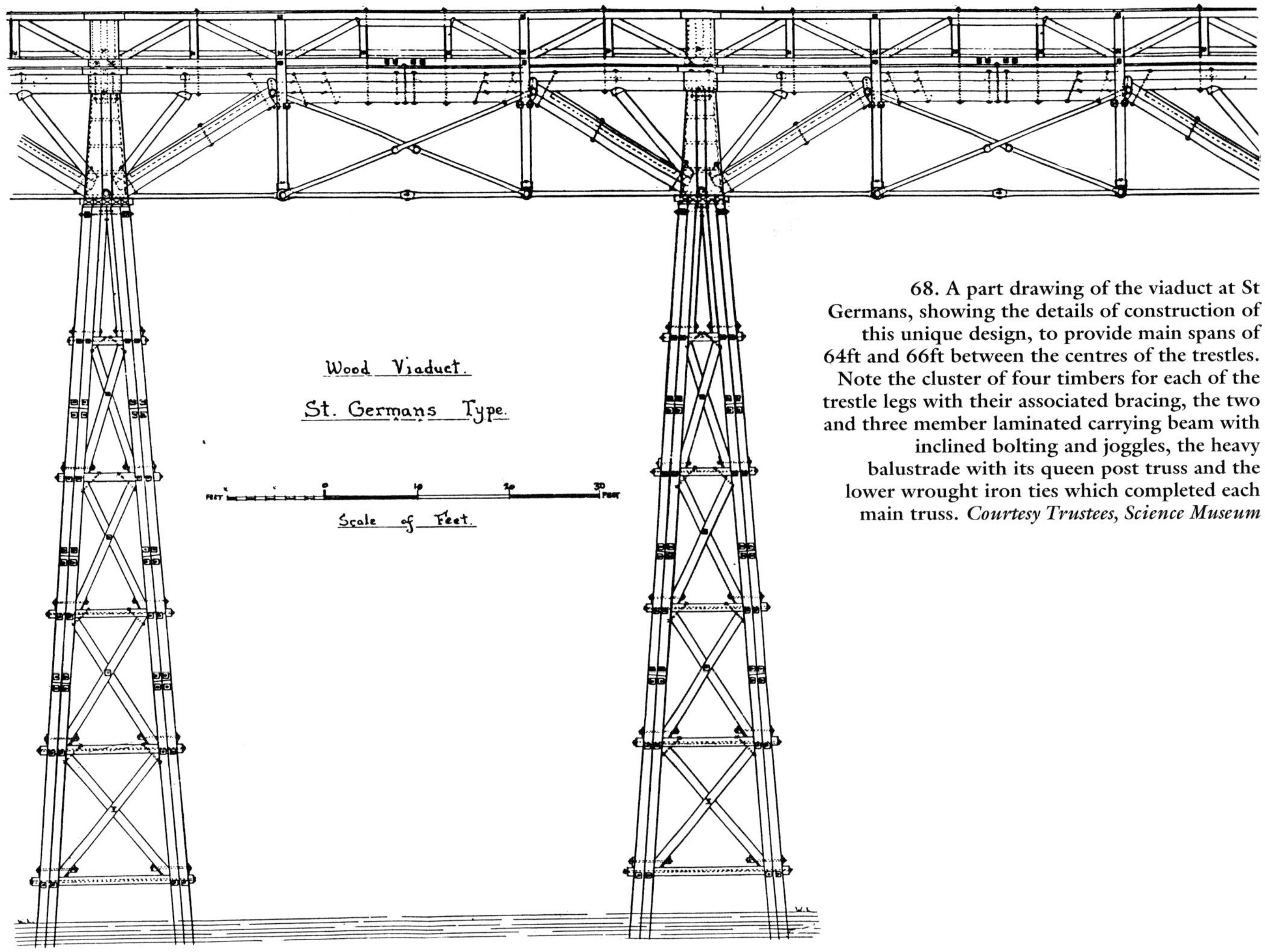

68. A part drawing of the viaduct at St Germans, showing the details of construction of this unique design, to provide main spans of 64ft and 66ft between the centres of the trestles. Note the cluster of four timbers for each of the trestle legs with their associated bracing, the two and three member laminated carrying beam with inclined bolting and joggles, the heavy balustrade with its queen post truss and the lower wrought iron ties which completed each main truss. *Courtesy Trustees, Science Museum*

It represented a striking example of a composite timber structure, developed to accommodate the increase in span compared with that of the Class C viaducts. From the above original drawing, dated 1858, it is possible to establish the details of construction, all as shown in Fig.68. Each girder was built up from a massive cast iron seating, located on the cill timbers of each trestle, 15ft below rail level. From there sprang a vertical leg, an intermediate raking leg and finally, a 14in × 24in composite raking strut, all formed from a series of 14in × 12in timbers. The upper ends of each composite strut seated in cast iron strap brackets, which served the dual purpose of end locations for a horizontal straining piece, also of 14in × 12in section, and as the upper anchor points for the diagonal wrought iron ties.

This arrangement of a substantial timber framework, supported the horizontal carrying beam, formed from a laminate of two 14in × 12in timbers, which incorporated the usual hardwood joggles, wrought iron wedges and inclined bolts. These were located immediately adjacent to the ends of the central straining piece, where similar joggles etc were inserted between this latter member and the lower member of the beam. It will be seen, therefore, that this arrangement provided a laminated beam, the central portion of which was 3ft deep over a 30ft mid length. Its ends were supported at each trestle by the 12in × 14in upright timber, located in the casting on top of the cill timbers and fitting in a second casting under the beam, this overall construction providing a superstructure nearly 15ft deep. The intermediate raking legs, which also sprang from the cill castings, provided additional support at each end to the horizontal beam over its inner length.

Below the junction of the upper end of each intermediate raking strut and the intermediate straining piece, vertical 12in × 12in timbers dropped to form locations for middle cill members, of section 12in × 7in, which in turn provided the lower bracket supports for the wrought iron ties. In addition, at this cross section, an outside 12in × 10in timber extended from this lower cill to the top of the parapet.

The horizontal beams supported the 8in decking, which carried a 12in × 10in bottom rail surmounted by a $2\frac{1}{2}$in × 4in ballast board and a 8in × 5in fender, similar to other structures. This provided the trough for the ballast and set the rail height 1ft 2in above deck level. The top of the 14in × 10in parapet rail was 4ft 6in above rail level, being carried on 12in × 8in posts at approximately 9ft centres, with diagonal strut pieces of similar section, which thus formed the balustrade. Over the central 10ft length of this parapet, an additional 12in × 8in member acted as a straining piece for the adjacent diagonals, its ends seated in cast iron shoes. At four locations across each span, vertical through bolts, $1\frac{1}{4}$in dia, extended from the top of the parapet through the horizontal beams, and served to clamp the component parts together, to form the complete girder. The distance between the inner faces of the parapets was the usual 14ft, while at the trestles and two mid positions of each span, $1\frac{1}{8}$in dia lateral tie rods linked the two girders at deck level.

Below deck level, the two girders were connected by pairs of 9in × 7in walings and 9in × 9in cross bracing between the composite raking struts and the vertical timbers at the appropriate sections, while the cill castings of adjacent trestles were also connected by wrought iron ties of section 6in × 1in, jointed at the intermediate

69B. A close up view of some of the trestles and the composite timber and wrought iron trusses of St Germans. *L G Booth Collection*

cill brackets. Likewise, the latter points were linked to the strap brackets of the horizontal beam straining piece, by means of diagonal wrought iron cross ties, of section 5in × $\frac{7}{8}$in.

An analysis of the timber content of this structure indicates a total of over 2,200ft^3 in each span, exclusive of the trestles, to give a figure of 34ft^3/ft of span for the superstructure, for comparison with the other Classes summarised in Appendix 1. In illustration, Fig.69B is a close up of the western set of trestles and spans while Figs.11A and 69A give an excellent impression of the overall size and grandeur of the structure.

While undoubtedly a fine example of timber design showing typical Brunellian ingenuity, it had the great disadvantage from the maintenance engineer's point of view, that repairs could not be carried out to the superstructure without the breaking up of a complete truss. Gibbons reported in 1899 that since the opening of the line, major renewal work through the viaduct had been carried out twice, and that a further such operation would soon be required unless the structure was replaced. In the event, of course, this did not prove necessary because of the introduction of the 1908 deviation.

The first renewal took place in 1872/3, when the queen trusses and trussed parapet above the cills were entirely renewed. Yet by 1886, examination of the timbers showed that a further renewal programme would be necessary which was put in hand the following year. The extent of all this work was partly reflected in the 1860–1882 maintenance cost of £8,514 — the highest figure recorded on the line. However, when this amount is set against the total timber content of the structure, including trestles, which amounted to over 60,000ft^3 then the annual cost at £6.42/1,000ft^3 compares favourably with that of the other classes.

It is interesting to note that in order to effect the renewal work, a wrought iron bow-string girder was placed inside the parapet, which supported the flooring on one side of a span so that the timber truss could be taken away and a new one framed up to take its place. In this operation, as there was bare clearance between the girder and a passing train, great care had to be observed while this work was in hand. No mention is made of whether this was a piecemeal operation or the removal of the trussed girder as a complete unit.

With regard to its overall replacement, Margary recommended in 1880 that:

> '...in consequence of the method adopted in the formation of the piers, the substitution of cast iron for timber would be extremely difficult, but they can be easily repaired piecemeal with timber. Therefore, I would suggest in the reconstruction of this viaduct, that the present piers be left standing and that wrought iron girders and decking be substituted for the present timber trusses and floor'.

However, Brunel's original structure was to continue in service for nearly a further 30 years, until the replacement viaduct (Fig.11B) was brought into use on the new deviation, in 1908. It is a splendid masonry structure, built mainly of granite on a graceful curve, downstream of and at a level higher than that of the original which it replaced. The contactor was Relf & Son, with W Y Armstrong as Engineer and J C Inglis, Consulting Engineer — these details being recorded on a suitable stone let into the parapet brickwork, commemorating the date of completion, 1907. The new line was opened for goods traffic on 22nd March 1908, over a single track from the west side of the new Nottar viaduct, crossing the old alignment by means of a temporary bridge, and so into St Germans station. Passenger traffic followed on 19th May 1908, while the route was doubled from 31st May 1908.

All that now remains of Brunel's original masterpiece is the substantial abutment in the woods on the Truro embankment, together with the footings for the masonry pier and the masonry plinth, which formed the seatings for the timber trestle located on the west bank of the river. However, the course of the original alignment can be clearly followed on the Plymouth side of the estuary, as the line came in bordering the shoreline from Saltash.

70. An 1898 view of Tresulgan from the south, showing the piers of the replacement viaduct under construction. The simple trestle running the length of the works, with the attendant derrick cranes, appear to be the only equipment in use. Materials for this construction would have been brought by rail; those for the original timber viaduct would have had to have been hauled to this remote site from the half mile distant Liskeard–Saltash road. *From the Clinker Collection, Brunel University Library*

Tresulgan to Liskeard

From St Germans the line finally left the shores of the Lynher River and the Tamar Estuary, to climb away across the southern slopes of the spine of Cornwall for some five miles, to reach the first of the inland 'Fan' type viaducts in the County at Tresulgan, to cross a tributary of the Seaton River, and thus set the pattern for the remainder of the route to Truro.

10. Tresulgan — Margary Class A — Figs.70 and 71
Location 260/72 — Length 525ft — Maximum height 93ft

Margary describes the structure as Class A and length 508ft, while the 1895 Parliamentary Session drawing quotes a length of 532ft. Unfortunately, the only photographs to come to light are those taken during the building of the replacement masonry viaduct, (Figs.70 and 71), which show, as would be expected, that it conformed with its neighbours along this length of line as a Class A2 design. It was built on a left hand down side curve on six masonry piers, together with a fan set on a plinth on the embankment at each end, making a total of eight fans. From the information established in Chapter 2, it would appear to have been completed in 1857. Being located some distance from a main road, the access for the supply of materials must have posed many problems, since there is no evidence of a local quarry.

Margary originally recommended that the structure should be replaced by a new masonry viaduct while later, in his 1887 report, it is interesting to note that he records 'several of the original legs and a few old beams remaining. These will have to be changed when next the viaduct is under repair'. They had therefore achieved a lifespan of nearly thirty years, well in excess of that recorded for other viaducts in later years. The repair costs from 1860 to 1882 amounted to £2,316, giving an average annual cost over the period, based on a total timber content of over 16,800ft^3, of £6.27 per 1,000ft^3 — a favourable comparison. The structure continued in service until 1899, when the replacement masonry viaduct, built to accommodate a double track narrow gauge on the downside of the original, was first brought into service on 26th March as a single line, and then doubled later in that year. At the site today, the ivy clad stumps of four of the original piers are still standing.

71. A closer view of Tresulgan, at the time of building the replacement viaduct. This view shows the irregular formation of this Class A2 structure after nearly forty years' service, with the shores added to the piers, while men working on top of one of the new piers, building them without scaffolding, should be noted. *From the Clinker Collection, Brunel University Library*

72A. A distant view of Coldrennick which gives an excellent impression of its 790ft length and 138ft height, in its location adjacent to Menheniot station, carrying the line across this deep, wood covered valley of the River Seaton. This was the fifth highest structure in Cornwall and, sadly, was the scene of a serious accident in February 1897 when, during its rebuilding, scaffolding collapsed and twelve men fell to their death. *L G Booth Collection*

11. Coldrennick — Margary Class A — Figs.8, 72A, 72B and 73
Location 261/42 — Length 795ft — Maximum height 138ft

A mile further on from Tresulgan, the route crossed the valley of the River Seaton by means of this magnificent structure, built on a downside right hand curve on twelve fully buttressed masonry piers, and completed in 1858. The line was level across the viaduct which was located at the foot of two inclines. In order to raise the level of the rails, with a view to easing the affect of the two gradients, longitudinal trussed beams were introduced between the tops of the raking legs and the Class A2 superstructure, making yet another variation from standard construction. This additional formation is clearly seen in Fig.72B, and was built up from 12in square vertical posts and struts, between a 12in × 24in laminated bottom beam and a 12in square top member. The outer frameworks incorporated 12in × 6in vertical posts extending from the top of the parapet to the bottom beam.

The date of the introduction of this modification has not been established; it was probably at the time of original construction, since a contemporary report[12], commenting on the progress of the construction of the line, refers to 'the balustrade being added to the viaduct'. For it to have been introduced once the line was in regular use would have posed a major operation, which can be envisaged from the general views of the structure given in Figs.8, 72A and 73. The presence of additional shores on two of the three piers shown in Fig.72B should be noted.

An appreciation of the scale of this magnificent timber structure may be gained from Fig.73, a view taken from the tops of the piers, some 100ft above the level of the bottom of the valley, looking towards Menheniot station. The lower trussed beams and Class A2 superstructure can be easily distinguished; compare them with the man standing in the refuge while a train crosses the structure. This photograph was taken shortly before work started on reconstruction.

In his 1880 report, Margary quoted the length as 790ft and height 134ft and recommended replacement of the timber structure by building up the piers to take wrought iron girders. Later, in 1887, he noted that as the structure had recently been under repair, very little of the original timber was still in place. The cost of repairs to 1882 totalled £4,738, giving an average annual repair cost of £6.80/1,000ft^3, in line with those of its neighbours.

Margary's recommendations were eventually put in hand in 1895 and completed on 23rd January 1898, the line between Tresulgan and Menheniot then being doubled. In carrying out this work, the procedure followed was similar to that previously adopted at St Pinnock. The piers were raised in brick to take latticed steel girders, slots being left around the timber legs to permit their later removal; in this instance, the depth of the lattice girder taking up the height of the timber trussed beam. Sadly, all this work was not completed without tragedy. During February 1897 a gang of seventeen men were engaged in fixing one of the new girders, working from a temporary platform suspended from the seventh span at a height of 130ft above the ground. A local newspaper report[13] gives a graphic account of how the platform:

> '...was fixed just below the permanent way, and, as far as can be gathered, consisted of a number of planks, the ends of which rested on scaffold poles, which were supported by the timberwork belonging to the bridge. The girder weighed about seven cwts, and whilst 13 men were engaged in shouldering it into position, the foreman and the ganger stepped on to another stage in order to watch operations. The girder rested upon a projecting portion of the pier nearest Menheniot station, and by slow degrees it was lifted upon the shoulders of the men, and levered forward to its intended resting place. Just as it was being carried to the farthest end, the platform, by some means, collapsed, and with the exception of Samuel Stephens, the whole of the men working on it were hurled into the ravine below. Stephens was standing at the other end, where the angle of fall and the force of gravitation were at the minimum; consequently he had a moment's advantage over his comrades, and that moment saved his life. He clutched at a

72B. A close up view of the unique construction of this viaduct showing the lower timber trussed beam construction, supporting the Class A2 decking and ballast troughing which effectively raised the track level by some 6ft. Note the additional shores introduced on two of the three piers, which appear to be very slender; they were in fact similar to those at Liskeard and following their raising to carry wrought iron girders in 1897, were later encased in granite as rein-forcement. ***L G Booth Collection***

cross-trestle, and hung in this terrible position until he was released by the foreman ganger, and others. The awful thud caused by the fall of the 12 men, and portions of the platform, was heard by those working in the immediate vicinity, and those who looked down into the valley saw the bodies scattered in all directions on the grassy slope beneath. Everyone rushed to the spot, horror stricken...'

Twenty five children were orphaned as a result of this accident, and as the navvies concerned were only casual labourers, no compensation was due to their dependants from the GWR. Nine of the men were buried in Menheniot churchyard and the remainder at Liskeard. The inquest, held at the *Sportsmans Arms*, adjacent to Menheniot Station, revealed that not only had the scaffold beam not been chained to the main viaduct structure, as required by the correct installation procedure, but that the beam itself, formerly a ballast fender from the original timber structure, was flawed. The Coroner recommended that in future, the Company should issue printed regulations regarding the correct procedures to be used in such instances and also ensure that the timbers being used were free from decay etc. Foremen and gangers were then to familiarise themselves with such directions.

In 1933 the piers were encased in granite, so as to provide a more substantial support, no reason being forthcoming for this work but doubtless considered necessary due to the curvature of the structure. Of all those viaducts on the main line incorporating Brunel's original piers, those at Coldrennick now appear by far the more solidly built.

73. A dramatic view of Coldrennick taken from the top of one of the piers, some 100ft above the floor of the valley, showing the relatively smooth curvature of the structure and its massive proportions in comparison with the figure standing in the refuge, as a down goods train trundles across the viaduct. This view gives an excellent impression of the conditions under which the workmen were involved in building up the piers for the replacement and fixing the new lattice steel girders. ***From the Clinker Collection, Brunel University Library***

74. Treviddo viaduct viewed from the south west, taken in 1895, yet another structure built on a curve and requiring additional shoring within the fan superstructure. These extra members can be seen fitted to all the piers. The design is Class A2, but the additional cross timber introduced on each linking span, had not been added at this date. ***L G Booth Collection***

12. Treviddo — Margary Class A — Frontispiece & Figs.74 and 75
Location 262/49 — Length 486ft — Maximum height 101ft

A mile after passing through Menheniot station, with the line still climbing, Treviddo viaduct was reached which crossed another tributary of the Seaton River. It was completed in 1857 and from the illustration in the frontispiece it will be seen that the structure was carried on five piers with, in addition, a fan set in the embankment slope at each end. Again, it was built on a curve and, as in the case of Tresulgan, only two of the piers were built with buttresses. The superstructure is identified as Class A2 while Margary recorded a length of 476ft compared with 487ft shown in the 1895 Parliamentary Sessions drawing.

The illustrations clearly show the queen post truss at each end, together with the presence of additional shoring on the piers introduced to counter the adverse lateral loading. Figure 74 is a closer view of the structure, taken in 1895, from which the detail of the extra shoring can be seen. Margary had in 1880 recommended that the viaduct should be replaced by a new masonry structure. However, in 1887 he was reporting that following examination of the timbers in January of that year, repairs had recently been completed and it was in good order. Again, it will be noted that maintenance costs over the earlier years were in line with the average, at £7.27/1,000ft^3 per annum.

However, it was a further eleven years before a new masonry structure, built on the up-side of the original viaduct, was finished and brought into service on 14th September 1898, the line being doubled in the following month. This structure in a part completed condition, on 28th January 1898, is shown in Fig.75 when it will be noted that underslung cross timbers had then been added to each linking span of Brunel's viaduct since the date of the previous photographs. At the site today, the five remaining ivy clad masonry piers of the latter are visible from the nearby A.38 trunk road.

75. The scene at Treviddo in 1898 when the replacement viaduct was partly completed, showing the timber arch supports for the new masonry in position on top of the new piers, with Brunel's original structure behind. This view, taken three years later than Fig.74, shows the addition of the underslung cross beams to the linking spans, and illustrates the difference in section between his buttressed and plain masonry piers, and how slender were the latter. ***From the Clinker Collection, Brunel University Library***

76. A view from the south of the replacement Cartuther viaduct in 1992, showing a single ivy clad pier on the left, all that remains of Brunel's original structure. *J R S Binding*

13. Cartuther — Margary Class A — Fig.76
Location 263/74 — Length 411ft — Maximum height 89ft

This viaduct, set in a delightful valley, carried the line across yet another tributary of the East Looe River, at a location not easy of access. While no photograph survives, it is believed to have been built on six masonry piers, including a fan set in the embankment at each end, and completed in 1857. The stone involved was probably taken from a quarry located immediately to the south of the line, at the Truro end. In conformity with its neighbours, it is identified as Class A2. Sadly today, all that remains of this structure is a pier footing in the Truro abutment, a single ivy clad plain pier and the remains of a buttressed pier, which thus establish the course of the original alignment. That all but one of the original piers have been dismantled could point to a weakness in their construction, particularly since replacement dates from 1882, whereas the neighbouring Treviddo saw service until 1898, where the original piers are still standing.

Compared with other viaducts, the cost of repairs from 1860 to 1882 was well below average, at only £5.81/1,000ft^3 per annum. However, this figure had significantly increased over the last 12 years to £8.89, which would appear to indicate that its early replacement was made for reasons other than problems due to the timbers; a deduction lending support to the foregoing conjecture regarding the doubtful quality of the masonry piers.

Margary quoted a length of 401ft and recommended a masonry viaduct as replacement, details of which were submitted to the Joint Committee at their meeting on 24th August 1880. He was authorised to proceed at an estimated cost of £8,500, subject to approval of the Great Western Company; and the new structure, shown in Fig.76, was completed in 1882 at a cost of £7,883. Comprising five segmental arches of 56½ft width and a rise of 20ft, it was located on the down side and the single broad gauge line diverted over it on 8th January of that year; the route being doubled in 1896

Disposal of the stones from the original Brunel piers appears to have been achieved by building them into a shallow embankment within the curtilage of part of the railway land beneath the new viaduct, the stream being culverted beneath this formation. Some were also used to construct a buttressed stone abutment at the Plymouth end of the new alignment. Over the years, the area has become grassed but the smaller size of stone as used in the Brunel piers are apparent within this overall arrangement in comparison with the larger individual stones of the new viaduct. The latter probably came from the Westwood quarry — as later discussed under that viaduct reference.

14. Bolitho — Margary Class A — Figs.77, 78A and 78B
Location 264/21 — Length 546ft — Maximum height 113ft

From Cartuther it was but a short distance to Bolitho viaduct, completed in 1858, a crossing of yet another deep valley of a tributary of the East Looe River. It was built on a left hand downside curve and incorporated six masonry piers, of which only one in three appeared to be buttressed, together with a fan support on the embankment slope at each end. Viewed from the depth of the valley, this must have been one of Brunel's most impressive timber structures and it is to be regretted that no photograph has been located of this viaduct as built. In line with its neighbours, it is identified as Class A2.

Margary quoted a length of 526ft and was sceptical regarding the condition of the masonry of the piers, since 'the viaduct has a tendency to lean over towards the North and has to be shored on one of the piers at its Eastern end where the curve changes'. It is not clear whether this referred to the inclusion of a shore within the superstructure (as was the case at Treviddo and others), or to the shoring of the actual pier itself. Surprisingly, the annual repair costs, 1860 to 1882, were below the average at £6.06/1,000ft^3 per annum, but this figure had increased to an average of £9.62 over the last twelve years of its life. Significantly, this viaduct was replaced some 15 years ahead of its neighbours at Liskeard and Treviddo, and in the light of this decision, again throws into question the quality of workmanship in the masonry piers; although from the records it would appear that all the viaducts between Liskeard and Coldrennick were built by the same contractor, Messrs. Sharp & Sons.

For a replacement, Margary recommended the construction of a new masonry viaduct on the south side of the original structure, which would also permit an improvement in the curve. Negotiations had commenced in 1880 with the adjacent landowner, the Bolitho family, for the purchase of the necessary additional land and to include the temporary lease of extra land immediately alongside the viaduct in order to accommodate the stores and machinery required during construction.

However, the tenant, a farmer by name of Moon, raised numerous objections to the overall proposal insofar as he was concerned, and in a statement[14] dated 20th February 1880 he detailed the inconvenience which he and his family would incur through some 150 men working on the project over 'at least three summers'. This fascinating document gives a contemporary account of farming life and the likely affect of the presence of a large number of men working in the area.

In the outcome, the small amount of additional land required was to be purchased at the rate of £200 per acre while, as compensation for his inconvenience, Mr Moon required a down payment of £300 before work started. These terms were so very far in excess of those anticipated by the Directors of the Cornwall Railway, that they were rejected out of hand and Margary wrote Mr Bolitho on 12th March 1880, declining to proceed with the scheme. The Board had agreed to go ahead with Margary's alternative plan, whereby the work would be confined to the Company's own land, by the building of a new masonry viaduct on the same alignment as the original line, construction being undertaken in two longitudinal halves, so as to keep the line open.

However, to maintain traffic in these circumstances inevitably posed considerable operational difficulties, while execution of the contract must have been under extremely trying conditions. Moon's letter details the problems that would have been involved with personnel movements and the provision of water supplies throughout the year, not to mention the removal of spoil and the supply of the materials of construction, at a location in a deep valley with very limited access. It speaks highly of the skill and adaptability of the workforce who carried out this work within the limited confines of the Company's own land, over a length of some 175 yards and working at heights of up to 100ft.

According to Gibbons, the plan was for the new piers to be built up to the level of the impost course, since he stated that they were not located opposite the original ones. However, examination of the site today, shows that each new pier was, in fact, built approximately a half pier width off both the centre and the centre line of each original; this will be apparent from Fig.78A and the detail shown in Fig.78B. Based on site measurement, the original piers were spaced at nominal 64ft centres. Half of each new pier width was thus built up to the impost course, from where a half arch was then formed for each span, wide enough to accommodate a temporary line of broad gauge track. On completion of this part construction, the main line was swung to this new alignment so as to maintain services, albeit over a somewhat confined crossing, doubtless traversed by traffic at very low speed.

77. A 1992 view from the north east of the replacement viaduct at Bolitho, which was built in two longitudinal sections on the alignment of the original Brunel structure. ***J R S Binding***

78A. **A view of the Bolitho piers, showing the remains of the Brunel piers at their base, the new masonry having been built half on the centreline and half on the longitudinal centre of the original, so as to maintain as closely as possible the then existing alignment.** ***J R S Binding***

78B. A close up view of the remains of one of the original piers, showing its relationship to the new structure. Bearing in mind the 113ft height of this viaduct, we can but admire the skill and dedication of the workmen who built the replacement within the limited space available to them. ***Author***

This arrangement then allowed the timber structure to be dismantled and the original piers stripped to ground level, following which the new piers were built up to their full width. The second longitudinal half of the masonry arches was then added and the viaduct finished, eventually to take double track, narrow gauge. Great care would have been taken to ensure that, as part of the building procedure, the two sections of the arches were carefully toothed together since, from examination of the masonry today, it is not possible to distinguish the line of construction between the two halves. However, on some of the piers it is possible to discern the outline of the original Brunel masonry. All this work was completed at a cost of £9,188, with the final alignment of the single broad gauge line made across the structure on 8th January 1882, in conjunction with the alterations at Cartuther on the same date. The route was eventually doubled in 1896.

The original piers having been reduced to mere stumps, disposal of the stones again posed a problem in this deep, inaccessible valley. It appears that they were built into a shallow embankment beneath the new viaduct, over part of its length, the stream being culverted beneath this formation. Over the years, saplings have become established on this area so that it is only in winter, with no leaves on the trees, that this feature becomes apparent. Some of the stones were also used to strengthen the embankment at each end of the new alignment.

15. Liskeard — Margary Class A — Figs.10, 48, 79, 80A to 80E Location 264/49 — Length 720ft — Maximum height 150ft

Liskeard viaduct, Fig.10, was crossed immediately before the station of that name, a magnificent structure spanning this wide, deep valley. Its eleven sets of timber fans were supported on nine fully buttressed, solid masonry piers, constructed from local stone, together with a masonry plinth set in the embankment at each end. Although of dimensions similar to those of Moorswater and St Pinnock, the piers did not include the gothic openings of the latter.

In his 1880 report Margary refers to it as a Class B structure 706ft in length. However, from all the available photographs it was clearly a Class A2 design, generally similar to the superstructure of Coldrennick, without the additional trussed beams. Repair costs over the period to 1882 totalled £3,349, to give an average of £6.61/1,000ft^3 per annum; a figure lower than the overall average, probably due to it being a straight viaduct, coupled with the affect of the high timber content of our analysis.

The 1880 report recommended reconstruction by raising the piers to carry wrought iron girders, but no immediate action was taken since a report seven years later commented that there were then a few legs and beams which required changing. However, apart from normal maintenance, and the introduction of underslung cross beams on the linking spans, it was not until 1893 that steps were taken to provide a replacement, when work commenced on building up the piers in brickwork, following the method previously adopted at St Pinnock. When raised, the piers were sufficiently wide to permit two main girders to be placed upon them, 18ft 6in from centre to centre, and outside the single line timber structure.

79. A close up view of Liskeard viaduct believed taken in the mid 1890s, viewed from the south west. Note the cross member at the mid point of the longer linking spans, slung from the decking, the details of the Class A2 superstructure and the similarity of the piers with those of Coldrennick (Fig.72). With a height of 150ft from the bottom of the valley to rail level, this was the second highest in Cornwall and these original massive piers, without the reinforcement subsequently applied to those at Coldrennick, still carry the main line across this deep valley and into Liskeard station. ***Liskeard Museum***

We are fortunate that this whole operation was photographed through its various stages, to furnish an excellent record of how the work was carried out — see Figs.80A to 80E.

Referring to the relevant paragraphs under the description of St Pinnock, it will be seen that pockets were left in the new brickwork for the timber struts, while each pier was capped on both sides by granite bedstones (Fig.80A and Fig.80B) to receive, not wrought iron girders as the replacement, but lattice steel girders. Prior to installation, these prefabricated members were brought to Liskeard station yard, following which each was then carried by two steam cranes (Fig.80C) and pulled by a locomotive to the appropriate location on the viaduct. There it was lowered on to the granite bedstones prepared to receive it (Fig.80D). Once the new girders were in place, the floor could be temporarily supported and then the raking timber legs withdrawn; the pockets being infilled and the structure finally completed (Fig.80E).

It should be remembered that this work was carried out in the space above the original pier levels, at heights in excess of 100ft above ground level, working with the minimum of safety precau-

80A. The piers have been built up in brickwork around the raking struts and a granite bedstone is being lowered from a mobile crane into position on top of a pier, ready to receive the new lattice steel girders; the bedstones being already in position on the adjacent piers. ***Liskeard Museum***

80B. Liskeard viaduct with the piers raised and capped, showing the original structure still supported by the raking legs.

80C. (below) Two travelling cranes lift one of the new girders at Liskeard station before being towed to the viaduct.

80D. (centre left) Lowering girders into position. Flying scaffolding will be seen on spans already replaced to facilitate manual insertion of cross girders and steel decking, following which the timberwork will be dismantled and the slots in the brickwork infilled. *Liskeard Museum*

80E. (below) The replacement viaduct now in service, with all trace of the Brunel superstructure removed. It is interesting to note that the early onset of corrosion necessitated the replacement of these first sets of steel girders in 1929. *All Liskeard Museum*

tions. We cannot speak too highly of the men involved in the planning and execution of these operations, while at the same time, apart from Sunday occupation, normal traffic continued to cross the viaduct. Photographs of the structure before modification show balustrade type handrailing, yet at the time of rebuilding, the diagonal strutting had been removed; presumably to assist in reconstruction.

This rebuilding was completed in 1894, with doubling of the route following in 1896. The original lattice steel girders remained in service for some 35 years and then in 1929, owing to excessive corrosion of some of the steelwork, a further reconstruction of the viaduct took place, to instal new steelwork. Significantly, Brunel's original masonry piers with their extended brickwork continued in use, as they do to this day. We cannot help but wonder what were the problems which, in 1855–1856, caused him to suspend all work on the masonry of both this and the neighbouring viaducts. Apart from the details which follow concerning Moorswater, the records have failed to reveal any answer.

16. Moorswater — Margary Class D — Figs.9, 22, 41, 42, 47, 81, 82, 83, 84 and 85
Location 265/38 — Length 954ft — Maximum height 147ft
(Margary quotes a length of 960ft)

From Liskeard station the line swung to the south west on a downward gradient of 1 in 60 followed by a reverse curve to the west, as it approached and crossed Moorswater viaduct on the level, before climbing away towards Doublebois on an incline of 1 in 60. Thus, trains travelling in either direction, tended to cross the structure at speed, a factor which, in conjunction with its curvature, could have had a significant influence on its history.

Of all the Cornish viaducts Moorswater, by virtue of its size and location, was surely the most spectacular, crossing the wide, open valley of the East Looe river by means of this lofty structure, set on a graceful curve throughout its length. Twelve imposing fully buttressed piers, each pierced by up to four gothic arched openings, together with a masonry plinth built into the embankment at either end, formed the bases for the fourteen sets of double fans of the Class D timber superstructure. Although each fan comprised the four massive legs of this design, in combination with the longitudinal tie beam on either side of the structure, they gave an overall impression of a delicate tracery supporting the trussed timber beams, which carried the flooring and permanent way. This will be apparent from Fig.82, a photograph taken in April 1879, when work was under way on the replacement masonry structure.

Sadly, Brunel's viaduct was in service for only 22 years, and its history is something of an enigma. Its neighbours at Liskeard and St Pinnock were both of comparable height, with their superstructures resting on masonry piers of similar construction, yet they were built as Class A2 and Class B designs respectively, the former seeing service through to 1894 before it was replaced. For reasons so far not found in the records, Brunel adopted yet a further variation for the Moorswater superstructure by incorporating the heavier Class D design; with the legs of each fan springing as distinct pairs from castings located at the outer corners of the masonry piers, instead of from their centreline as in other designs. They were seated on a pair of 12in × 8in transverse cill timbers, which spanned the buttresses on either side of each pier, and overhung the latter at their outer ends to provide the location for these castings. In turn, the cill timbers were supported at their ends by vertical struts or shores, each comprising a massive cluster of four 12in square timbers, scarfed and bolted together. These were located in the four outer corners formed by the adjacent buttresses of each pier, to which they were through bolted. They extended down to the pier footings, presumably with the intention of relieving the piers themselves from the direct loading of the superstructure. The arrangement of these details can be seen from an examination of the accompanying illustrations; Fig.9 a photograph dating from c1860, Figs.41 & 42 of the timber fans and longitudinal timber tie beams, Fig.83, which gives an excellent general view of the structure taken from the south east in the late 1860s, and Fig.84.

This overall form of construction, which apart from the method of reinforcing the support for the fans, conforms to the description given in Chapter 4, was originally shown in a drawing (Fig.81)[15], of which Fig.41 is an extract. Believed dated c1860, it could have been prepared after the completion of the work, but there is no evidence to suggest that the viaduct was not, in fact built to this unique design; as opposed to having been modified at a later date. Whether this form of construction was adopted because of the suspected weakness of the piers or because Brunel, from later experience, sought to increase the lateral strength of the design, is open to conjecture. No record has been discovered to shed light on this aspect, but the inclusion between the piers of heavy longitudinal timber tie beams in place of the usual wrought iron tie bars, points to Brunel's concern regarding the overall strength and stability of this particular structure.

82. A splendid photograph of Moorswater taken in April 1879 from the south east showing the timber original with construction of the new masonry viaduct in progress alongside. All fourteen fans are included in this view and on some of the piers, the horizontal struts which were fitted between the buttresses can be seen. An appreciation of the size of the structure can be gained from the two men standing on the horizontal tie beam at pier No 5, numbered from the left. Note also the strapping which is partly visible on pier No 7. It is also interesting to observe that the piers of the new viaduct are being built with hardly any scaffolding — a practice no doubt dating from Brunel's time. ***J R Rapson — Liskeard Old Cornwall Society Collection***

83. Moorswater viewed from the south east, believed taken in the late 1860s, showing the massive timber struts, set into the corners of the buttresses of each pier, together with the longitudinal tie beams linking the piers on either side of the structure. In the valley can be seen the track of the Liskeard Looe line, with the route of the original canal hidden by the bushes in the foreground while in the distant background is the extant building of the limekiln, beside the East Looe River. *R.I.C.*

However, from such records as do exist it is possible to piece together something of the background history of this viaduct. According to Allan[16], the piers were partially built by 1856. It will be recalled that they had been condemned by Brunel in 1855, presumably due to the collapse of two of the piers, and work on their building suspended. At a meeting of the Board[17] on 23rd November 1855, it was noted that no further report had been received:

> '...from Mr Brunel respecting the reconstruction of the Piers of the Moorswater viaduct and the masonry works on the viaducts on the Eastern part of the line being entirely suspended'.

(Again this would seem to point to the quality of all the masonry work on this part of the line being suspect).

At the half yearly meeting of the Company in March 1856, the Chairman commented[18]:

> 'With respect to those pillars of the viaduct near Liskeard, which fell down, some suppose it to have happened from one cause, and some from another, and many think it was caused by the electric fluid [sic]. But whatever was the cause of their falling, there is no doubt that they can be rebuilt in a manner sufficiently substantial, so as to make the viaduct perfectly safe. There is, indeed, no question about it; and so far as regards the pillars that remain standing, they will be minutely inspected by Mr Brunel and the engineers, and will either be left to stand and the wood-work be placed upon them, or, if it be required, they will first be made substantial, and rendered perfectly satisfactory and secure'.

Brunel's report of 27th February 1856, presented to the same meeting, spoke of:

> 'A few weeks of fine weather will enable us to rebuild the two piers of the Liskeard [sic] viaduct'.

However, by a meeting[19] of the Board of 23rd May 1856, no action seems to have been taken in this matter, as it was resolved:

> 'That a letter be written to Mr Brunel stating the desire of the Board that the Piers at Moorswater be proceeded with as soon as it can be properly accomplished'.

By August 1856, Brunel was reporting[20] that 'the piers of the Moorswater viaduct have been nearly re-built, and will soon be finished', while in February 1857 he noted[21] that:

> '...all the works between Truro and Liskeard are completed ready for the stations and permanent way, except the erection of the timberwork of the Moorswater viaduct, which will be proceeded with in a few weeks, as soon as the season improves'.

However, it would appear that for some reason completion of this work was delayed, since sixteen months later Bush reported[22] on 3rd June 1858, that the building of the timber superstructure was then in hand, ten spans having been completed by that date. This would seem to indicate that Brunel was now prepared to accept the quality of the masonry work of the piers, but fearful of their further failure, he had resorted to the use of the heavier Class D design superstructure, reinforced by the four massive vertical struts which were incorporated in each pier. This arrangement also included the insertion of timber baulks between some of the buttresses, which can be seen in Figs.82 and 83. With the pair of longitudinal tie beams extending on either side throughout the length of the structure at cill height, the viaduct as finally built was indeed a massive structure in comparison with its neighbours.

According to the evidence given by J P Elms, Engineering Department Accountant of the Cornwall Railway, to the Arbitration Hearing, the viaduct in its final form included a total of 60,043ft^3 of timber[23], an amount exceeded only by the unique structure at St Germans. However, it is a sad reflection on its construction that, according to the same source, within a relatively short life of 22 years, no less than 29,059ft^3 had been renewed.

The operations involved in this work must have led to a general weakening of the superstructure. No evidence has come to light to account for this high proportion of timber replacement, all the more remarkable when it is realised that the timbers in some of the early viaducts achieved a life in excess of 30 years.

The total cost of repairs between 1860 and 1880 amounted to £6,560. This was the highest of any of the Cornish viaducts at that time, to give an average annual rate of £5.92/1,000ft^3, based on the author's estimate of total timber content. That this figure is lower than the overall average could be accounted for by the high timber content of our analysis. However, over the period from 1868 to 1880 this average rate had increased to £8.96/1,000ft^3, indicating a deterioration in the condition of the overall structure.

With the legs of each fan springing from the outer corners of the piers, their base was of sufficient width to provide a batter of 1/5, compared with 1/15 on the usual Class A and B designs. This arrangement should have materially contributed to providing increased lateral strength, but it would appear that its height of 147ft, in combination with the curved length of 954ft, presented what was probably the most extreme loading on any of the Cornish viaducts. It could be this factor, taken in conjunction with the location at the foot of two inclines, a weakening of the framework due to the high proportion of timber replacement and the circumstantial evidence of suspect masonry piers, that gave rise to ongoing problems in service, reflected in the above repair costs.

In spite of all Brunel's efforts to construct a substantial timber viaduct at Moorswater, it seems to have been dogged with problems. A drawing[24], produced in 1876, details the layout at the base of each of the piers and numbers them from the Plymouth end; which identification is used in the following context. Apart from what would appear to have been an ongoing replacement of many of the timbers, in 1867 the top 12/14ft of masonry of pier No.5 had to be taken down and rebuilt[25]. This must have been a major operation and sadly no details of how the work was carried out

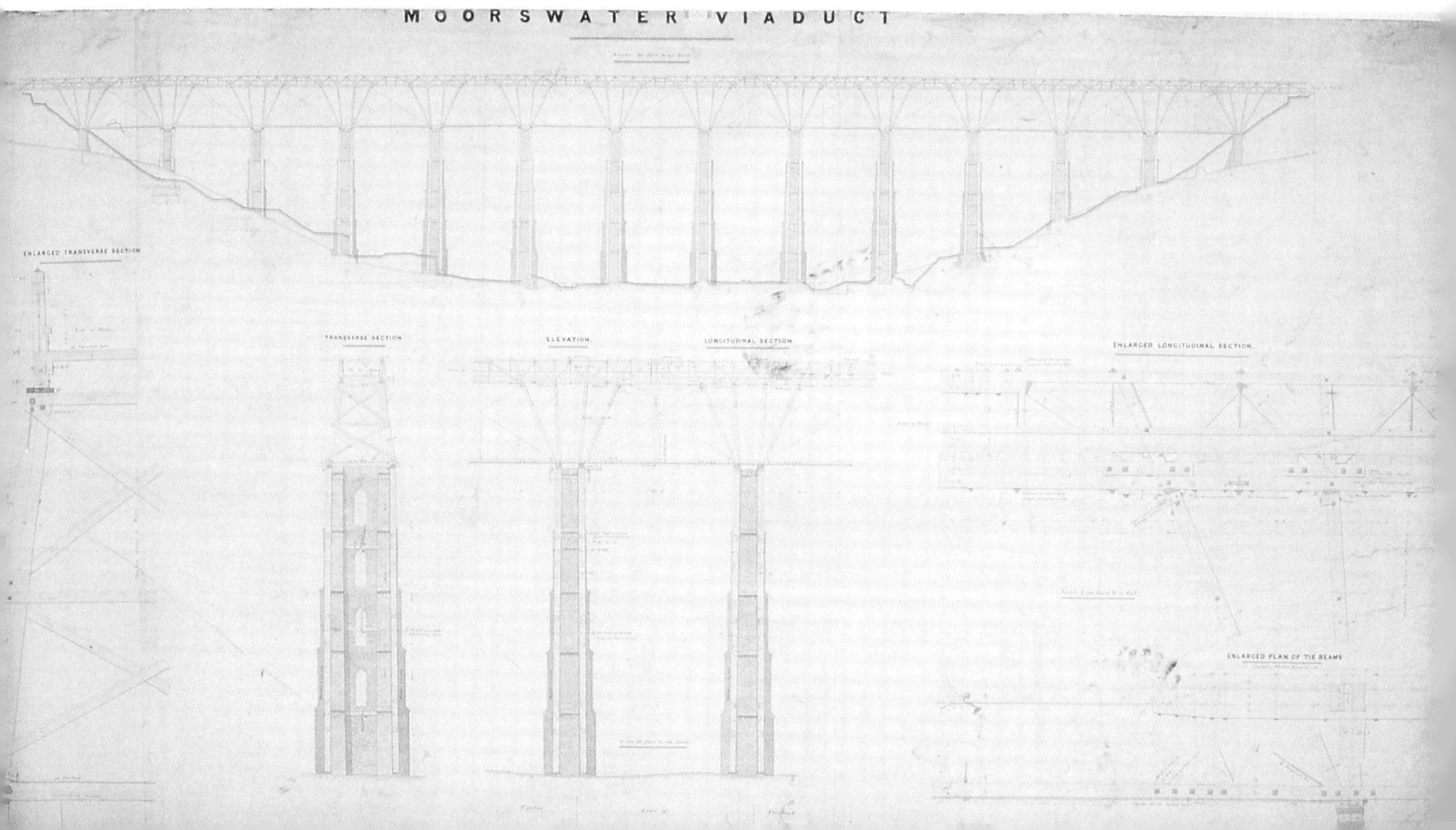

81. A reproduction of a drawing of Moorswater viaduct, believed prepared c1860 following the building of this magnificent structure to a unique design based on the Class D configuration. While not as high as Liskeard — only 147ft — its greater length at 954ft compared with 726ft and being built on a curve, gave an aura of majesty all its own. It will be seen from the drawing that no details of the curvature were provided, from which it can be inferred that the dimensional differences within the legs and beams to provide a smooth profile to the finished structure, were worked out at site. It is also interesting to note that no details of foundations are given and in the absence of bed rock seating, this could account for the settlement of two of the piers which later occurred in service. The four vertical timber struts which were through bolted to the buttresses of each pier, provided the support for the feet of the raking legs of each fan. *PRO RAIL 134/47*

84. A view of Moorswater from the north in the early 1870s, certainly later than Fig.83, since pier No. 7 has been 'strapped', presumably due to some weakness in the masonry, and this strapping is shown still in place in Fig.82, taken in 1879. In the foreground, below the slope of the hill, can be seen the buildings and chimney of what are believed to be the Cheesewring Granite Company while beyond can be seen the cottages beside the viaduct pier which are still standing today. ***Cornwall Local Studies Library***

have survived. When the viaduct was eventually taken out of service, this pier was razed. Significantly, the same report referred to one or two of the other piers as showing symptoms of settlement. Later, a weakness became apparent in pier No.7 as subsequent photographs show strapping around the masonry.

Then in 1878 a letter[26] appeared in the local press expressing in no uncertain terms, the concern of one passenger at the state of 'the portentious [sic] pile of indifferent masonry and flimsy woodwork, which at a giddy height, spans the valley at Moorswater'. Written under the pseudonym 'Prudens', his letter made an alarming attack on its safety, 'the viaduct was never a decent or reputable structure'. Significantly, he appeared to be mainly concerned with the quality of workmanship and stability of the masonry piers, which he alleged were in a state of disintegration. He spoke of one of the tallest piers near the centre of the viaduct showing signs of weakness and being:

> '...bound round and supported, at a considerable height from the ground, by a vast bandage of timber and splints (like a man's broken leg)'.

The next pier to the eastward had shown similar signs of breaking up and was secured in the same way while, from his own examination of the piers, there was evidence of the pointing being shaken out from 'between the stones which compose their wretched rubble masonry'.

Such was his alarm, he had made up his mind never to go over it again; he would 'systematically leave the train at Liskeard and post to Doublebois and vice versa'. However, he appeared equally concerned for the safety of those who continually used the route, in particular the Bishop of Truro, who travelled on the line 'a score or so of times to the ordinary passenger's once'. He went on to question the advisability of even building a new viaduct, suggesting it would be more desirable to divert the line north of Liskeard, thus avoiding 'the worst part of the great chasm altogether'.

Fortuitously, the Cornwall Board had their regular half yearly meeting shortly after the publication of this letter, when the Chairman expressed his regret at the feeling of alarm which it had obviously caused. Couched as it was in exceedingly sensational language, the danger suggested was quite imaginary. He could do no better than repeat what the engineer reported to the Board; namely, that:

> 'The Moorswater viaduct is in a perfectly safe state, in which he is confirmed by the engineer of the Great Western Railway, and will be so maintained so long as it is used for traffic'.

We do not know whether in the light of these remarks 'Prudens' still continued to take the chaise from Liskeard to Doublebois, but these remarks, taken in conjunction with the other reports regarding the piers, would seem to confirm that the overall structure was not entirely satisfactory. Examination today of the remaining masonry piers at Moorswater and comparison with those still standing at St Austell, certainly points to the superiority of the latter. Despite the Chairman's confident report, 'Prudens' concern regarding the quality of the masonry piers may well have been justified.

Meanwhile, it had already been reported in the local press of 31st March 1877[27], that survey work had started for a new masonry viaduct; and went on to express relief that action was at last being taken, rather 'than to let things go on until a serious accident occurs'. The inference is obvious although, as in the case of many of the other viaducts, no actual defect reports have come to light to confirm the exact state of the structure.

At their meeting of 15th March 1878, the Joint Committee[28] considered a total of seven tenders which had been submitted for the rebuilding of the viaduct; these ranged from £56,969 down to £35,810. The Committee's recommendation was for the Company's own Engineer to carry out the work at a cost of £28,520, subsequently confirmed on 29th March 1878 and approved by the Great Western Company on 12th April. Significantly, work started almost immediately, negotiations for the purchase of the additional land which was required, having been concluded during the previous year. H G Cole was appointed Resident Engineer under Margary, at a salary of £400pa. Apparently, his responsibilities also extended to the reconstruction generally of the viaducts on the line. Sadly, in October 1878, he was killed when a steam powered travelling-crane overturned while unloading stone from a truck at the site. He was succeeded by T H Gibbons, who at the lesser salary of £350pa, carried through the construction to its completion and in due course became the Great Western Divisional Engineer at Plymouth.

The design for the new viaduct called for eight arches each of 80ft span, which were constructed of sufficient width to carry two tracks of 4ft $8\frac{1}{2}$in gauge. Margary[29] gives a very detailed account of its building and in particular that the new piers and abutments were set on foundations at an average depth of 12ft below the level of the adjoining ground. The materials for the new viaduct were delivered by rail to the embankment top, much of the stone coming from Westwood quarry. After unloading, the material was run down an inclined plane to the pier where required, there to be set in place by one of four Scotch derrick-cranes worked by steam.

These stood on 70ft high stages so that they could handle materials for the stonemasons at a height of 120ft above the ground. Although of 3 ton swl, the loads were not allowed to exceed 2 tons. As soon as the centres were fixed, an overhead road, at a level of 2ft above the crowns of the main arches was set up, to carry travelling cranes which were used to handle the materials for building arches, spandrils and upper works. As a comment on contemporary life, in July 1878 a Temperance House was erected at the site, for the benefit of the workmen which, on completion of the contract, was purchased by Lord Robartes.

This new structure was completed at a final cost of £30,368 and passed for service on 25th February 1881, which year is carved in the stonework of the up side parapet and can be seen in the view of the viaduct decking in Fig.85. Although initially laid for a broad gauge single line, following the gauge conversion in 1892, it was doubled with effect from October 1893 and this view clearly shows the reverse curve approach to the new structure at the Liskeard end. There was obviously a sharper curve into the original timber viaduct from that end. Conversely, it should be noted that the new alignment involved a sharper curve in the approach to the western end of the masonry viaduct. It is reported that this situation often caused quite an experience on the footplate of 'Mogul' type locomotives on an up train; and is even evident in the cabs of modern diesels.

At the site today, alongside the splendid masonry viaduct, stand the remains of Brunel's masterpiece, in the form of six complete masonry piers (Nos.3, 4, 9, 10, 12 and 13), together with the cropped stumps of Nos. 6, 7, 8, and 11. As noted above, pier No.5 was reduced to ground level while pier No.2, high on the slope at the Plymouth end, has been toppled over and remains as large chunks of masonry on the hillside. The foundations for fan Nos.1 and 14 remain at their respective ends of the old alignment, set in the original embankment slopes.

As will be seen from Fig.22, the piers could be considered constructional marvels in their own right, despite the condemnatory remarks of 'Prudens' in 1878. They were built from local stone on a simple rectangular base (the remains of the quarry are still evident on the south side at the Truro end). The three buttresses at each side, stepped according to height, were in the form of a crucifix, the centre of which normally provided the location for the cast iron seatings of the raking legs. This arrangement follows the description by Brunel's son of the St Pinnock viaduct, in his biography of his father, the loading thus being concentrated at the centre of the three buttresses. In the case of Moorswater, however, it will be apparent that this arrangement was varied as described above, but the formation of the masonry piers was similar, with gothic openings incorporated in the central walls, presumably with the intention of reducing the weight on their foundations.

Allowing for the height of masonry above ground, then the total weight of the tallest pier would have been about 2,400 tons, giving a bearing pressure of around $6\frac{1}{2}$ tons/ft^2, excluding the loading due to the timber superstructure and the live load. This figure compares with a bearing pressure of 6 tons/ft^2 for the piers on the South Devon viaducts[30]. As already noted, when the new masonry viaduct was being built, a good foundation on slate rock was found at an average of 12ft below the surface of the ground and it is questionable whether the piers of the original timber structure extended to that depth, in view of the earlier comments regarding settlement.

That six piers have been left standing while, at best, the remainder have been reduced to mere stumps, lends support to the previous conjecture that the original quality of materials and workmanship on some piers was unsatisfactory. For reasons of safety, these particular piers could not be left complete, even after the viaduct was taken out of use, so they were progressively dismantled over the years, to leave the present ruins. Nevertheless, they stand today in tribute to the memory of their brilliant engineer.

85. A 1990 view of the viaduct decking and track, showing on the left the date '1881' inscribed in the parapet, commemorating completion of this replacement structure. At the other end, the track can be seen descending from Liskeard station and curving on to the new viaduct; originally it would have had to curve further round to approach Brunel's timber viaduct and then enter a reverse curve to cross the structure, the old alignment coming into this picture on the right of the fencepost in the foreground. *Author*

The Glynn Valley

From Moorswater the line climbed steadily for almost the next three miles to reach its highest level in Cornwall, at Doublebois, at the head of the Fowey River or Glynn Valley. From there, clinging to the southern slopes of this beautiful tree-lined valley, with its path carved out of the steep valley side, the line dropped steadily for nine miles, to Lostwithiel. During the first four miles it crossed no less than eight viaducts, which spanned several side valleys, some of quite considerable depth. In springtime the masses of wild rhododendrons added a spectacular splash of colour to the route.

17. Westwood — Margary Class A — Fig.86
Location 269/12 — Length 372ft — Maximum height 88ft

This structure was set high up in the woods on the valley side, and was completed in 1857; according to Margary, of length 363ft. No photograph or drawing has yet come to light, but it is believed to have been a typical curved Class A1 structure, built on three plain piers constructed from local stone, with a fan springing from the embankment at either end. Access to the site must have posed considerable difficulties to the personnel engaged in its construction, since the surrounding hillsides are steep, with only a mud track to provide access from the Bodmin-Liskeard road. This would have made the conveyance of the materials, including some 10,000ft^3 of timber, involved in the viaduct's construction, an onerous task.

It was fortunate, therefore, that the local stone comprised a hard, durable, shale rock with flat natural beds, suitable for the masonry piers, superior to that found in other locations along this stretch of the line. Considerable amounts of stone were quarried from a site immediately adjacent to the viaduct for the piers of both a number of the original timber viaducts and also, later, for the replacement masonry structures. The valley under the viaduct and adjoining the quarry proved to be a convenient place for tipping 'deads', for much of the initial excavation was not suitable for building stone. However, rubble from the quarry was also used for filling up embankments, and for building dry walls at the ends of the new viaducts. In its heyday, the site was an extensive quarrying operation, which included its own storage sidings, with a downside connection to the mainline[31], controlled by Westwood signal box. This can be seen from the 1882 site plan (Fig.86), the box superseding an original situated 650ft to the east.

The original viaduct was of modest proportions in comparison with many others on the line, and was in fact the second Class A1 structure to be replaced; even though the cost of repairs from 1860 to its demise was only £857, giving an annual cost of £4.43/ 1,000ft^3, well below the average. Over the later years of its life, this figure had only increased to £6.51, so that the decision to build a replacement must have been influenced by factors other than maintenance cost. From its location, as with the other structures on this length of line, the deleterious affects of the speed of down trains could have been the deciding factor, coupled with possible weakness of the piers, in the absence of any buttresses.

As part of the plan to replace all the timber viaducts on the Glynn incline, work on this replacement was put in hand in two stages. Firstly, in order to save excavating through some of the original debris from the quarry which had been deposited adjacent to the viaduct, a contract was let in 1874 for the erection of the eastern abutment and pier for the new viaduct, and placed with the contractor working on the Draw Wood realignment, at a cost of £600[32]. Later, there was a further addition to that contract of a second masonry pier, authorised in 1875 at a cost of £300.

In April 1878, the Joint Committee approved the final plans for the new viaduct at an additional cost of about £3,000, this work to be carried out by the Company's own staff. On its completion, the working of the Company's quarry at that site would be considerably improved. Apparently, it was necessary to purchase additional land for the new structure, at a rate not exceeding £75 per acre on the south side and £25 per acre on the north side[33]. (These figures should be compared with the £200 per acre involved in the original Bolitho replacement). As completed, the new viaduct comprised four segmental arches of 50ft span, and a rise of 13ft 6in, built at a cost of £3,958, and brought into use from 14th December 1879. It is interesting to note that, at the Joint Committee meeting of 30th January 1880, the BoT inspector had not yet inspected the deviation as it was considered preferable for the parapet to comprise a wall rather than iron handrailing, as had been previously recommended. In due course, this was put in hand.

Today, the site of the quarry is totally overgrown, with its eastern extremity a large lake, dank and almost inaccessible. On foot, the viaduct can only be reached with considerable difficulty, set as it is amid thick undergrowth reaching to the level of the top of the parapets. The overburden from the quarry working of later

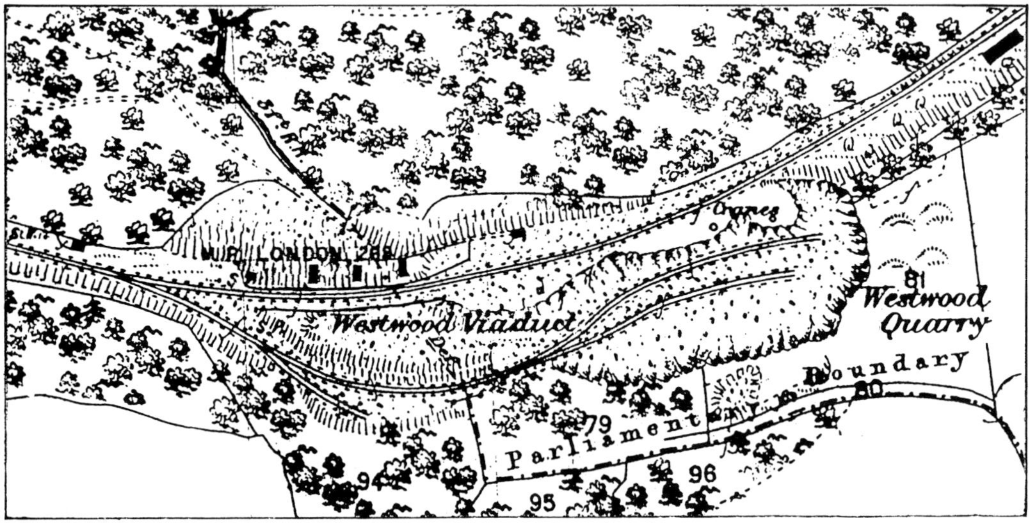

86. In the absence of a photograph of the viaduct at Westwood, this extract from the OS of 1880 shows the layout of the site shortly after the replacement masonry structure was brought into use, with details of the original piers, and the trackwork into the extensive quarry operation; note also the presence of cranes located at the quarry face. Today, the whole site is a mass of almost impenetrable undergrowth. ***Reproduced from the 1880 Ordnance Survey Map***

years was subsequently dumped on the slope under the replacement viaduct, to spill down and almost envelop the remains of the three original piers of Brunel's structure. Yet, the ivy clad stonework of these piers, complete with their plinth bedstones, is in remarkably good condition. There is evidence of the retaining wall which was built at its eastern end, presumably with a view to stabilising the ground for the building of the abutment of the new viaduct.

According to Gibbons, the last viaduct to be replaced using stone from Westwood quarry was that at Coombe St Stephens, completed in 1886. It would appear, therefore, that the quarry probably fell out of use shortly after this time, and the signal box closed. At the site today, the boundary fencing at the top of the quarry includes strutted end posts formed from light section flat bottom rail rather than the bridge rail used generally elsewhere for this purpose. It is possible that these particular rails were salvaged from the quarry sidings following their lifting during the late 1880s.

18. St Pinnock — Margary Class B — Figs. 87, 88 and 89 Location 269/40 — Length 633ft — Maximum height 151ft

Continuing further down the 1 in 88 incline for but a short distance the line crossed St Pinnock viaduct, a magnificent structure of straight formation, built on nine fully buttressed piers, incorporating gothic openings similar to Moorswater. These supported the Class B timber structure, which according to a report in *The West Briton & Cornwall Advertiser* of 7th March 1856 was, with Largin, the first viaduct to have been completed between Truro and Liskeard; their location close to the Bodmin–Liskeard road, such as it was, no doubt being a contributory factor in this respect.

Over the period 1860 to 1882 St Pinnock had incurred repair costs of £2,246, or £6.42/1,000ft^3 per annum, comparatively low considering its height. It would appear that, being straight, the absence of significant lateral loading could have had a beneficial affect on the structure. However, over the years 1869–1881 the annual maintenance cost had increased to £11.13/1,000ft^3 and no doubt this factor, coupled with the affect of speed, had some influence in prompting early action on replacement.

In 1880, Margary recorded a viaduct length of 613ft and proposed that, as the piers were well built and sound, replacement should be by raising them to carry wrought iron girders similar to his report's proposal for Liskeard. The necessary details had been submitted to the Joint Committee at their meeting of 30th January 1880, and prices for the wrought iron work were considered at their meeting of 13th February 1880. A total of thirteen companies submitted tenders, with prices varying between £13 and £18.15s per ton for the main girders. Margary was authorised to proceed with the reconstruction, at an estimated cost of £11,200 — but the work was finished in September 1882 at a cost of £9,284.

We are fortunate that soon after its completion, Margary presented a paper[34] to the Institution of Civil Engineers, giving a detailed description of the work involved. He estimated that the cost of the whole of the work amounted to less than half that of building a new masonry viaduct alongside the existing one but, as

87. This drawing, from Margary's paper to the Institution of Civil Engineers in 1882, shows the detail of construction of the Class B superstructure at St Pinnock and also illustrates the method of building up the piers to take the replacement wrought iron girderwork. ***Courtesy Inst.Civ.Engrs.***

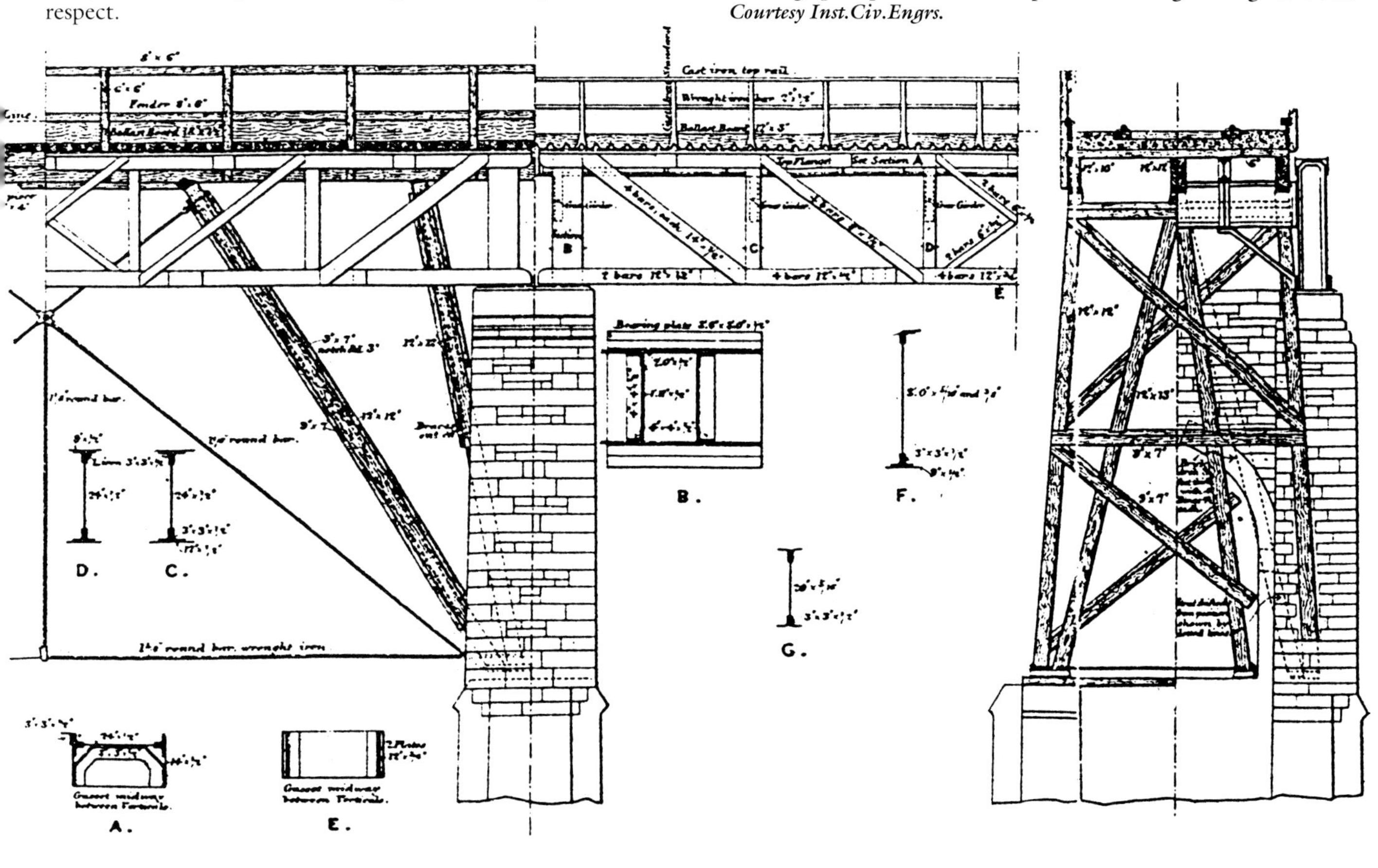

88. A picturesque view of the replacement St Pinnock viaduct from the north east, believed taken soon after its completion. The Bodmin–Liskeard road is just visible in the foreground but what is now the Trago Mills site is covered in trees while the valley sides include extensive woodland, all of which must have made not only the original construction, but also work on the replacement, a difficult operation. ***Great Western Trust***

a method, 'is economical only in the case of viaducts exceeding 120ft in height, and where the piers are of thoroughly good masonry and are buttressed'.

His proposals required the addition of 23ft of new masonry to the top of each of the existing piers, so as to provide support outside the timberwork for the wrought iron girders, which carried a floor wide enough for two lines of narrow gauge trackwork. It was the first occasion where this type of reconstruction had been attempted, and required that the pairs of raking legs of the two centre fans be moved nearer the centre of the piers, together with the removal of the diagonal bracing from the outside struts. This preparation will be understood from an examination of the drawing from Margary's paper (Fig.87). The additional masonry was then built up so as to enclose the outside legs, but to leave pockets for their later withdrawal. By building an arch over the centre of the new work on each pier, the whole of the masonry could be built up at one time without interfering with the timberwork supporting the railway above. In order to transport this stonework for the piers, from a dump alongside the main line, a standard gauge track was cantilevered out on each side of the viaduct, at the same level as the main line. Along this a light travelling crane was used to carry stone, up to one ton in weight, out to the appropriate location and lower it down to the masons working on the pier below.

At the top, on either side of the new masonry, a granite bedstone was set in place to support the ends of the new main girders. Each of these stones weighed 5 tons and was positioned by a travelling crane, operating from the broad gauge main line. Reference to Figs.80A to 80E, which illustrate the scope of similar operations carried out at a later date at Liskeard, will facilitate an understanding of these operations.

89. An appreciation of the height and majesty of Brunel's original piers can be gathered from this 1990 view of the replacement structure, completed in 1882. The original wrought iron girders are still in service after nearly 110 years. The precision edges of the masonry of the original piers shows quite clearly in comparison with the rather rough stonework of the extensions, which were later built on top of the piers to carry the present girderwork. ***Author***

Thus, apart from occasional occupation of the main line in order to position the bed stones, the masonry work could proceed without interruption to traffic. Margary makes no mention of the use of scaffolding for this work, and the absence of any scaffolding in the illustration of Keyham (Fig.53) for a similar operation carried out at the time of the modification of that viaduct, implies that the men worked on top of the piers without any such staging.

With the bedstones in place, the new wrought iron girders could be positioned. Each main girder weighed 15 tons, and was carried from the jib of a travelling crane at each end, hauled by a locomotive from the storage siding a quarter of a mile from site, along the main line to its location. There, it was swung over the side of the timber viaduct and lowered into position on the bedstones. It was possible for this operation, covering the positioning of two girders, to be completed in less than one hour, so that interruption to traffic was minimal. The cross girders then followed, being initially located on the bottom flange of the main girders, before being hauled up into place under the floor of the old viaduct. The supporting rail girders, which were to rest on these cross girders, were then lowered through the old floor and put into position by hand. The main girders were placed close to the old timberwork, so as to keep the weight over that part of the pier where it was originally located. However, as the timberwork was not always in a true line throughout the viaduct, it was necessary in some places to cut half through a timber strut in order to get the main girders exactly in line. In those instances the main girders, cross and rail girders were riveted together, as nearly in place as possible, and then, in the intervals of time between trains, the original timber beams were cut out and the combined girder work jacked into exact position, so that the timber floor was supported on the rail girders. By progressively removing the timber decking in lengths of about 10ft at a time, the new Barlow rail decking could be inserted and thus complete the replacement support. The addition of new iron handrailing and iron ballast edging strips completed the work, ready to receive the ballast for the single track broad gauge permanent way. Figure 88 shows the new viaduct in its tree lined location soon after completion.

While the girderwork of the other viaducts on the mainline, which were reconstructed in a similar way — Keyham, Coldrennick and Liskeard — has subsequently been replaced, the original wrought iron girders of St Pinnock (and Largin) are still in daily use. Apart from routine maintenance, the replacement of the decking and some local strengthening, they remain as installed in the 1880s. Viewing the site today (Fig.89) Brunel's original masonry piers still carry the main line to Penzance, singled since 1964 in the interest of economy, across the deep valley which is now the site of an out of town shopping centre known as Trago Mills. It is, thus, not impossible to imagine the awe with which the height and majesty of the original timber structure (it was the highest on the line) must have been viewed by the passing traveller on the nearby Bodmin–Liskeard road; and the nervousness felt by passengers, due to the inevitable creaking and groaning from the timbers, as the broad gauge trains sped down the 1 in 88 incline westwards to their destination.

19. Largin — Margary Class B — Figs.90 and 91
Location 269/69 — Length 567ft — Maximum height 130ft

With the line still falling at 1 in 88/89, the gradient eased to 1 in 146 as Largin viaduct was crossed after just a further 29 chains, a Class B structure similar to St Pinnock (although of less height) and completed in 1856. It was built on eight fully buttressed piers, incorporating gothic openings like Moorswater, and set on a curve. Figure 90, although taken from an early photograph, gives a good idea of the terrain of the Glynn Valley, with the surrounding tree lined slopes. It will be noted that the landward spans comprised queen post trusses, seated on embankment slopes with no abutments.

Margary quoted a length of 544ft, and in his 1880 report recommended reconstruction by a method similar to St Pinnock while repair costs between 1860 and 1882 totalled £2,615, to give

90. Although the original photograph is of poor quality, this view of Largin from the north, c1860, had to be included as the only record of any of the viaducts in the Glynn Valley. It shows the extensive woodland of the area and confirms the Class B construction of this fine viaduct, incorporating a trussed beam in each landward span. ***R.I.C.***

91. A view of some of the original masonry piers of Largin taken in 1990, clearly showing the massive buttresses, the Gothic arch openings and the top extensions built to carry the wrought iron girders of the replacement structure. These original piers and girderwork still carry modern traffic loads, although the line has been singled since 1964. Viewed today, we can only marvel at the skill and bravery of the workmen constructing these piers and working on the superstructure with only simple jib cranes to lift their materials into position, and with little or no safety precautions. *Author*

an average annual cost of £6.99/1,000ft³. A replacement structure was estimated to cost £9,000 and, following much consideration, instructions to put this work in hand were given by the Joint Committee in 1883, along with the replacement of Coombe St Stephens.

However, this action sparked off the dispute between the Joint Committee and the Board of the Cornwall Railway, which culminated in the Directors of the Company demanding arbitration; details of this action follow in a later chapter. Margary's evidence to the hearing contains some illuminating comments on the state of the structure at that time. In particular, the curvature was far from smooth, attributed to inferior workmanship at the time of the original construction — a circumstance also confirmed in the evidence given by the consulting engineer Harrison Hayter, and by Col. William Yolland, the BoT Inspector. In his evidence, Yolland pointed out that of the original 128 timber legs installed in the structure at the time of building, by the end of 1883 only 14 remained.

It is interesting to note that Brunel's original drawings, in general, show a width between parapets varying between 13ft 6in and 15ft, whereas in his evidence, Margary considered 15ft 6in to be the desirable figure; since on a curve, the lower width could give rise to an open door on a passing train fouling the parapet. When asked if this dangerous situation was due to the original construction or to wear of the structure, Margary replied 'I think it is original construction'. However, in corroborating this statement, Harrison Hayter added that he considered the enormous error in the structure was due to something else — distortion brought about by the action of passing traffic. Significantly, the evidence also revealed that despite these problems due to the curvature of the structure, no shores had been introduced to counter any lateral movement; no doubt the Class B superstructure, with its inverted 'V' leg support to the centre beam, proving its superiority in this situation. Furthermore, no mention was made of any movement or settlement of the piers. When further questioned regarding the use of timber for such structures, 'when no question of money were involved', Margary replied that the material should be avoided. In the outcome, as will be seen, reconstruction of Largin was allowed to proceed as originally planned, but thereafter, further viaduct replacement work was delayed for some five years.

Figure 91 is a view of the completed replacement structure, from which the additional height added to Brunel's original piers can be clearly distinguished, the pattern of reconstruction following that of St Pinnock. The work was completed on 16th January 1886, suitable for double track, narrow gauge, but the line was not doubled until December 1893. Like its neighbour, the track has subsequently been singled since 1964 in the interest of economy, the original wrought iron girders remaining in service.

Continuing its downward course, the line crossed a further three viaducts in a distance of just over a half mile, then within the next mile and a half, another two. Sadly, few records have come to light regarding the design of all these structures and, regrettably, no photographs; but the Minutes of the Joint Committee do record the timing and cost of the action taken with regard to their replacement. These details have been extracted under the appropriate Public Record Office reference in order to furnish the following information.

20. West Largin — Margary Class A
Location 270/21 — Length 315ft — Maximum height 75ft
(Margary quoted a length of 324ft)

With no drawing or photograph available, we can only conjecture that West Largin was built as a Class A1 structure, of straight formation. Examination of the site today shows that it was built on three masonry piers, the central one being buttressed, and with two fans located on the embankment slopes. It is significant that this viaduct was the first of its class to be rebuilt, although maintenance costs amounted to only £336 over its useful life of sixteen years, to return a low annual maintenance cost of £2.74/1,000ft³. This could point to speed being the major factor which determined its early replacement. While it is possible that the damp environment of the surrounding woodland could have brought on a serious rate of timber decay, we should have expected that problem to have been reflected in a higher maintenance charge.

Plans for its replacement, together with the neighbouring structure at Draw Wood, were first approved at the meeting of the Joint Committee on 11th July 1873, at a total cost of £8,000[35]. Terms for the purchase of the additional land were agreed at their

August meeting while eleven tenders, varying in total from £15,000 to £7,648, were considered on 24th October 1873. The lowest, from a Mr Pethick was accepted, and a new three arch masonry structure was brought into use on 26th September 1875. However, the BoT were not officially notified of this change until October 1875, to include the work at Draw Wood and Probus. Official approval was given on 1st January 1876[36].

21. Draw Wood — Margary Class E — Fig.92
Location 270/39 — Length 669ft — Maximum height 42ft
(Margary quoted the length as 681ft)

Again, no photograph has confirmed the details of this curved Class E structure, but it is believed to have been built on 17 local stone stub piers and was completed in 1857. Despite this being a light structure (and Crispin mentions that it was 'very modified' but gives no details)[37] maintenance costs over the period of its relatively short life of 16 years amounted to £593, to give an annual figure of £2.41/1,000ft^3. However, this figure had nearly doubled over the final seven years of its life to £4.68/1,000ft^3.

In August 1872 the Joint Committee approved the construction of an embankment and massive masonry retaining wall, at an estimated cost of £4,000 in substitution for the timber viaduct, while later in the month they considered a suggested deviation of the line which would 'admit of the abandonment of one or two more viaducts'. This proposal was apparently not pursued as by the following year, replacement was linked with that of West Largin within a single contract, as already noted above. The new embankment and masonry retaining wall (Fig.92) were brought into use on 23rd April 1875. The cost of all these works — including West Largin viaduct and the provision of the retaining wall and pier at Westwood — came to a total of £11,563.

92. With no photograph of the original Class E timber structure at Draw Wood coming to hand, this 1958 view of No 6940 *Didington Hall* at the head of a north bound train shows the massive buttressed retaining wall which was built to contain the embankment that replaced the viaduct in 1875. Set high up on the valley side construction of both the original and its replacement must have posed many difficulties to the contractors. *Anthony Fairclough Collection*

93. The viaduct at Derrycombe in 1991, with the remains of three piers of Brunel's original structure standing in the foreground, ivy clad and forlorn monuments to a bygone age. *Author*

22. Derrycombe — Margary Class A — Fig.93
Location 270/75 — Length 369ft — Maximum height 77ft

While no photograph of the original structure is available, it is believed that, in common with its neighbours in the Glynn Valley, it was built as a Class A1 viaduct and completed in 1857. The five fans were carried on three piers, of which the central one was buttressed, with a fan on the embankment slope at each end. (Margary confirmed the length at 369ft). Significantly, maintenance costs during its short life of twenty one years amounted to £1,058, giving a below average annual rate of £5.53/1,000ft^3, although this had increased to £8.97/1,000ft^3 over the final eleven years.

Approval for the building of a replacement masonry structure, suitable for double track narrow gauge, was given by the Joint Committee at their meeting of 15th August 1879, at an estimated cost of £5,600. It comprised four segmental arches of 56½ft span with a rise of 20ft, and was completed at a final cost of £5,107. It was brought into use from 8th May 1881, as a single broad gauge line; the route not being doubled until 1893.

At the site today, close to the Bodmin-Liskeard road, three of the original piers are still standing (Fig.93) and their centres measure a nominal 66ft. The old alignment can be traced on the adjacent embankments, to include in the western slope the remains of the plinth. Based on the indicated length of 369ft, the structure would have included four spans of 66ft, together with a trussed beam in each of the landward spans. It is of interest to compare the stonework in Brunel's original piers with that of the later replacement; the latter comprises large shale type stonework while the former was formed from smaller, flat stones, probably taken from the earlier surface workings of Westwood quarry.

94. A 1991 view of Clinnick viaduct, showing the buttressed and one of the plain piers from the original timber structure still standing. Years of ivy and sapling growth had been recently cut back to reveal this attractive site. *Author*

23. Clinnick — Margary Class A — Fig.94
Location 271/46 — Length 330ft — Maximum height 74ft

Continuing its downward path, the line crossed a tributary of the River Fowey by means of Clinnick Viaduct. In the absence of documentary evidence, we can only assume that this structure followed the pattern of its neighbours, and was completed in 1857 as a Class A1 design. It was built on three masonry piers, the centre one buttressed, together with two landward fans seated on the embankment slopes; Margary confirmed the length as above. Two of the piers still stand today (Fig.94) with the cropped remains of a third, together with a plinth in the western embankment slope, all of which clearly establish the course of the original alignment. The pier centres are measured at 57ft — yet a further variation from the nominal standard of 65ft.

Little is known of this structure other than since 1860 maintenance charges had reached a total of £475, to give an exceptionally low average figure of £2.77/1,000ft^3 per annum over 20 years. However, for the last 10 years this had nearly doubled to £4.78, still lower than average, but reflecting a deteriorating situation. The approval of a replacement masonry structure was given by the Joint Committee in June 1877 and by 16th March 1879 the single line had been slewed to the new structure, built on the downside of the line. Of more elaborate construction than other replacements, it comprised six semi-circular arches of 34ft span and incorporated decorative architectural features in local Devonian stone, together with an iron railing parapet. According to Crispin, these features could have been demanded by a local landowner as a stipulation of sale of the additional land involved. The BoT inspector required that a check rail should be provided and that future viaducts should incorporate a parapet wall of stone or brick, in place of the iron railing. The final cost of this replacement amounted to £5,019.

24. Penadlake — Margary Class E — Fig.95
Location 272/20 — Length 426ft — Maximum height 42ft

This was the last viaduct of the group in the Glynn Valley and having regard to its relatively low height of only 42ft, it was completed in 1857 as one of the lighter type Class E structures (Fig.95). Built on a curve of approximately 2,000ft radius, Margary recorded a length of 396ft, which is probably the more accurate. The ten sets of light double fans each sprang from low masonry plinths, set just above the level of the surrounding ground. Maintenance costs over the period 1860 to 1878 amounted to £669, to give an average annual charge of £4.08/1,000ft^3, increasing to £6.48 for the period 1869 to 1878.

A firm proposal to build a masonry replacement first came before the Joint Committee at their meeting of 1st October 1875, which was approved at a cost of £5,000. Significantly, it was minuted that half of this cost was to be 'charged to Capital and half to Revenue, in accordance with the principle laid down in Minute No 102 of May 1874'. This aspect was again raised in January 1877, when the Revenue charge was fixed at £250 pa, as 'approved by the Shareholders at their meeting in August 1875'. This statement should be borne in mind when we later come to consider the details of the Arbitration Hearing.

The Fortesque family was prepared to let the Company have the necessary land for this project (presumably at no cost, since no terms were mentioned at the April 1876 Meeting at which it was discussed), and the replacement was brought into service on 7th October 1877. It comprised an eight arch masonry viaduct, with segments of 30ft span and a rise of 9ft, built on the downside, at a cost of £4,444. Today, apart from being able to trace the course of the original alignment through undergrowth, there is no evidence of the remains of the timber structure.

95. With no photograph available, this drawing from Whitley's 1931 article in the *Railway Engineer* is the only record to survive of the Class E viaduct at Penadlake. As he wrote that article at the time he was a member of the GWR Engineers' Office at Plymouth, when he would have had access to the drawings which doubtless then still existed, we can assume it to be an authentic reproduction. *Whitley*

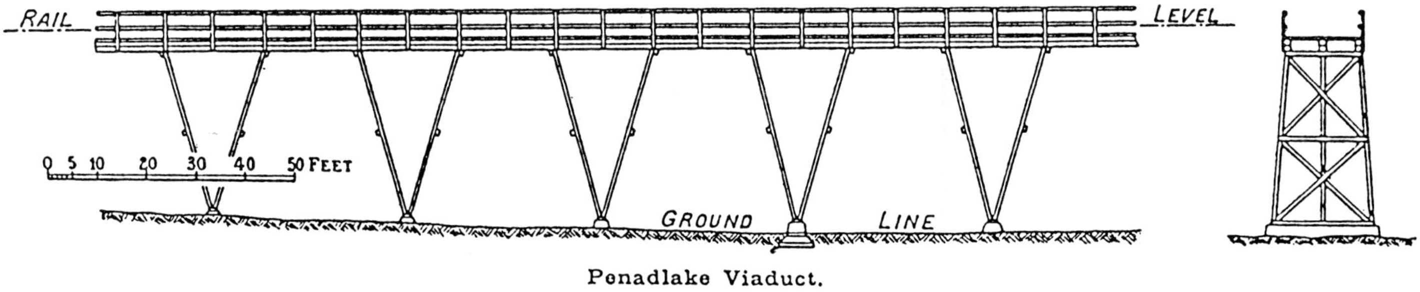

96. A view of the work of building the replacement viaduct at Milltown, taken in 1895. The formation of the original timber structure forms the background of the preparations for the new masonry viaduct. The simple jib crane has been erected on staging across the valley and will be used to lift men and materials to the top of the piers, as they slowly take shape. The standard gauge track in the foreground had presumably been laid in from the engineer's siding alongside the mainline, for the conveyance of materials. *From the Clinker Collection, Brunel University Library*

From the foregoing, it will be evident that during the period of the original building of the line, considerable work was in hand on this three mile stretch. This involved the employment of many hundreds of men, together with supporting cranes and equipment for the transport of the stonework and haulage of the timber baulks from the sawmill at Lostwithiel. Fortunately, the Bodmin to Liskeard road, such as it was, followed the route of the railway in the lower reaches of the valley and doubtless facilitated the operations. Nevertheless, the magnitude of the task involved over those years should not be underestimated. It is also interesting to note that for the five viaducts, West Largin to Penadlake inclusive, the overall average annual maintenance cost per 1,000ft^3 during their life was reported as significantly lower than that which generally applied for other similar structures on the line. Yet, they were among the earliest to be replaced but the records provide no ready explanation for this apparent paradox.

The line continued to fall for a further five miles, passing through the station at Bodmin Road, until reaching Lostwithiel, where almost at sea-level it crossed the Fowey river at location 277/50. This involved a bridge comprising both a wrought iron span of 82ft and up to a total of four 29ft spans formed from trussed timber beams. The crossing, built on a skew, was completed in 1857, its timber construction being similar to that employed at Wivelscombe. It is interesting to note that an original drawing[38] of the timber span shows the trussed beam on the north side of the span to have been in timbers of heavier section than those used on the south side.

Milltown to Truro

25. Milltown — Margary Class A — Figs.20 and 96
Location 278/49 — Length 501ft — Maximum height 75ft

From Lostwithiel, the line climbed along the side of the Fowey valley at 1 in 70 to cross a steep sided river inlet by means of Milltown viaduct. This was a Class A1 structure built on a curve and incorporating five masonry piers, of which two were buttressed. In addition, the two landward fans sprang from footings on the embankment slopes at each end, believed to have included timber platforms. Unusually, the landward spans were not comprised of queen post trusses, the ends of the horizontal carrying beams resting on timber platforms on the top of the embankment. These features will be clear from Fig.20, study of which would indicate that the viaduct length, based on pier centres of 66ft, was probably not more than 484ft, although Margary quoted a figure of 491ft. The average annual maintenance cost over the period 1860 to 1882, at £6.61/1,000ft^3, compared favourably with the overall average.

In 1880 Margary proposed a masonry replacement, but seven years on it was recorded that the structure still included a number of the original timbers which were then being renewed. Although the viaducts on the Glynn incline had been replaced by the 1880s, no action was taken with regard to this structure until 1893, despite it being on a 1 in 70 gradient and, therefore, subject to the adverse affects of trains speeding in the up direction. Work then commenced on building a masonry replacement on the up side.

97A. **This well known view of St Austell shows the Class A1 viaduct curving over the head of the Trenance Valley, some 100ft above the cottages below. The superstructure was carried on a landward fan at the Truro end set in the embankment, seven slender masonry piers, of which only two were buttressed, and the skew piers and special fans which supported the span that crossed the St Austell to Bodmin road. Surprisingly, despite its height and curvature, this viaduct was not replaced until 1898, although towards the end of its life additional cross timbers were added to the linking spans**

Figure 96 is a general view taken early on in the construction, showing the staging for the steam crane and a railway track in the foreground. The purpose of the latter is not clear, but it could have acted as a feeder from the engineer's siding which had been laid in to the west of the viaduct from December 1893.

Construction was completed in 1896 and the line was then doubled between Lostwithiel and the viaduct from May 1896, to connect with the realigned and doubled line between Milltown and Par, which had been completed by December 1894.

26. St Austell — Margary Class A — Figs.21, 97A, 97B, 98, 99 and 100
Location 286/60 — Length 720ft — Maximum height 115ft

Built on a sweeping curve, as will be seen from Fig.97A, this Class A1 structure carried the line high above the cottages nestling at the head of the Trenance valley, adjoining the town of St Austell. Its actual length is open to question since, compared with the above figure, Margary quoted 706ft while the 1894 Parliamentary Sessions drawing recorded 713ft. Surprisingly, having regard to its height and curvature, the eight masonry piers were of the lighter type with only two buttressed, as will be apparent from a study of Fig.21 and the splendid view of the structure in Fig.98. From this it will be seen that the fan at the Plymouth end sprang from a masonry plinth built alongside and parallel to the St Austell to Bodmin road, which passed under the structure at an angle to the line of the viaduct.

Consequently, this plinth was not normal to the line of the structure and hence, required the immediately adjacent pier to be of unusual construction. It was built with its Truro face normal to the viaduct and its Plymouth face parallel to the roadway, and was therefore of a triangular formation. Accordingly, in place of the usual fan arrangement on this pier, it comprised a southernmost one of six legs, the centre pair of legs being in the form of an 'A' frame, while the (outside) northern fan was of the usual four leg variety. The construction of the centre fan is not clear from the photographs but in all probability, having regard to the loading of the centre carrying beam, it also included a centre pair of legs in the form of an 'A' frame. Coffin pieces were included on the middle legs of each outer set, while the arrangement of these two plinths, meant that the inclined legs supporting the structure on either side of the roadway, were staggered across the width of this particular span; a most unusual configuration, which will be apparent from Fig.99. This formation meant that the braces were notched at an angle to the raking legs, while in order to provide sufficient headroom where the roadway passed under the structure, the horizontal wrought iron tie bars, which normally linked the cills of neighbouring piers, had to be omitted at this location. Finally, springing from the embankment slope behind the roadway plinth was a set of two leg fans which provided intermediate support to the landward span, brought about by its exceptional length due to the staggered main plinths. The Truro end landward fan was also seated on a masonry plinth within the embankment slope, with the end of its short landward span resting on top of the embankment.

97B. A close up view of the two buttressed and two of the plain piers of this viaduct which shows the detail of the superstructure, including two of the man refuges and the sagging wrought iron ties referred to in the text. *Both British Rail*

98. (below) A magnificent view of St Austell, taken from the adjoining hillside in the broad gauge days of 1890. It shows the St Austell to Bodmin road on the left, the viaduct crossing it on the skew, with the landward pier built parallel to the road and the adjacent special pier having one face also parallel to the road and the other normal to the viaduct; thus requiring a special set of fans. The slender slab sided piers accentuate the frailty of the overall structure. *R.I.C.*

99. This aspect of St Austell, taken in the mid 1880s from the St Austell to Bodmin road, shows the special six legged fan on the pier behind the house and the skew pier on the extreme right hand side, with its raking legs staggered across the span. Note the absence of horizontal wrought iron ties across the road between these two piers. ***R.I.C.***

At an average annual figure of £8.55/1,000ft^3, the maintenance costs for this viaduct worked out higher than the overall average, doubtless due to its curvature. If we refer to Margary's 1880 report, we find he comments that this structure did not include diagonal rods, referring to the ties between adjacent fans. However, all the available photographs show these rods as being present, and he may well have meant the horizontal members linking the piers across the above roadway. Today, study of Margary's reports show that he was not always consistent.

The recommended replacement was for 'enlarging some of the piers and raising all of them to carry wrought iron girders in substitution for the present timber'. However, despite its height and curvature, the original structure continued in service until the new masonry viaduct was brought into use in 1898, built on the up side. Figure 100 shows this work in hand in 1897, alongside the original timber structure. It will be noted that at least two of the latter piers incorporated shores.

At the Plymouth end, it was not possible to acquire sufficient width of land to build the new structure alongside the old, and hence the new viaduct overlapped the original timber structure at this point. Consequently, the original roadside masonry plinth formed part of the abutment of the new structure, as can be seen at the site today, while the northern face of the original triangular plinth abuts the pier of the new arch. This meant that the southernmost part of this span was completed after the old viaduct had been dismantled, single line working across the half finished section being involved during that time, until the line was doubled to Burngullow from 26th March 1899.

100. Work in progress on the building of the replacement viaduct at St Austell c1898, with a group of engineers surveying the site from the adjacent crane platform. Note the complete absence of scaffolding around the new piers during their construction, the excellent masonry on the left hand pier of Brunel's original structure, the extra shores added to increase the lateral strength of this viaduct and the cross timbers added to the linking spans. ***British Rail***

An interesting advertisement appeared in the 'Situations Vacant' column of *The West Briton & Cornwall Advertiser* for 29th June 1896:

> 'Wanted, for St Austell and Gover viaducts, twenty five Granite Cutters and twenty Trowel Masons; wages 7d (2.92p) per hour; from 12 to 18 months' work. Week-end railway tickets at half-price'.

These figures give some idea of the numbers of personnel engaged in the building of a masonry viaduct at that time, bearing in mind that each skilled man would require the supporting services of several unskilled workers.

27. Gover — Margary Class A — Figs.4, 101A, 101B, 102 and 103
Location 287/37 — Length 690ft — Maximum height 95ft

Before reaching its second highest point between Plymouth and Truro, at Burngullow, the line had to cross the Gover Valley, a mile beyond St Austell. Here a splendid curved Class A1 structure was built on eight piers of which only two were buttressed. In addition, the landward fans at each end sprang from masonry plinths on their respective embankment slopes (Figs. 101A and 101B). The 1894 Parliamentary Sessions drawing confirmed the above length but Margary quoted a figure of 679ft. Measurement at site today gave nominal pier centres of 65ft, and in the absence of trussed beams in the spans at the landward ends, according to available photographs, Margary's figure was probably the right one.

At £7.64/1,000ft^3 the average annual maintenance cost over the first 22 years of its life compared favourably with the overall average and in his 1880 report, Margary recommended that:

> '...as the masonry of the piers of this viaduct seems to be of a doubtful quality and only two piers out of ten being strengthened with buttresses, I would suggest erecting a masonry viaduct alongside the present structure'.

Again, he mentions the absence of diagonal rods, which nevertheless, appear in the photographs.

However, even by 1887 no action had been taken with regard to providing a replacement, as the viaduct was then under repair, with defective timbers being removed. It was not until 1895 that

101A. Gover viaduct from the south west, shortly before work commenced on building its replacement. Again, it will be noticed that of the eight piers (excluding the plinth on each embankment slope) only two were buttressed, despite its curvature and height (95ft). This view, together with that of Fig.4, give an excellent appreciation of this typical Brunel Class A1 structure.

101B. A closer view of Gover, showing the additional cross timbers of the linking spans together with the extra shores and the detail construction of the two buttressed piers. Both *British Rail*

102. This view of Gover from the south east, taken in 1896, shows men working on top of the pier in the foreground and gives an appreciation of the scale of not only that work, but also of the original piers, which had probably been built by similar methods more than forty years earlier. A shore can be seen within the superstructure of the right hand pier, just behind the top of the jib of Relf & Son's crane, and the stirrup supporting one of the linking span cross timbers. *British Rail*

work commenced on building a masonry replacement on the down side, which was completed and brought into use in 1898, the line between Burngullow and St Austell being doubled early in the following year.

Despite its apparent frailty, as will be apparent from Fig.4, this viaduct, together with St Austell, saw service for nearly forty years; a record all the more remarkable when their timber content per foot of span is compared with that of Moorswater, which had a much shorter life — 26ft^3 and 39ft^3 respectively. However, during their lifetime, as will be seen from the illustrations, additional shores were incorporated in the superstructure, while in their latter years the linking spans were strengthened by the addition of underslung cross timbers.

Figure 102 shows work in hand on the building of the new viaduct, while Fig.103 is a splendid view taken in 1898, shortly after the single mainline track had been diverted over the new viaduct. Again, this illustration provides a striking comparison between the scale of the old and the new, even taking account of the double track status of the latter, and illustrates just how frail were Brunel's masterpieces.

103. Gover, on 8th August 1898, on completion of the replacement masonry structure, which well illustrates the diminutive size of Brunel's original viaduct in comparison with its handsome new double track masonry successor. The mainline has been diverted from its original alignment, as yet only single, the double track not coming into service until March of the following year. The timber viaduct shows obvious signs of wear and distortion while it awaits dismantling and the site is still covered with the inevitable builders debris. *From the Clinker Collection, Brunel University Library*

28. Coombe St Stephens — Margary Class A — Fig.104
Location 291/16 — Length 738ft — Maximum height 70ft

Considering that this viaduct figured so extensively in the evidence given to the Arbitration Hearing, it is remarkable that no photograph has yet come to hand which would have shown the exact configuration of the structure. In conformity with its neighbours, it was probably of Class A1 construction, built on eleven masonry piers, including one set in the embankment at the Plymouth end. From an examination of the site today, it appears that they were at 64ft nominal centres and only two were buttressed. Margary quoted the length as 721ft (probably correct) in 1880 and considered that as the masonry of these piers was of doubtful quality, the line should be deviated to the north over a replacement masonry viaduct.

During the above Hearing, much evidence was presented regarding the fact that the original viaduct incorporated an 'S' curve — a construction roundly condemned by Margary, who was strongly supported by Harrison Hayter and Col. Yolland. A study of the alignment today, shows that the line from Plymouth approached the viaduct on a right hand curve. On reaching the landward span the curvature changed to left hand to cross the structure, a configuration which, while far from desirable, was perhaps not so acute as the evidence presented to the Hearing would lead us to believe. However, Margary pointed out that shores had been introduced on both sides to counter the adverse affect of trains crossing this 'S' configuration.

For these reasons, he was anxious to have the viaduct replaced. Coupled with total repair costs between 1860 and 1882 amounting to £3,513 (giving a higher than average annual cost of £8.52/1,000ft^3) his report to the Joint Committee of 31st July 1883 urged that action should be initiated without further delay. At their meeting of 11th January 1884, it was resolved to proceed with the replacement of this viaduct, and also the one at Largin. This decision was instrumental in the Cornwall Company seeking arbitration, and work was delayed for several months while the legal process followed its course. Eventually, replacement was allowed to proceed with the construction of a masonry viaduct on the up side, able to accommodate a double line of narrow gauge, with a realignment of the track to remove the 'S' curve. The broad gauge single line was diverted over the new structure from 11th July 1886. As will be seen from Fig.104, a view of the site in 1990, the ivy covered stumps of the original viaduct still stand alongside its successor.

29. Fal — Margary Class A — Fig.105
Location 291/59 — Length 570ft — Maximum height 90ft

According to Margary this viaduct was of length 573ft and included nine openings, thus being built on eight piers, although today there is no evidence at site to confirm this configuration. Again, like its neighbours it is assumed to have been of Class A1 design, but no drawing or photograph is available for verification.

104. (right) A 1990 view of the redundant piers of the viaduct at Coombe St Stephens, ivy clad and derelict with the replacement masonry structure behind. Among the Class A1 viaducts, this was one of the lowest at 70ft but the inclusion of an 'S' bend within its length severely tried the design necessitating the inclusion of a number of shores on both sides. ***Author***

105. (left) All that remains today of the timber viaduct at Fal is this lone masonry pier, close alongside its 1884 replacement; it is believed that the remaining piers were demolished at sometime in order to recover their stone, as the site is easily accessed from a nearby road. Like its neighbour at Coombe St Stephens, the original timber structure was built on an 'S' alignment which gave ongoing problems in the face of increasing traffic. ***Author***

Based on these data, the landward spans would certainly have needed to be trussed beams, each probably of 33ft span. According to Margary, it included a 'very sharp 'S' curve' and repairs between 1860 and 1882 amounted to £2,886, to give an average of £8.85/1,000ft^3 per annum — again higher than the average.

Following his 1880 recommendations, these factors combined to prompt construction of a replacement masonry viaduct on the up side. At an estimated cost of £12,000, this would allow realignment to remove the 'S' curve, and accommodate double track, narrow gauge. The single broad gauge line was diverted across the new structure from 24th August 1884. All that remains of Brunel's viaduct at the site today is the solitary pier shown in Fig.105.

30. Probus — Margary Class E — Fig.23
Location 295/30 — Length 435ft — Maximum height 43ft

Having crossed Fal viaduct, the line climbed steadily to a peak at Grampound Road, and then descended for a distance of over two miles, before reaching Probus viaduct. No photograph of the structure has been discovered, but Crispin has produced a helpful sketch of what it is believed to have looked like, which is reproduced in Fig.23. It was built on eleven stub masonry plinths from which sprang the light Class E double fans, to support the superstructure. Situated at the foot of two inclines, each of a gradient of about 1 in 100, led to trains crossing at speed. This factor is believed to have been the major reason which determined that it should be the first of the timber viaducts to be replaced[39].

In his evidence to the Arbitration Hearing, Margary confirmed that this viaduct was subject to exceptional strain since trains ran very fast over it. Being of weak construction, 'it was out of repair', although repair costs from 1860 to the date of its replacement had amounted to £455, or an annual average over its short life of £4.14/1,000ft^3. Rather than carry out the requisite heavy repairs, it had been considered preferable to arrange replacement by means of an embankment, incorporating a culvert. This work was put in hand in 1869, additional land being purchased to enable the new alignment to be formed clear of the original viaduct. It was completed on 16th July 1871, thus giving the original structure a life of just over twelve years.

106. Tregarne viaduct, viewed from the south east in 1898, was built on seven masonry piers, three being buttressed, together with a fan located in the embankment at each end. Close study shows that most of the piers incorporated a shore, but at this date the linking spans had not yet been strengthened. ***L G Booth Collection***

31. Tregarne — Margary Class A — Fig.106
Location 296/52 — Length 606ft — Maximum height 83ft

From Fig.106 this structure can be identified as Class A1. It was built on a sweeping curve and supported by seven masonry piers, of which only three were buttressed, with an additional fan support at each end, carried on the relevant embankment slope. According to the drawing prepared for the 1894 Parliamentary Session, that at the Penzance end rested on a timber platform while the Plymouth end unit sprang from a masonry plinth. This drawing also gave the length as 8·80 chains or 581ft, while Margary quoted a figure of 584ft. However, according to a GWR site plan, the pier centres were 62ft and with a trussed beam in the landward span at the Plymouth end, the latter figure was probably the correct one.

Over the period from 1860 to 1882, the cost of maintenance totalled £3,352, giving an average of £10.04/1,000ft^3 per annum, an exceptionally high figure with no obvious explanation. As a replacement, Margary recommended a new masonry viaduct to the north, with a view to improving the alignment. However, in his 1887 report, apart from a few pieces showing signs of decay, the timbers of the original viaduct were recorded as being in good order. Although located at the foot of an incline of 1 in 66 and built on a curve — factors which could well have influenced its life-span — no action was taken apart from the introduction of shores, until it was decided to proceed with the building of a masonry replacement in the late 1890s. Work then commenced on the construction of a viaduct suitable for double track on the down side, contrary to Margary's original recommendation. This was completed by 1st September 1901 when the single line was diverted across the new structure, followed by doubling in March of the following year.

107. This Class A1 viaduct at Tregagle was carried on four sets of fans, two on light masonry piers and one located on the embankment slope at each end. The latter were seated on timber platforms which incorporated timber wedge supports. Note the additional cross member slung from the mid point of each linking span which provided extra support for the centre carrying beam. This view is dated 1898. *L G Booth Collection*

32. Tregagle — Margary Class A — Figs.39 and 107 Location 297/07 — Length 315ft — Maximum height 69ft

Again, we are fortunate to have a photograph of this viaduct and thus identify it as Class A1, built on two masonry piers, with the addition of two fans springing from the embankment slopes at each end. These details will be apparent from Fig.107, from which it will be noted that both landward spans were composed of queen post trusses, while the Plymouth embankment fan was certainly supported on a timber platform (Fig.39). Margary recorded a length of 303ft, all but confirmed by the 1894 Parliamentary Session drawing at 304ft.

Over the years 1860 to 1882 a total of £1,400 was spent on maintenance, giving an annual average of £8.08/1,000ft^3. Margary had recommended a masonry replacement, similar to Tregarne, to be built at the same time and thus allow an overall improvement in the alignment through these two structures. However, following the repairs carried out in 1885, his 1887 report showed the timbers to be in good order, with few pieces showing signs of decay. Even though this original structure was situated on an incline of 1 in 66, it continued in service, with the addition of shores and in its latter years, an under slung cross beam for each of the linking spans. Thus, it was not until 1896 that work was put in hand for a new viaduct, which was built for double track, on the up side. The replacement was completed in time for the single line to be diverted across it from 2nd February 1902, with doubling of the route following in March.

33. Truro (Moresk) — Margary Class A — Figs.108, 109, 110 and 111 Location 300/09 — Length 1,329ft — Maximum height 92ft

Having crossed Tregagle viaduct, the line continued to climb until reaching Buckshead Tunnel (320 yards), after which there was a long drop at 1 in 70, easing to 1 in 84 to reach Truro viaduct; sometimes known as Moresk. From the illustrations, it will be seen to be a Class A1 design and was the longest structure in Cornwall. Compared with the above length, Margary quoted 1,392ft [sic] while the 1894 Parliamentary Sessions drawing recorded 1,310ft.

In his article on the timber viaducts, Gibbons[40] included a sketch of the viaduct, showing it to comprise 20 masonry piers. Examination of available records, photographs and site survey indicate that four of them were buttressed, while apart from a span at each end of 52ft, the pier centres were 66ft — a foot longer than the usual maximum of Class A1. This would indicate that the length of 1,310ft was probably correct.

The approach from Plymouth was on a right hand curve and Figs.110 and 111 show the inclusion of shores on the piers supporting that part of the structure. From this initial curved approach it then continued in a straight alignment, and having regard to its length, albeit of modest height and curvature, it is quite remarkable that this original structure saw service through until 1904 — a life of 45 years. During its latter years, the linking spans were strengthened by the addition of underslung cross timbers. These are visible in Figs.110 and 111 but missing from Fig.109, a view from the south, taken in the late 1870s, before the stream in the foreground was bridged.

In 1880 Margary commented to the effect that:

> '...the piers generally although apparently constructed with sound masonry are not of sufficient height nor of such dimensions as to render the adoption of wrought iron girders advantageous; and therefore in reconstructing [this] viaduct I would suggest erecting alongside [it a] masonry structure'.

108. Truro, or as it was sometimes called, Moresk viaduct, was the longest in Cornwall, at 1,329ft. It was supported on no less than 20 masonry piers, of which only six were buttressed. The absence of additional cross members under slung from the mid point of the linking spans dates this view in the 1880s. ***R.I.C.***

Maintenance charges to 1882 totalled £5,480, which work out to an annual average of £7.31/1,000ft^3. Further heavy repair work was carried out on the original timbers during the first half of 1886 so that the 1887 report showed it to be in very good order. Consequently, it continued in service for a further fifteen years and steps were only initiated to build a double line replacement viaduct in 1898. Figure 111 is a close up view of the structure taken in 1901, with the new works in hand alongside, which shows excellent detail of the original timbers and wrought iron ties. The new viaduct was built on granite piers and abutments with the arches and balustrades from Staffordshire blue bricks, with a pronounced torus mould outside the arch rings. The single main line was finally diverted over the new route from 14th February 1904, and the line doubled in the following May.

Today, this impressive granite and brick structure forms a fitting contrast to Brunel's original slender masonry piers, fourteen of which still stand alongside as tribute to his memory.

109. (above) A charming view of Moresk from the south, c1870, with no shores or additional cross members in place. *R.I.C.*

110. (left) Taken from almost the same location as Fig.108 this later view of Moresk dates from the start of work on building the masonry replacement, c1901, the apparatus of construction and heaps of stone being visible in the background. Note also the addition of the extra cross member to each linking span. *Royal Cornwall Polytechnic Society*

111. A 1902 view of work on the construction of the replacement viaduct at Truro, with the original Brunel structure behind. Note the shores incorporated in the fan sets on several of the lefthand piers, and the underslung cross members fitted to each linking span. Otherwise the timberwork appears to be in good order, despite its length of service. *L G Booth Collection*

112. A view of Carvedras viaduct, looking down St Georges Road, c1890, with a broad gauge goods train crossing. The masonry and timberwork appear in good order and while a shore has been fitted to the left hand pier, which was of plain construction, the linking spans had not yet been strengthened. Of its 13 piers, only four were buttressed. Not until 1902 was a masonry replacement brought into use, after 43 years' service. *R.I.C.*

34. Carvedras — Margary Class A — Figs.112, 113A and 113B Location 300/39 — Length 969ft — Maximum height 86ft

A short distance beyond Truro viaduct, the line crossed Victoria Gardens on another fine structure, as shown in Figs.112 and 113A, which identify it as a Class A1 design. The piers comprised three buttressed and eight plain, supporting the centre group of fans, while a double pier at each end carried a set of fans each comprised of six legs. The landward spans linked to masonry abutments and included additional short strut supports. Compared with the quoted length of 969ft, Margary gave a figure of 1,011ft and the 1894 Parliamentary Session drawing 966ft. The main pier centres measure 66ft and taking account of the special end pier formation, the length of 969ft appears correct.

The maintenance cost from 1860 to 1882 amounted to £4,248, or an average of £7.38/1,000ft^3 per annum. Again, in 1880 Margary's recommendation for this replacement was similar to that for Moresk, and while his 1887 report spoke of 'several legs and beams that should be changed before very long and a great many planks will have to be renewed next time this viaduct is under repair', it continued in service into the twentieth century. Significantly, at some stage, shores were introduced on some of the piers, particularly those adjacent to St Georges Rd. This is confirmed by Fig.112, a view taken in the early 1890s, showing a broad gauge train on the viaduct. The linking spans were also strengthened towards the end of its life, while according to a photograph, c1892, of the Carvedras Tin Smelting Works (Fig.113B), which was located alongside this structure, it will be seen that a granite pier had been built to support one of the linking spans at the western end.

That together with its neighbour Moresk, these two structures should have achieved such long service, compared with those in the Glynn Valley, would appear to indicate that the speed of traffic crossing the viaducts must have been a significant factor in determining their useful life. The location of Truro station close to both Carvedras and Moresk meant that trains would either be slowing for the station or would have only just started their journey, so that their speed would not have been excessive. By the turn of the century, work was in hand on building a replacement structure for Carvedras, similar to the one at Moresk, which was completed in 1902, the single main line being diverted over it on 17th August of that year. Today, there are five piers still intact, standing within the picturesque setting of Victoria Gardens, providing another fitting tribute to Brunel within this capital city of Cornwall.

113A. (left) Carvedras viewed from the south east in 1899, before work started on its replacement. It will be seen how well the overall structure had by this time mellowed into its surroundings. Note the addition of a cross timber to each linking span.
L G Booth Collection

113B. (below) The Carvedras Tin Smelting Works c1892 with Carvedras viaduct in the background, showing the granite pier built under the mid point of the left hand linking span — a sure sign that the structure was in trouble. *R.I.C.*

West Cornwall

From Truro, after passing through Higher Town Tunnel, the main line swung away to the west at Penwithers Junction. It then traversed the route of the original West Cornwall Railway, leaving the Cornwall Railway to continue as a branch to Falmouth. It will be recalled that the former line had originally been built to narrow gauge and that the broad gauge rail was added in 1866, following takeover by the Great Western Railway. This conversion involved a considerable amount of work — alteration to earthworks, supply and laying new permanent way and, relevant to our story, following the recommendations of the BoT's Inspector, Col. Yolland, renewal and alteration to the timbers and strengthening of the viaducts. A report[41] of the scope of all these alterations was made by Bush in February 1867, which included an amount of £9,657 for 'alterations of bridges and viaducts', and estimates of £4,000 for 'masonry piers Penwithers, Chacewater, Blackwater & Redruth viaducts' and £2,500 for 'parapets and coffin pieces of viaducts'.

Sadly, with a few exceptions, original information on the construction and history of the nine structures between Truro and Penzance has not come to light. Both Gibbons and Whitley refer to them in broad terms and their details, together with those from MacDermot, and the interesting notes and sketches compiled by Crispin, enable the following histories to be compiled.

43. Penwithers (Sometimes referred to as Penweathers) — Class Y — Fig.114
Location 302/03 — Length 372ft — Maximum height 54ft

According to both MacDermot and Crispin, this viaduct followed the original Class Y construction, built on a left hand curve from Truro. Based on the above length, it would have been carried on seven sets of supports, with a landward span at each end of 21ft; although no photograph has been traced from which to verify the details. Initially, each pier would have comprised upright timbers braced together, similar to those shown in Fig.7, and seated on either stone footings or timber planking. From the tops of these supports sprang the three sets of radial legs which carried the superstructure. The viaduct was originally completed in 1852 while the timber supports were replaced by masonry piers, in accordance with the above Bush report, in 1869.

A replacement masonry viaduct, suitable for double track narrow gauge, was built in granite and completed in 1887, as recorded on a commemorative stone in the parapet. It comprises seven arches of 45ft span and 15ft rise, with a central height of 68ft, and was located on the down side, the track being realigned between the new viaduct and Penwithers Junction. At site today it is just possible to trace the original alignment, as shown in Fig.114, a view taken from the north east, but there are no traces of the piers of the original structure.

114. The site at Penwithers on the West Cornwall main line in 1990, showing the replacement masonry structure on the left, dating from 1887, with the alignment of Brunel's original timber viaduct on the right. Over one hundred years since it was taken out of service there are no remains at site to show where the structure once stood — only the wide embankment slopes at each end. *Author*

44. Chacewater — Class Y — Fig.115
Location 305/46 — Length 297ft — Maximum height 52ft

Again, with no photograph from which to verify the details, we are dependant on MacDermot and Crispin's report that this was also a Class Y structure. Built on a downside left hand curve and at the above length, it would have originally incorporated six timber piers on either timber planking or stone footings. These were

115. A similar view of Chacewater, which dated from 1888, with the former alignment in the foreground. Regrettably, no illustration of either of these two viaducts has been discovered. *Author*

116. Of all the original Class Y viaducts in West Cornwall, only Blackwater, shown here, has the remains of one of the original masonry piers still standing, which enables the alignment of Brunel's structure to be clearly determined, including the embankment slopes at each end. Like so many of his viaducts it was built on a curve but no photograph has survived. The masonry replacement, shown here, was completed in 1888. ***Author***

replaced in 1869 by masonry piers, the material probably coming from a small quarry on the Penzance side.

The replacement masonry viaduct, again built in granite wide enough to accommodate double track narrow gauge, was sited on the down side and completed in 1888 — as recorded on a stone let into the parapet. It includes five arches of 45ft span and 15ft rise, and a central height of 55ft. As will be seen from Fig.115, viewed from the north east, the site today, apart from the embankment slopes, shows little evidence of the original formation or remains of the piers.

45. Blackwater — Class Y — Fig.116
Location 305/68 — Length 396ft — Maximum height 68ft

This structure was crossed shortly before reaching Chacewater station, built according to MacDermot as a Class Y design on a downside right hand curve. It was carried on eight sets of timber supports, and completed in 1852, but once again no photographs are available from which to verify these details. Having regard to its height, it is thought that the landward fan at each end sprang from the relevant embankment slope, while the original timber piers, similar to those at Penwithers and Chacewater, were replaced by masonry in 1869. The remains of a small quarry on the Truro side was probably the source of the stonework involved.

A double track narrow gauge replacement masonry viaduct was built on the down side and opened in 1888, which date is again recorded on a commemorative stone in the parapet. The seven arches of 45ft span and 15ft rise, are all in granite, with a central height of 70ft. Today, the original alignment can be easily traced as this is the one location on the West Cornwall line where there are the remains of one of the 1869 replacement piers (Fig.116).

46. Redruth — Class Y — Figs.7 and 117
Location 309/79 — Length 489ft — Maximum height 61ft

This fine structure, of which we are fortunate to have several photographs, carried the railway high across the town of Redruth, to link the Hayle-Redruth section with the Redruth-Truro line. It was completed in 1852, and is an excellent example of the Class Y design carried on ten piers, originally of braced timber like the other viaducts in this Class. Set in a downside right hand curve, Fig.7 gives a good general view of the viaduct formation, a photograph taken in the early 1860s before the timber piers were replaced. Meanwhile an appreciation of the frailty of these structures can be obtained from Fig.117, which shows a broad gauge train on the viaduct in the late 1870s. Although Bush speaks of the addition of parapets and coffin pieces to the Class Y viaducts, we are at a loss to know what he had in mind with regard to those entries. Examination of these two photographs, which would have been taken respectively, before and after the broad gauge strengthening, does not reveal any significant differences regarding these features.

In his Report, Bush chose to consider the work associated with these four viaducts as a single entry, so that it would seem reasonable to assume that their design followed a similar pattern. Hence, the photographs which we have of Redruth could be taken as representative of the group, and therefore, go some way to verify the earlier comments relating to Penwithers, Chacewater and Blackwater.

The replacement by masonry for the braced timber of the piers was completed in 1869 and the viaduct then continued in service for a further 19 years, attracting in 1881 a most critical report[42] in the local press. This questioned:

> '...how much of the timber used in building the Redruth viaduct, about 30 years ago, remains in its place to this day. Years ago rumour spoke of the shaky condition of this viaduct; yet by dint of continual attention, and frequent visits from gangs of navvies, with a new piece of timber here, another piece there, and masonry rests at two or three places, it still stands, and bears up the heavy loads which daily go over it. Navvies have been, for the last week or two, engaged repairing it, the scene of operations being, for the most part, at Penryn-street, where some two or three 'legs' of old timber have been replaced by new ones, and whilst this has been doing a temporary 'prop' from the ground has done its part to share the burden, and keep the structure up. May we ever expect to have a new viaduct at Redruth, or must we still put up with the present one?'.

117. A broad gauge goods train crossing Redruth viaduct in about 1880, a view which, although previously published, could not be omitted since it gives such a clear impression of a typical West Cornwall train on one of the original Class Y viaducts. *R.I.C.*

It was to be another seven years before that question was answered, by the completion in 1888 of a new masonry viaduct. Wide enough to carry double track narrow gauge, the replacement was formed by seven arches of 56½ft span and 20ft rise, and one span of 60ft over Penryn St. Because the original line of railway passed directly over the town, there was not the space available alongside the route to build the new structure. Accordingly, it was erected substantially on the original alignment, similar to the procedure carried out earlier in the decade at Bolitho. Thus, construction was made in two longitudinal sections; the first being just wide enough to accommodate the single broad gauge track, which was diverted over it on completion. The timber viaduct was then dismantled, allowing the second half of the new structure to be built, the two sections being carefully toothed together, to form the splendid granite structure which spans the town centre today. Although provision had been made for these four replacement viaducts to accommodate double track, narrow gauge, it was not until the early 1900s that action was taken to double the line west of Truro — but the rebuilding work carried out in the late 1880s had paved the way for this improvement.

47. Penponds — Class Z — Figs.6, 25, 26, 27, 28, 29 and 118
Location 314/49 — Length 693ft — Maximum height 45ft

The details of construction of this viaduct have already been fully described in Chapter 4, and the design identified as Class Z (Figs.25 to 29 inclusive). It was completed in 1852, having been built on the embankment of the original Hayle Railway, which had been carried across the valley in combination with the Penponds incline; the original drawing giving a total length of 739ft. At its western end, a farm track passed under the embankment, through a small tunnel, which is still in use today. The whole area is now overgrown with trees and bushes so that it is difficult to follow the original alignment.

In 1861, a third central leg was added to the two-leg supports over the Penzance length of the structure. Shortly after that date, the timber seatings and masonry plinths incorporated in the original design, were replaced with dwarf stone piers. At the same time, the embankment at the Penzance end was extended by some 60ft, these alterations being shown on the later drawing[43]. These modifications thus reduced the overall length of the viaduct to 693ft, and arose from the recommendations of Col. Yolland at the time the line was adapted to the broad gauge; the above drawing shows the track formation as mixed gauge. However, despite these alterations, the structure retained a most fragile appearance which drew much local criticism, as exemplified by the comments of a correspondent in *The West Briton & Cornwall Advertiser* of 30th March 1882, who asked:

> 'And how about the viaduct at Penponds? It is in a miserable state, and I really regret to see the piles of timber alongside of it, which show that it is to be patched up. These 'West Cornwall' viaducts are inferior altogether to the not very desirable erections of the same kind on the Cornwall line; they were built for narrow gauge engines and trains, and are now subject to the tremendous burden of the broad gauge, for which they were not intended and are not calculated'.

Nevertheless, the structure continued in service until 1900 and, apart from Penzance, it was the last timber viaduct in West Cornwall to be replaced. Work was put in hand in the late 1890s to build a masonry viaduct on the downside of the original structure, constructed of granite piers with Staffordshire brick arches, spandrel walls and parapets and wide enough to accommo-

118. The replacement viaduct at Penponds under construction in 1898, viewed from the south east, which clearly shows Brunel's original Class Z timber structure built on the embankment of the old Hayle Railway. The absence of scaffolding around the new piers will be noted, together with the narrow gauge construction line built on piles at the base of the original viaduct. ***From the Clinker Collection, Brunel University Library***

date double narrow gauge track. It was completed at the end of the century and the double line from Camborne to Gwinear Road introduced to traffic from 21st January 1900.

Figure 118 taken in 1898 shows the start of work on the replacement viaduct, with in the background the original Hayle Railway embankment and Brunel's timber structure. Again, the comparison of its slender supports with the massive new masonry piers illustrates better than any words, the frailty of his original design and we can but marvel that it remained in service for all those years without calamity.

48. Angarrack — Class Y — Figs.31 and 119
Location 317/52 — Length 798ft — Maximum height 100ft

Of all the viaducts in West Cornwall, this must have been the most impressive and it is sad that no photograph appears to have survived to record what must have been a quite remarkable structure. We do have an illustration from Whitley (Fig.31) while both MacDermot and Crispin record that it was similar to the other Class Y structures on the line.

Construction commenced in 1851, and according to a contemporary report[44], was:

> '...built wholly of timber on stone footings. The piers were formed of upright timbers brought together and...were fifty feet apart, the longitudinal beams of the railway being supported at three points'.

However, there appeared to be much doubt among the public as to the safety of this remarkable structure and there was a report in the *Royal Cornwall Gazette* of 31st October 1851 (before the line was opened) which noted:

> 'It is satisfactory to learn that several practical men of science in the Western part of the county have satisfied themselves by scientific enquiries and calculations that the viaducts in course of construction on the [West Cornwall Railway] line have been planned and are being constructed on principles which offered a guarantee of their safety and stability. Unscientific observers however, still regard the works with feelings of doubt and alarm'.

In the light of the analysis of Chapter 3, the extent of the deliberations of these men of science is open to conjecture.

The viaduct was built to a 30 chain radius, on 15 piers; those at the landward ends being formed from two sets of raking legs in conjunction with vertical legs while the middle piers followed the usual Y Class construction. A newspaper report[45] spoke of local inhabitants:

> '...who had gazed at it in wonder and apprehension while in course of construction...and viewed from below or from either of its roadway ends, the seeming intricacies of its supporting timbers — horizontal, upright and diagonal presented a singularly beautiful and most fairylike appearance'.

Indeed, so fairylike was the appearance of the new viaduct having regard to its height of 100ft and relatively narrow width (at the base, probably not more than 30ft over the footings), anxiety regarding its safety is quite understandable. The inevitable creaking of the timbers as a train crossed the structure would only have added to that anxiety.

However, it was duly examined and accepted by the Government Inspector, Captain Laffens, who 'highly commended' its construction and expressed the opinion that, in common with all the West Cornwall structures, it was sufficiently strong. According to a local newspaper report[46] the cost of this viaduct was quoted as £4,000, compared with a figure of £30,000 for a masonry viaduct and £18,000 to have built an embankment across the valley. However, this figure of £4,000 should be compared with an estimated cost of at least £6,500, as calculated from the data of Appendix 1. Nevertheless, by his design, Brunel was able to achieve a remarkable saving in first cost.

In 1862 steps were taken to replace the underground timber portions of the piers by masonry. In the period 1864/5, this was followed by the building of masonry piers up to the level of the horizontal timber ties, thus providing a masonry cill for the springing of the raking legs. In this condition the structure continued in service for a further twenty years, until the decision was made in 1882 to commence the building of a masonry replacement on its up side, suitable for double track, narrow gauge.

This evoked a letter[47] to the local press, to the effect that the correspondent was:

> '...thankful to find that the Great Western Railway Company intends at once to rebuild the Angarrack viaduct. Not a day too soon. It ought to have been condemned before. A poor man was on it the other day when a train went over, and he was quite horrified by what he felt and saw'.

Although the contract for its erection was initially secured by a Mr Phillips, of Plymouth, because of his departure to Scotland to work on the Forth Bridge, the project was completed by a Mr Henry Stevens, of Ashburton. Granite for the structure was quarried at Tregenhorne, St Erth and transported to the site by road. The construction was not without incident; a number of fatal accidents occurred, including one through a crane overturning and crashing some 60ft to the ground and another when a block of stone fell from a crane killing two men. On 3rd March 1885 the 68 stone cutters and 40 masons employed on the site went on strike, following discontent among the men due to their loss of earnings when bad weather prevented work. They maintained that the shelter provided in those circumstances was inadequate but the management refused to provide additional facilities and threatened dismissal of the strikers — which threat was duly actioned. However, a number of the skilled men involved sought work elsewhere so that management was forced to provide better shelter, a return to work being secured on 19th March.

Figure 119 is a view of Angarrack, seen from the south west, taken shortly before the new structure was finally completed in 1885, its eleven arches of 56ft 6in span with a rise of 20ft, dominating the village nestling in the valley below. The timbers of the original structure can be discerned through the arches. The line remained single until 19th December 1901, when doubling to Hayle was introduced. Following the dismantling of the original timbers, the masonry piers were undisturbed for a number of years until they also were removed, it is believed in order to provide the stonework for the sea wall protection at Penzance. Today, there is no evidence at site of the original structure, just the wider embankment slopes at each end enable its alignment to be determined.

119. The only photograph to come to light of Angarrack, taken at the time the replacement structure was nearing completion. The original timber superstructure can be seen through the arches, seated on masonry piers, which was finally taken out of service in 1885, after a life of thirty three years. *R.I.C.*

49. Guildford — Class Y — Fig.32
Location 318/25 — Length 384ft — Maximum height 56ft

From Angarrack the line dropped at around 1 in 80 to cross Guildford viaduct, the final Class Y structure on the route to Penzance. It was built on a downside right-hand curve of 24 chain radius, on seven timber piers, and completed in 1850. Some of the details of construction can be seen from Fig.32, taken at the time the replacement masonry viaduct was being built. In common with other similar structures, the timber footings of the piers had been replaced by masonry in 1862, and stub masonry piers added in 1869.

This viaduct continued in service until the completion of the masonry replacement, on the down-side, in 1886. This was built of granite, wide enough to accommodate double track, narrow gauge. Having six arches of 45ft span and 15ft rise, it was first opened for single line traffic, but the line was not doubled until 19th December 1909. Other than the embankment slopes, there is no evidence at site today of Brunel's viaduct, the foundations for the new Hayle by-pass passing under the existing structure having removed any trace of the original piers.

50. Hayle — Modified Class Z — Figs.5, 120 and 121
Location 319/39 — Length 831ft — Maximum height 34ft

The West Cornwall line crossed the town of Hayle by means of this long, low structure, partly built on a down-side right hand curve. According to MacDermot, its construction was similar to that of Penponds or, in our notation, Class Z. Regrettably, no photographs or drawings of the original formation appear to exist so that its story is very much a matter of conjecture.

Gibbons reported that the viaduct comprised 'thirty six spans of about 20ft each, and two spans of 40ft'. A view of Hayle in an early lithograph (Fig.5) shows the viaduct supported on piers each of only two legs. Therefore, it would be reasonable to assume that they were similar to the two-leg supports of Penponds (Fig.26) which formation we know from photographic evidence, was also used for the viaduct at Penzance. This interpretation is thus in conformity with MacDermot's statement regarding the similarity between these three structures. However, it would appear that in the case of Hayle viaduct, a number of spans at the Penzance end, where it crossed Harvey's foundry, were in fact carried on 2ft thick masonry piers, at 20ft centres, 'to prevent destruction by fire'[48]. This is confirmed from the details of the piers shown on a drawing[49], prepared in 1880, of the modifications required for the 'Proposed Hayle Viaduct' to accommodate double track narrow gauge. This called for those piers to retain their original thickness but they were to be widened to accommodate the increased width of the new structure.

In the absence of any details of the timber superstructure, it must be assumed that it followed closely the Class Z construction, similar to that of Penponds. However, the two spans of 40ft were doubtless of a trussed beam formation. Furthermore, the location of the supports across the length of the viaduct appears to have been most irregular which leads to the belief that it was a far from perfect design that drew considerable criticism from the public at large. A correspondent to *The West Briton & Cornwall Advertiser* wrote on 30th March 1882 'such fabrics as those which cross over the houses at ...Hayle are scandalously dangerous, and in no wise adequate to the strain of broad gauge traffic'.

120. A 1989 view of the rebuilt viaduct at Hayle, showing the remains of the original masonry plinths in the middle distance, opposite the pedestrian; the reinforced masonry piers in the background and the leaning pier in the immediate left hand foreground. It was beneath one of the plinths that the remains of one of Brunel's original piles was exposed in 1990. *Author*

121. A general view of Hayle, taken from the north west in 1989. It is difficult to realise that, when the original viaduct was built in 1852 on this same alignment, the whole of the area beneath the structure on the right comprised the foundries and workshops of the famous engineering firm of Harveys of Hayle. Since that time, the viaduct has been rebuilt to carry a double track, narrow gauge and the original piers reinforced by means of the additional brickwork seen in this modern day photograph. *Author*

In 1864/5 dwarf stone plinths were built for the timber piers, the masonry seating on the timber piles, but there is no evidence to indicate that a third, central leg was ever introduced at these supports. At a nominal 20ft length, the spans were slightly less than those of Penponds, so that based on our earlier stress analysis, using the Landore loading, they would have been less highly stressed. However, the partial curvature in the structure doubtless added to its problems in service and influenced the decision of 1883 to proceed with a replacement.

As already mentioned, the line of railway passed immediately over the buildings of Harvey's works at Hayle, and this consideration determined that the new structure, which was to be built wide enough for two lines of narrow gauge track, should be substantially on the existing alignment. Because of its low height, the timber superstructure was to be replaced by wrought iron girders carried, in general, on masonry piers, with a timber decking.

However, its location meant that the modifications involved were not straightforward, a conclusion which can be drawn from the details of the above drawing. Firstly, where land was available, the six existing masonry piers at the Penzance end were widened by 7ft on the down side. Then, where there were numerous buildings immediately beneath the structure, a more difficult modification was involved. Here, the increased width on the downside was obtained by erecting seven cast iron pillars, generally spaced at double the normal span, to carry a series of heavy wrought iron girders. These in turn supported wrought iron cross members linked to the adjacent normal spans, thus providing the increased width. These pillars were mounted on substantial masonry footings, each built up from a 3ft 6in square granite bed stone (2ft thick) seated on a 4ft 6in square masonry plinth which, in turn, was seated on a similar plinth, 5ft square.

The masonry piers adjacent to the south road crossing were strengthened, and where the original structure had been supported on the two-leg timber piers, new masonry piers of the increased width were built on their plinths, amounting to a total of ten such modifications. The difference in masonry work can be clearly distinguished at site today. The north road crossing abutments were strengthened and increased in width while the remaining six piers to the Truro abutment, believed also to have originally been of masonry, were increased to the appropriate width.

Gibbons reported that the timber superstructure was replaced 'bit by bit with one of wrought iron', by the Company's own staff while the rest of the work was let by contract. The line was finally doubled across the structure from 10th September 1899. In November 1990, trial excavations were made around some of the central masonry piers, in connection with the laying of a storm water drain under the viaduct. This revealed the remains of a timber pile beneath the end of the 1864 plinth of one pier, outside the present contour of the viaduct on the up side, while on the widened downside, the pier was supported by a concrete raft. These plinths extensions will be noted from Fig.120, which is of the viaduct in 1989.

It is also interesting to note that one of the rebuilt piers adjacent to the north road bridge has settled at one end, on the up side, by as much as 12in; the wrought iron span being packed to adjust and so level the track. The viaduct has continued in service in this condition for a number of years without further deterioration. A general view of the structure (Fig.121) taken from the south west in 1989 reveals that the original piers at the Penzance end have been strengthened in brickwork (this work also included encasing the cast iron columns in brickwork), while all the original buildings which occupied the site have now been demolished.

Before finally reaching its destination, Penzance, the line crossed the Hayle River at location 320/35, near St Erth, by means of a simple wooden span, believed similar to that of Lostwithiel. It was replaced in 1883 by a steel girder bridge, supported on granite piers and abutments.

52. Penzance — Class Z — Figs.122, 123, 124 and 125
Location 326/10 — Length 1,041ft — Maximum height 12ft

Situated on the exposed south east shore of Mounts Bay, this long low structure finally carried the railway into Penzance. Having regard to its low height, the first construction was of light timber, and consisted of 51 spans averaging 19ft in length, and with a clear width of 12ft 6in at rail level. The location of the viaduct was such that there was no effective natural breakwater for its protection from heavy seas and soon after the opening of the line, the great storm of 27th December 1852 inflicted considerable damage. Unfortunately, it was the period of spring tides, and during the gale the whole of the scaffolding and wood-work erected for the work involved in extending the southern arm of Penzance pier, were totally swept away. This scaffolding was carried by the heavy seas against the railway viaduct with such force as to wash away sixty yards at the western end. Figure 122 gives a graphic impression of the resulting damage, albeit with artist's licence. However, the structure was repaired and continued in service, although according to Bennett, it was necessary each winter to close the line during the worst of the winter storms.

122. An engraving from the *Illustrated London News* of January 1853, showing the storm damage to the first Penzance viaduct, following the great storm of that year. There has been a degree of artist's licence employed as the timbers are obviously out of scale to the personnel standing on the beach but the extent of damage incurred is well illustrated.

123. A double headed train leaving Penzance after the gauge conversion, showing the close proximity of the rebuilt viaduct to the beach, there being no protection from the south easterly gales. The masonry supports at the western end are clearly shown, with the reminder of the structure built to a modified Class Z timber design. ***Cornwall Local Studies Library***

Then, on the last day of 1868, a violent south easterly gale, with the tide 'at its height and an immense body of water ... beating against the timbers', destroyed more than half of the structure and covered the line between Penzance and Marazion with sand and shingle to a depth of two or three feet. Services were temporarily restored by laying down an inland diversion of the track, until a new viaduct was built and opened on 28th October 1871.

On the original viaduct, the floor, in common with the other viaducts in Cornwall, was close-decked and consequently there was no means of egress for the volumes of water and shingle hurled against the structure during a storm. For the new structure, the deck timbers, of section 8in × 8in, were laid with about a 4in gap, the longitudinal timber baulks of the permanent way being carried directly by this decking. This arrangement was intended to break the force of the storms, and interestingly, the deck timbers were underslung from the laminated horizontal carrying beams. They were carried on longitudinal wrought iron sections supported by $1\frac{1}{4}$in dia through bolts spaced generally at 2ft pitch. Their securing nuts and square washers on top of the two 12in × 12in laminated beams, together with the pairs of joggles incorporated in the latter, can be clearly seen in Fig.125. These latter beams were supported by a pair of 4in × 8in cross members attached to the 12in square piles of each pier, while an outside stiffening piece was through bolted to each pile and extended to the top of the beams. According to Butland[50], the structure was situated on the site of what was believed to have been a submerged forest, which presented difficulties with regard to obtaining a solid foundation. This required the timber piles to be driven to a considerable depth. Thus in construction, the viaduct conformed generally to the Class Z design, with double-leg timber piers throughout the greater part of its length, and the addition of nine granite piers supporting the spans at the western or station end.

In 1895 the structure was strengthened by the addition of a pair of 12in × 5in rolled steel joists, spaced 11in apart and carried on short 6in × 5in stub joists at each pier, supporting the decking under the centre of the track. This arrangement was in turn supported from a pair of 12in × 9in angled timber struts, let into each pile with a 6in × 12in locating piece through bolted to the piles. These supports can be seen within the piers of Fig.124, a view of the overall structure c1920.

124. A view of Penzance viaduct taken in 1921, shortly before the timber structure was replaced by a new line protected by masonry sea defences. Again, the exposed nature of the site is clearly illustrated while the 'A' frame support added to the double timber leg piers, to support the central carrying beam, can be easily distinguished. ***British Rail***

125. A close up view of the Penzance viaduct, taken at the time work had started on the new sea wall defences. The formation of the timber structure shows the laminated carrying beams supporting the underslung decking, with the cross timbers spaced to provide drainage. The hardwood joggles of the laminated beam, and their associated inclined bolting can be seen, while in the foreground is the temporary trackwork used to convey the large boulders of the seawall defences into position. ***From the Clinker Collection, Brunel University Library***

The position of the viaduct remained exposed to the south easterly gales in Mounts Bay, the line virtually running along the beach, as will be apparent from Fig.123 By the early 1920s, its single line formation was proving inadequate for the weight of the new locomotives coming into service, and thereby an obstacle to the full development of traffic to and from Penzance. Accordingly, it was decided to replace the timber viaduct with a granite-faced embankment, surmounted by a parapet on the seaward side, raised to a height of three feet above rail level. The land to the north of this new protection was infilled so as to accommodate a double line of track. Suitable openings were provided at the western end to permit access to the beach and drain the hinterland. All this work was completed in 1921, and the temporary track in the foreground of Fig.125 was laid in connection with the building of these sea defences. It is believed that many of the granite blocks used for the embankment came from the redundant masonry piers at Angarrack and the other viaducts in West Cornwall, which could account for there being no remains at those sites west of Truro, apart from a single pier at Blackwater.

126. Penwithers, Falmouth Branch, viewed from the south east, probably taken shortly before work commenced on the replacement embankment. Note the inclusion of a shore within the superstructure of the left hand pier while all the linking spans include the additional underslung crossmember. The embankment fans spring from buttressed plinths. Today, with the embankment a mass of undergrowth, it is difficult to visualise the scene as shown here. ***L G Booth Collection***

The Falmouth Branch

At Penwithers Junction, the original Cornwall Railway left the alignment of the West Cornwall main line, and continued down to Falmouth; the route, under the aegis of the GWR, eventually becoming a branch, which incorporated the following viaducts.

35. Penwithers — Margary Class A — Figs.126, 127 and 128A & B
Location 301/43 — Length 813ft — Maximum height 90ft

Initially, work commenced on this viaduct under the original 1853 Garratt contract and by the time work ceased at the end of 1854, four of the ten masonry piers had been partly built. No further action ensued until Brereton recommenced construction of the line in 1861. A drawing dated 27th June 1861[51], shows the Class A2 superstructure, which he adapted for all but one of the Falmouth branch viaducts, supported by ten piers spaced at 65ft centres. In addition, there was a landward fan on each embankment slope which appeared as if supported on a timber platform. However, from a study of other contemporary drawings they were in fact mounted on additional masonry piers, with the embankment graded to match the level of their cills.

127. Another view of Penwithers, or as it was sometimes called, Penweathers, taken in 1900 and seen from the north west, with a Falmouth bound train crossing the viaduct. Judging by the number of men on the structure it was obviously in the hands of a repair gang. *R.I.C.*

128A. Building the replacement embankment at Penwithers, showing the work nearly completed in early 1926. The date '6/23' painted on the two beams to the right of the workman, shows that they had been renewed in 1923, while the stirrup carrying the underslung crossbeam can be seen above his left shoulder. This is an excellent illustration showing the details of the timber construction of the viaduct, the joggles on either side of the lefthand raking strut with its cast iron shoe locating the laminated beam.

According to the above drawing, every third pier was of section 10ft thick × 22ft wide and buttressed, while the straight piers were of the same width but just 6ft thick. Each landward span was formed from a pair of the usual queen post type trussed beams, with their ends seated on the top of the embankment. These details will be apparent from Fig.126, and indicate an overall length of 821ft compared with the above MacDermot figure and 800ft included in Margary's report.

As part of his 1880 reconstruction proposals, Margary recommended that a new masonry viaduct should be erected on the south side of the existing structure. Yet, by 1887 the viaduct was undergoing full repair and it was, in fact, to remain in service for a further thirty nine years until replaced in 1926 by a massive embankment. Figures 128A and 128B are two views taken while this latter work was in progress, the original masonry piers being buried within these earthworks, while some of the timbers were removed for further use. Crossing the site today, with the embankment slopes submerged under a mass of trees and vegetation, it is difficult to envisage the handsome timber structure that originally spanned this valley.

128B. Taken in October 1926, this photograph of Penwithers shows the embankment nearly completed. Eventually, the timbers will be removed, to leave the track carried on the embankment but with the masonry piers buried within. *Both R.I.C.*

129. Ringwell photographed in March 1932, shortly before work commenced on building the replacement embankment, similar to that at Penwithers. It was completed the following year. On the left a narrow gauge line has been laid, in preparation for this work but repair work on the structure is still in hand with flying scaffolding in position between the two righthand fans. *L G Booth Collection*

36. Ringwell — Margary Class A — Figs.129 and 130
Location 304/01 — Length 366ft — Maximum height 70ft

This relatively small structure was built as part of the 1861 contract. A drawing[52] dated 27th June 1861 shows three masonry piers, of section 22ft × 6ft, at 66ft centres, with a landward fan at each end apparently sited on the embankment slope. These details indicate a length of 370ft but Margary quoted a figure of 356ft, with height 72ft. Again, like the other structures on the Falmouth branch, these landward fans did in fact spring from additional masonry piers, each set in their respective embankment slope which was then graded to the top of the pier (Brereton had thus abandoned Brunel's cheaper alternative). The viaduct was, of course, a Class A2 design.

Margary had recommended a deviation of the line, in 1880, to cross a new masonry viaduct to the north. However, an inspection in 1887 confirmed the structure to be in good order — 'only one or two important pieces show signs of decay' — and the viaduct continued in service well into the twentieth century. Figure 129 is a view from the north east, taken in 1932, while Fig.130 is of the viaduct under repair; note the inclusion of shores on each pier and additional cross beams under each linking span. The balustrade over the centre fan has been dismantled and temporary joists attached to the legs, in preparation for the work.

By the early 1930s it was decided to replace the viaduct by means of an embankment with a culvert, similar to Penwithers. This was opened to traffic on 17th September 1933 and, at the site today, it is difficult to visualise a seventy foot high viaduct curving across the landscape, the embankment having mellowed into the local scene.

130. An earlier view of Ringwell, with major repair work in hand over the centre fan. The balustrade and much of the handrailing have been removed, together with the ballast boards, indicating major timber replacements. Note the inclusion of shores within all the fans and the underslung cross timbers of the linking spans. *L T George Collection*

131. **A spectacular view of Carnon viaduct in 1922, showing the buttressed piers, with their additional shoring, and the strengthened linking spans. The valley carried the effluent from the mine workings up stream, in contrast to the present day scene of a dried out valley.** ***R S Carpenter***

37. Carnon — Margary Class A — Figs.131 and 132
Location 304/26 — Length 756ft — Maximum height 96ft

On a falling gradient of 1 in 68 within a short distance of leaving Ringwell viaduct, the line faced the crossing of the deep valley extension above Restronguet Creek. Here a part tidal inlet, having a layer of sand 21ft thick[53], collected the drainage of silt etc from the mine workings higher up the valley, which was not an ideal foundation for a 96ft high viaduct. No work had been carried out at this location under the original contract and a first drawing[54], dated 1st July 1861, proposed the construction of a Class D superstructure, generally similar to the viaduct at Coombe by Saltash.

It was to have been supported on twelve piers, of which six were formed from piled timber trestles, spaced 66ft apart. At the Truro end, there were to be three masonry piers, spaced at 57ft centres, and one trestle supported on a masonry plinth while, at the Falmouth end, two masonry piers, at 66ft centres, completed the supports. This arrangement would have resulted in a structure some 792ft in length.

When work commenced at site, Brereton arranged for a trial pit to be dug. Arising from this investigation, he recommended to the Joint Committee at their meeting of 29th November 1861[55], that masonry piers should be built in place of driving piles as originally proposed. He estimated that this modification would incur an extra cost of £1,200 and considered the change to be well worthwhile. The Committee duly approved this alteration, 'on the express condition that the Contractor enter into an engagement that the increase of cost including all contingencies shall not exceed £1,200'.

Consequently, no further work was carried out on the original proposal, as a later drawing[56], dated 7th December 1861, showed a Class A2 superstructure of length 766ft, carried on only eleven masonry piers. Part of this second proposal was to extend the embankment at the Truro end in order to achieve this reduction in length. However, Margary quoted a length of 775ft.

Having regard to the soft sandy bottom of the valley floor, the foundations for the fully buttressed piers posed a problem. This was overcome by sinking at each location[57] a pair of cast iron cylinders, each 16ft diameter, cast in segments and bolted together. They were weighted and sunk through the sand until they reached the rock; the sand was then excavated and water pumped out. This enabled, within each cylinder, a foundation to be built up to the level of the sand of section 8ft thick by 13ft wide. The cylinders were then withdrawn by hydraulic jacks and an arch

132. This well known photograph of Carnon, dated c1912, with the track of the Redruth & Chasewater Railway in the left foreground and a '3521' Class locomotive hauling a Falmouth-Truro train across the viaduct, could not be omitted. The additional shores can easily be seen on some of the piers. ***M Messenger Collection***

turned to connect the two sections and form the base on which each pier was then constructed. This arrangement applied to the central five piers, situated in the floor of the valley, the remaining piers being formed on conventional masonry foundations.

When Margary came to recommend replacement, he considered the masonry in the piers to be of good quality and that they should be built up so as to carry a wrought iron superstructure in place of the timber. However, the 1887 examination reported a satisfactory condition, apart from some initial decay in a few legs which would require renewing when the viaduct was next under repair. Consequently, no action was taken with regard to Margary's proposals and this original structure continued in service. A 1922 view of the viaduct is shown in Fig.131, while Fig.132 is the classic illustration of the structure spanning the marshy valley with the track of the Redruth & Chasewater Railway passing beneath a Truro bound train.

In the early 1930s, work was eventually initiated on a handsome nine arch masonry replacement, built on the southern side of the original. It was completed at a cost of £40,000[58], and opened for traffic in June 1933. At the site today, the piers of the original viaduct still stand but the mineworkings are derelict, their tips graded to match the surrounding landscape and the valley is a wide open space, with no evidence of the marshy wastes of earlier years.

133. Perran viaduct, buried deep in the countryside, between Tregellas and Chyvogue farms, was replaced by a masonry viaduct in 1927. This view shows additional shores within the original superstructure, but with shortened linking spans of only 14ft 9in no extra cross timbers have been added to those spans. ***From the Clinker Collection, Brunel University Library***

38. Perran — Margary Class A — Fig.133
Location 305/70 — Length 339ft — Maximum height 56ft

According to an original drawing[59] dated 22nd February 1854, the superstructure was to be built to Class A1, with six masonry piers, of section 6ft thick × 22ft wide, spaced at 59ft centres, one at either end being buttressed and within the embankment slope. The raking legs were to support the horizontal beams at 14ft 9in centres — a variation from the normal Class A1 dimension of 15ft — while each of the landward spans was to incorporate a queen post truss of 30ft span. However, apart from building four of the piers, no further work was completed on this site at the time the contractor stopped operations in late 1854.

A subsequent drawing[60], dated 26th June 1861, showed the superstructure to be Class A2, with the raking leg supports at 15ft 4in centres, the pier centres at 59ft and the linking spans only 13ft. The viaduct, generally to this design, was completed in 1863 but was based on five piers with an overall length, according to Margary, of 343ft, as shown in Fig.133. This is a view in its later days when three of the piers incorporated shores.

The status report of 1887 recorded it to be in good general condition while in his replacement proposals, Margary had in mind to extend the embankment at each end and construct a short masonry viaduct on the northern side. Nevertheless, it continued in service with additional shoring as shown, but by the mid 1920s work was started on building a replacement masonry viaduct, which was completed and brought into use in 1927. According to Crispin, this viaduct was sometimes called Trewedna, presumably after one of the local farms in the area.

39. Ponsanooth — Margary Class B — Figs.13, 40, 134 and 135
Location 306/74 — Length 645ft — Maximum height 139ft

This, the highest viaduct on the branch and the fourth highest in Cornwall, carried the line across the lower valley of the River Kennall. According to an original 1854 drawing[61], it was intended to follow the usual Class B construction, like St Pinnock. There were eight massive fully buttressed piers, which incorporated gothic openings, six spaced at 66ft centres, one at each end at 63ft together with an embankment pier at 43ft centres. As in the other viaducts on this section of the railway, the end spans incorporated a 30ft queen post truss in the parapet, resting on a timber platform on each embankment, which was graded $1\frac{1}{2}$ to 2.

Under the original contract, four of the masonry piers were completed and five partly built at the time Garratt ceased work in 1854. Then, it was not until 1861 that a new drawing was issued to cover the completion of the structure. This called for the balustrade to be strengthened to a Class A2 design, but retained the Class B leg formation (Fig.40) thus making it unique. In addition, the gothic openings in the piers were to be infilled,

134. Taken in July 1929, this view of Ponsanooth viaduct from the north west includes excellent detail of Brunel's timber structure alongside its masonry replacement, then under construction. Details of the Class B superstructure, reinforced by the heavier Class A2 balustrade which made this viaduct unique, can be clearly seen, together with the fully buttressed Moorswater type piers including their infilled gothic openings. The new viaduct is taking shape and it is interesting to note that this is the first site to show limited scaffolding erected alongside one face of each of the new piers. ***L G Booth Collection***

135. **A typical Falmouth branch train on Ponsanooth viaduct, which gives a dramatic appreciation of the lightness and frailty of the structure when compared with the train. The additional cross timbers of the linking spans are clearly apparent in this 1920s view.** ***Cornwall Local Studies Library***

which modification can still be detected today in the redundant piers standing alongside the masonry replacement structure. A view of the timber viaduct taken in 1913, is represented by Fig.13, while Fig.135 shows a typical Falmouth branch train crossing the structure.

It is believed stone for the original piers was taken from a local quarry, the remains of which is evident in the hillside of the Falmouth slope. Margary, while quoting a length of 660ft, was of the opinion that their quality was suitable for the piers to be raised to carry wrought iron girders in substitution for the timber superstructure.

Despite a gloomy status report of February 1887, to the effect that a:

> '...good many legs of this viaduct...require to be changed soon especially towards the western end, and a few beams. After Penwithers...this viaduct will be taken in hand. This viaduct has 16 legs on each pier, supporting the load generally carried by 12 legs in the other viaducts',

the structure continued in service until work was put in hand in 1927 for a double line replacement masonry viaduct, at an estimated cost of £68,500. For this project[62], additional land of 1 acre $2\frac{3}{4}$ poles had to be acquired. A view of this work is shown in Fig.134 which also reveals much of the detail of the original timberwork, together with the partly completed masonry piers for the new viaduct. It is interesting to note, that this illustration is the first of a site to show scaffolding being used in the building of the piers; hitherto, it would appear that construction followed the original (and less safe) method of lifting men and materials to the tops of the piers, from which position they built up the masonry. The new alignment was brought into use in 1930, and with the completion of this viaduct, the more important structures on the middle section of the Falmouth branch between Perranwell and Penryn stations were suitable for two tracks, should they be required.

40. Pascoe — Margary Class A — Figs.136 and 137
Location 307/19 — Length 390ft — Maximum height 70ft
(Margary quoted a length of 386ft and height 71ft)

Under the original Falmouth contract some work was carried out for this viaduct in building the six masonry piers, 22ft wide × 6ft thick. They were to be spaced at 58ft centres, with a buttressed one set in the embankment at each end and the embankment sloped $1\frac{1}{2}$ to 2 in line with the top of the piers. The original drawing[63] for this arrangement also showed the raking legs supporting the carrying beams conforming to the A1 configuration at 14ft 6in centres — yet another variation — and each landward span comprising a 30ft queen post truss in the parapet.

However, under the final contract, a drawing[64] dated 27th June 1861 called for a Class A2 construction, with the leg supports at the usual 15ft 4in centres, pier centres at 58ft and 12ft linking spans. In 1880 Margary was of the opinion that a masonry viaduct should be built alongside as a replacement, while by 1887 a number of the original timbers required renewal, which work was to be carried out on completion of the repairs at Ponsanooth. Figure 136 is a view of this viaduct from the south west, which remained in use until 1923. By that time work had been put in hand to build a substantial culverted embankment on a new alignment to the west of the line, the partially completed work being shown in Fig.137, with a Falmouth train crossing the old viaduct.

136. Pascoe viaduct set in the countryside, just over a quarter of a mile beyond Ponsanooth, a Class A2 structure carried on six fans, spaced at 58ft centres. Despite this dimension being shorter than that of other Class A2 viaducts, the balustrade still retained eight sets of posts for each span, with a queen post truss at each end. *From the Clinker Collection, Brunel University Library*

At the site today, the cutting and embankments within the curtilage of the railway have become a most attractive copse, with the ground in springtime a carpet of bluebells. The original route, although overgrown, can be followed on each side of the valley to the ends of the embankment slopes of the original viaduct site. Within each slope are the remains of the masonry plinth, while the four main piers have been demolished to heaps of jagged masonry.

137. A Falmouth bound train crosses the Brunel viaduct in this early 1920s view of Pascoe, showing the new alignment being built over the embankment on the left with the new cutting in the background. This work was completed in 1923 and the old viaduct removed. Today, the whole site is a mass of trees and undergrowth but the original alignment can still be traced. *L G Booth Collection*

138. **Penryn viaduct, another Falmouth branch structure replaced by an embankment in 1923. Again, the route was realigned to the east and the adjoining Penryn station rebuilt.** ***From the Clinker Collection, Brunel University Library***

41. Penryn — Margary Class A — Figs.138 and 139
Location 308/69 — Length 342ft — Maximum height 83ft

As shown on a drawing[65] dated 27th June 1861, the superstructure of this viaduct was again Class A2 supported on five masonry piers, spaced at 59ft centres with the centre one buttressed and the others of plain section. The slope of the embankment at the ends of the viaduct was graded $1\frac{1}{2}$ to 2, in line with the tops of the end piers, and the landward spans were 30ft trussed beams, all as shown in Fig.138. Margary quoted a length of one foot longer than the above figure.

A further view in Fig. 139, taken in the early 1920s, shows the viaduct before work had started on the replacement embankment which altered the line of the track to the east. This alteration was completed in 1923, as an alternative to Margary's original proposal to build a new masonry viaduct. It is interesting to note that at the 1887 inspection the structure was reported to be in good condition, with but a few important pieces showing signs of decay, in spite of a good deal of the original timbers still being in the viaduct.

139. **A 'Duke' class locomotive hauls a goods train over Penryn viaduct in 1920. Note the inclusion of shores in the left hand and central piers, missing from Fig.138, which would place that photograph at an earlier date.** ***A J Fellows***

140A. The classic view of Collegewood viaduct from the north west, the last of Brunel's timber structures to remain in service in Cornwall. It shows a Falmouth-bound train, comprising an interesting collection of rolling stock, hauled by a 4575 Class 2-6-2 Prairie tank. With an all up weight of 61 tons, this class was one of the heaviest to work the branch at that time. Note the repair work in hand on the right hand fan, and the replacement viaduct under construction in the background, which dates the illustration in the early 1930s.

Collection of Richard Angove; Dr Ian C Allen. Courtesy Pendon Museum.

42. Collegewood — Margary Class A — Figs.1, 140A and 140B
Location 309/32 — Length 954ft — Maximum height 100ft

This was the last viaduct on the line into Falmouth and was built on a sweeping downside left hand curve. It did not form part of the first Falmouth contract, as it will be recalled that Brereton devised an alternative to Brunel's original route in taking the line down to the docks. Accordingly, within this design he incorporated the experience from all the timber structures that had been built at that time. It was carried on fourteen masonry piers, all fully buttressed and spaced at 66ft centres. The Class A2 superstructure comprised horizontal beams laminated from 12in × 14in timbers[66], compared with the usual 12in square sections. The raking legs supported the beams at 15ft 4in centres, with the centre legs of 14in square timbers. The linking spans were 20ft while the 30ft landward spans comprised the usual queen post trusses in the parapet. Again, the embankment slopes were graded $1\frac{1}{2}$ to 2, conforming to the tops of the end piers. These dimensions accrue to a length of 964ft while Margary in separate reports quoted 927ft and 957ft — so much for consistancy.

Although as early as 1880 Margary had recommended replacement of this viaduct, by raising the piers and substituting wrought iron girders in place of the timber superstructure, this was the last structure in Cornwall to be replaced. The 1887 report spoke of there being 'a great many original legs in this long viaduct. Next time it is under repair most of these will have to be changed'. Apparently, at that date there were not many of the original beams still in place.

An impression of its majesty and the delicacy of the timber superstructure will be appreciated from Fig.1, which is an 1890s view of a Falmouth-bound train crossing, while a similar view taken some 40 years later is shown in Fig.140A. Here, notwithstanding the fact that building of the replacement viaduct has been started, repair work is in progress on the right hand fan, where the balustrade has been removed and the legs tied together with temporary timber ties. This train, also Falmouth-bound, comprises an interesting collection of rolling stock hauled by an unidentified 4575 Class 2-6-2 Prairie tank, which has slowed to traverse the length under repair.

Figure 140B, a view taken in October 1933, shows construction work proceeding on the piers for the new viaduct, with the extensive use of scaffolding compared with its absence on earlier replacement contracts. It also offers an excellent view of the original timber superstructure, including the additional shores and underslung cross timbers of the linking spans.

As recounted in the opening paragraph of Chapter 1, this structure continued in service until the 1930s, when the new masonry viaduct, built on the downside, was completed and put into use on 22nd July 1934, the original timber unit having then completed seventy-one years' service.

140B.Taken in October 1933, and viewed from the south, this photograph shows the start of work on the replacement viaduct at Collegewood, with the extensive use of scaffolding around the piers, a feature missing from previous similar constructions. The presence of additional shores within the Class A2 superstructure of the old viaduct and the underslung cross timbers of the linking spans can be clearly distinguished, together with the horizontal and diagonal wrought iron ties linking the fans of adjacent piers. The pier centre distance is quoted at 66ft but the balustrade still retains eight sets of posts over each complete span, matching the number included for shorter spans in other Class A2 viaducts. ***L G Booth Collection***

Chapter 9

THE PATTERN OF REPLACEMENT

IT MUST HAVE BEEN generally accepted by the Directors of both of the Cornish Companies that, while Brunel's recommendation to use timber in his viaduct designs would reduce their initial cost, and thus enable the lines to be completed within the limited cash resources then available, in due course they would incur increasing ongoing costs for maintenance. This was to prove to be the viaducts' Achilles' heel, and the problems arising from this use of timber were an ever present anxiety to the managements of both Companies and their successor, the Great Western Railway, during the remainder of the life of these picturesque structures.

Problems became particularly apparent in the inland or fan type viaducts, and arose from a combination of one or more of the following:

1. Inadequate timber protection, leading to the onset of decay
2. Insufficient lateral strength of those viaducts built on a curve (and in the case of two locations, built with an 'S' curve)
3. At certain locations, the speed at which trains crossed the viaducts.
4. The facility to allow speedy replacement of defective timbers which, in practice, actually led to a weakening of the original framework.
5. The inadequacy of the wrought iron tie bars, under the affects of dynamic loading, in a multi-bay structure.
6. The overall lightness of the Class E design, which was quite unsuitable for main line operation.

A further factor which was to manifest itself in relation to Largin and Coombe St Stephens, concerned their unsatisfactory original layout, in combination with poor workmanship at the time of their construction; a situation which emerged at the Arbitration hearing[1]. These allegations do not accord with Brunel's reputation for painstaking attention to detail in his designs and his usual rigorous examination of completed works, and call for some further explanation.

Apart from the burden of ongoing maintenance cost, the tidal viaducts appeared to be far less of a problem, probably due to their trussed beam construction which precluded intermittent replacement of decayed timber members; as components decayed, then the complete truss had to be dismantled and rebuilt. While a more inconvenient practice than the piecemeal replacement arrangements of the inland structures, it did mean that they were able to continue in service for a longer period.

In reviewing the timing and order in which the viaduct replacements took place, it is not apparent at first sight that there was any systematic approach to the overall problem. However, on closer study, it would appear that replacement broadly followed a logical sequence covering, firstly, those of known weak design, such as the Class E structures. It then dealt progressively with those viaducts where speed was proving to have a deteriorating affect, (particularly in the Glynn Valley). Finally, with the viaducts at Moorswater, Bolitho and Cartuther, where circumstantial evidence points to, among other problems, the masonry piers themselves were not of sound construction. However, as we shall see, the overall programme was subject to a serious interruption, which delayed its timely completion.

It would appear that in their early life all the structures were able to accommodate the then level of train loads without distress. However, as traffic built up through the 1860s with faster and heavier trains, problems began to appear, particularly with some of the lighter designs. Following the death of H S Bush in 1868, P J Margary had been appointed Engineer of the Joint Committee and he immediately addressed this matter insofar as it affected the Class E design at Probus; situated at the foot of two inclines, it had suffered badly from trains crossing at speed while maintenance work had weakened the structure to the point at which replacement was essential. As already recounted, the problem was resolved by building an embankment adjacent to the original alignment, which was completed in 1871.

This, then, was the start of the replacement programme, which, with several interruptions, was to proceed through the following sixty three years, until final completion in 1934. The works were actioned in the following order and, with an eye to the future, the new constructions on the main line were built wide enough to accommodate two narrow gauge tracks:

> The three light Class E structures, at Probus, Draw Wood and Penadlake; completed over the period 1869–1877.
> Five of the remaining six viaducts in the Glynn Valley; West Largin, Westwood, Clinnick, Derrycombe, and St Pinnock; completed over the period 1873–1882.
> The three structures at Moorswater, Bolitho and Cartuther; completed over the period 1878–1882.
> The viaducts at Fal, Largin and Coombe St Stephens; completed over the period 1882–1886.
> Seven of the viaducts on the West Cornwall line were replaced between 1885 and 1888.
> In 1889 a contract was placed for a masonry replacement at Coombe by Saltash, which was completed in 1894.
> Following the broad gauge conversion in 1892, a massive programme was put in hand through to 1904, to replace the remaining main line inland viaducts.
> Weston Mill was replaced in 1903.
> The remaining tidal viaducts were abolished by the inland diversion of the main line between Saltash and St Germans, which was opened in 1908; with new masonry structures at Forder, Nottar and St Germans. Stonehouse Pool was also being rebuilt in that year.
> In 1921 Penzance was replaced.
> Finally, between 1923 and 1934, the viaducts on the Falmouth Branch were replaced.

It seems that speed was a significant factor which affected all the viaducts in the Glynn Valley. Following the replacement at Probus, a contract was placed in 1873 for the replacement of the similar Class E structure at Draw Wood, again by means of a deviation over a new embankment, complete with a masonry retaining wall, which was finished by 23rd March 1875. As part of that same contract, work was put in hand on two further projects: the first being to replace the Class A1 structure at West Largin. That this, one of the shorter viaducts, should have been replaced as early as 1875 calls for comment, particularly in view of its small maintenance cost[2]. While its location in a heavily wooded area, may have made it prone to excessive timber decay, it is more likely that commercial considerations determined its early replacement.

The difficulties with access and close proximity to Draw Wood, made it sensible for one contractor to work on both locations at the same time, the replacement being completed on 26th September 1875[3]. The second project included in this contract was to build the eastern abutment, together with the first pier of a new masonry viaduct at Westwood. The stone for all this work was taken from the quarry at the latter site where the masonry viaduct, partly prepared by the above contract, was completed by the Company's own staff on 14th December 1877[4].

Having now commenced in earnest to tackle the problems of the timber viaducts, the Joint Committee, under pressure from Margary, proceeded to put work in hand to replace the other viaducts in the Glynn Valley; completion being effected on the following dates[5]. Penadlake (the remaining Class E type), on 7th October 1877, Clinnick (Class A1) on 16th March 1879, and Derrycombe (Class A1) on 8th May 1881, were all replaced by masonry viaducts, suitable for double track, narrow gauge. Stone was taken from the Westwood quarry and the scope of all these works involved a total expenditure of £14,572.

On 12th February 1880, Margary had issued his comprehensive report[6], setting out in some detail his recommendations for the replacement of the remaining timber structures on the Cornwall Railway. For some unknown reason, the viaducts on the West Cornwall line did not seem to attract the same attention, presumably because they were being dealt with directly by the Great Western Company. Among his recommendations was the action to be taken with regard to the remaining two structures in the Glynn Valley, St Pinnock and its immediate neighbour, Largin. As already noted, both were to be rebuilt to incorporate wrought iron girders in place of the timber superstructure. St Pinnock was completed in September 1882, but instructions for similar action at Largin were not issued until March 1884, against the background of the dispute between the Cornwall Board and the Joint Committee.

That the problems of the timber viaducts was an ongoing concern of the Joint Committee is emphasised by a communication dated 6th October 1881 from the Great Western Railway[7]. This suggested substitution of masonry or iron for the remaining timber structures on the Cornwall line (following submission of the relevant plans to the Great Western). This was followed by yet another report[8] from Margary, dated 2nd November 1881, urging their replacement by more permanent structures, in which he reminded the Committee that he had:

> '...repeatedly placed before them my reasons for recommending the same course and would again repeat what I have said as to the desirability of following it. I would say in the first place that I have never recommended the reconstruction of the viaducts with stone and iron because of any great financial gain to be achieved but have more than once pointed out that the interest payable upon the amount of outlay would be nearly as much as the cost of the maintenance of the present structures...My advice in the matter has been given because of the engineering difficulties pertaining to the repairs of these viaducts and the desire for a greater measure of security'.

He went on to say that he had never presented the situation in an alarmist way, but had emphasised the elaborate precautions which were taken at all times to ensure safety when repairs were being carried out. It should be considered a matter of congratulation that no accident had so far occurred during this work, but with the viaducts getting older the attendant risks were becoming greater. Accordingly, having regard to the importance of safety and the fact that there would be little difference in expenditure, he urged the Committee to continue the work of reconstruction of the viaducts with iron or stone.

At that time, work was of course in progress on St Pinnock, Bolitho, Cartuther and Derrycombe and it was not until they had been completed that a further Minute was passed at the meeting of the Associated Companies[9] on 20th July 1883, which included the following instruction:

> 'That the Engineer be requested to furnish the Committee with a report upon the present condition of any of the remaining Wooden Viaducts which may appear to require special treatment with any recommendations he may have to make as to the replacement of such structures in stone or other permanent material'.

That this overall problem was very much in the forefront of Margary's mind may be gauged from the fact that he was able to report by 31st July, on the condition of the wooden viaducts on the Cornwall Railway — no mention of those on the West Cornwall line — in which he recapitulated the difficulties experienced with the structures in general. With his recommendation (yet again) that they should all be reconstructed in more durable material, he particularly drew attention to the viaducts at Coombe St Stephens, Coombe by Saltash, St Austell and Milltown. These he considered should receive precedence, 'in consequence of the framing to become distorted and pushed over...and which is now only kept in place by shores'. Within this same report he especially urged reconstruction of Largin, 'in consequence of the great irregularity in the lines of the viaduct as originally constructed it is impossible to maintain a true curve in the rails throughout the viaduct'.

By the date of this report, eleven of the original timber structures had been replaced, eight by masonry viaducts and two by embankments on new alignments, and one by substituting wrought iron girders on the existing piers. Meanwhile, work was in hand to build a new masonry viaduct on a new alignment at Fal. All this work had been carried out on the instruction of the Joint Committee, with the apparent agreement of the Cornwall Board, half the cost being charged to revenue and half to capital. This action should, however, be viewed against the background of the legal position between the Cornwall Railway and the Joint Committee, as expressed by the terms of the Lease between the parties. In addition, over the period 1880-1881, the Cornwall Directors, on behalf of their shareholders, had endeavoured to negotiate the absolute sale of the Company to the Great Western, but an offer by Sir Daniel Gooch of £4.10.0 (£4.50) cash for each £20 share, had been declined by the Directors at their meeting of 16th August 1881.

During this time, the subject of the reconstruction of the viaducts was assuming increasing importance in the deliberations of both the Cornwall Board and the Joint Committee — but for different reasons. On 16th November 1883, the Board, concerned at the growing cost of the work involved over which it seemed to have had no control, passed Resolution No.391 to the effect that 'the question of the reconstruction of the viaducts in stone or iron is one for the Board of Directors and not the Joint Committee'. Co-incidentally, the Joint Committee was meeting on the same date, at Plymouth[10], and by a majority of six votes to four, resolved to accept the recommendation in Margary's Report of 31st July 1883 to undertake forthwith the reconstruction of the whole of the Timber Viaducts in more durable material, and that the replacements should be of width sufficient for a double track, narrow gauge. Plans and estimates should be immediately prepared for the viaducts at Coombe St Stephens, Coombe by Saltash, St Austell, Milltown and Largin.

However, on 11th January 1884 the Joint Committee was again reminded of the above 16th November 1883 Board Resolution. Then at the Board Meeting of 18th January, the Directors' stance in this matter received further support, through a protest from the London shareholders on account of the viaducts being rebuilt to allow of a double narrow gauge line. Encouraged by this opposition to further expenditure on the viaducts, and following discussion among the members of the Board, a special meeting was convened on 10th March 1884, at which a resolution was carried to the effect that:

> 'The Joint Committee be informed that in giving instructions for reconstruction of viaducts with facilities for a double narrow gauge line they are exceeding their powers under the Lease and the Cornwall Railway directors have been advised that they would be justified in obtaining an injunction to restrain the Joint Committee from proceeding with the proposed works'.

At its subsequent meeting, the Joint Committee had yet another report from Margary, dated 17th January, dealing with the five viaducts mentioned in his earlier recommendation. Following a full discussion on the matter, it was resolved that he 'be instructed to proceed with the two viaducts, Coombe St Stephens and Largin, on the plans proposed by him'. The Cornwall Railway members of the Joint Committee immediately protested and matters then proceeded in accordance with the terms of the Lease to Arbitration, the works at the two viaducts concerned being suspended for two months, so that the matter could be dealt with accordingly.

We must now pause in order to consider the Term of the Lease particularly relevant to this situation. On 28th February 1884, in accordance with Article 67 Sir Daniel Gooch, the Chairman of the Great Western Railway and Mr R Tweedy, the Chairman of the Cornwall Railway, had jointly nominated the Right Hon Sir Arthur Hobhouse KCSI QC, Arbitrator for the year. The matter of the differences which had now occurred between the two parties was, therefore, referred to him to investigate and make an appropriate award, taking due account of the evidence submitted, having regard to the terms of that Lease.

What was essentially the commercial implication arising from an engineering problem was now to invoke the full panoply of the legal profession. Letters were exchanged between the respective solicitors representing on the one hand, the Cornwall Company and on the other, the Great Western Company, which was to act for the Associated Companies. Messrs. Smith, Paul and Archer, for the Cornwall Railway, had written on 17th March 1884, setting out their view, while Mr Nelson, for the Great Western Railway, had responded on 16th April 1884, with a similar but narrower approach to the problem. Meanwhile, at the Cornwall Board meeting of 5th April 1884, Mr E Clarke QC MP and Mr Tweedie were appointed to represent the Cornwall Company. For their part, the Associated Companies retained Mr Webster and Mr R S Wright. The Hearing was held on 28–29th April 1884 at the Westminster Palace Hotel and the transcript of the proceedings, amounting to 125 pages, was published on 13th June 1884, together with the details of the Arbitrator's award.

This fascinating document[11] records in considerable detail the legal situation affecting the replacement of the timber viaducts, in relation to the terms of the Lease existing between the parties. In addition, it also provides an excellent contemporary account of the state of the structures at that time, and the practical difficulties of keeping them in service in relation to the economics involved in their replacement.

The points of contention submitted by the Company were:

> '1. The necessity or propriety of construction
> 2. The power of the Joint Committee even if reconstruction be necessary to reconstruct viaducts so as to admit of their carrying a double narrow gauge line of rails
> 3. The power of the Great Western Company to charge the Cornwall Company with the cost of reconstruction'.

The Associated Companies submitted their view in slightly different terms, viz

> '1. The necessity for reconstruction of the two viaducts Coombe St Stephens and Largin at all at the present time
> 2. If such reconstruction is necessary whether they are to be reconstructed in timber or more lasting material
> 3. If reconstructed whether they are to be reconstructed of width and strength sufficient to carry only a single broad gauge line or a double line on the narrow gauge
> 4. Whether such reconstruction is to be paid wholly out of capital or how'.

In support of the case for the Associated Companies, Mr Webster presented a comprehensive historical review of all the circumstances; going on to question the justification for the Cornwall Directors now abandoning the discretion which they had previously exercised over the preceding 13 or 14 years; to point out the onus on all concerned regarding the safety of the travelling public; and to emphasise the commercial prudence of rebuilding structures wide enough for a double narrow gauge. His submissions were backed by the evidence of a number of expert witnesses. It does not appear that Mr Clarke called any witnesses of his own to present evidence on behalf of the Cornwall Company, but rather relied on cross examination of his opponent's, in order to make his case. This was to the effect that under the terms of the Lease, the members of the Joint Committee were not empowered to approve replacement structures suitable for double narrow gauge line.

The niceties of the legal arguments, so eloquently pleaded by learned Counsel of both sides, form no part of our story, but the terms of the award are material. In the outcome, Sir Arthur Hobhouse ruled that the Joint Committee might reconstruct the viaducts in stone or iron, and even for a double line, where ordinary prudence and foresight required it, but that without the consent of the Cornwall Railway, such reconstruction must be in accordance with Article 17 of the Lease, which required that the Cornwall Railway should be 'kept and maintained exclusively as a railway upon the broad gauge'.

While doubtless a technically correct interpretation of the situation, it was, in all the circumstances, practically absurd; but it did have the effect desired by the Directors of the Cornwall Company, of restricting expenditure on further viaduct reconstruction for the time being, since it would have been imprudent to waste money on building viaducts to take a double line of broad gauge, and shortsighted to construct new single track broad gauge structures. As MacDermot concludes, this foolish episode was closed by the parties agreeing to complete the reconstruction of Largin and Coombe St Stephens to the forbidden width, with no further work being undertaken for five years. In fact, as already noted, no further reconstruction was undertaken in the remaining years of the Cornwall Company, which was finally dissolved on 1st

July 1889. However, in its death throes, it was responsible for placing the contract to build the replacement masonry structure at Coombe by Saltash.

Included within the transcript were the contributions of several eminent witnesses, whose detail evidence is relevant to our study, presenting an unequivocal assessment of the generally parlous state of many of the inland structures at that time. Under cross examination, Margary again confirmed his opinion that the problems at Largin had arisen from the original construction. He considered that the use of timber for such a structure should be avoided, since apart from the onset of decay, their repair was always accompanied by risk, through trains crossing when the ballast had been removed and the track merely supported on wedges. He paid warm tribute to the care and attention which his men took in these repairs, but there was always the possibility that one day, through negligence, a train might come off the track on a viaduct with disastrous result.

In addition, with age, the risk attaching to the structures was increasing, not only through the deterioration of the timber but also due to a number of other factors. These included the age of the iron fastenings, the defective condition of some of the substructures and the increasing speed and number of trains run, all of which combined to cause growing anxiety. We cannot help but sympathise with Margary in these circumstances, in his ongoing worry throughout these years that one day, there could be a serious timber failure, leading to a major catastrophe.

He also pointed out that the viaduct at Coombe St Stephens was an 'S' shape, that it was propped up in many places, and that he had made it a practice as far as possible, to eliminate all such 'S' curves. Fal had a very sharp 'S' curve, and for this reason that structure had already been taken in hand. In response to questioning, he reported that a fire had occurred on one of the viaducts (as noted in Chapter 7) while, interestingly, he stated that the timbers of the viaducts were not creosoted.

A second witness, Harrison Hayter, a Member of the Council of the Institution of Civil Engineers who had been in practice for over 40 years, revealed that he had spent some nine hours inspecting the viaducts between Plymouth and Truro. In his opinion, they were 'in a very unsatisfactory state as regards shape, and as regards line'. He attributed the problems at Largin to:

> '...improper construction at the outset, and also the fact that the viaduct has been very much knocked over by the trains. It is quite evident that in going round a curve the tendency is to go in a straight line...tangentically, [sic] and therefore it exerts a force on the convex side, and there is a continual tendency to overturn the viaducts'.

He considered that all the curved viaducts were out of line, and the tendency to overturn was purely a question of velocity. His statements, in general, corroborated Margary's evidence and interestingly he pointed out that despite the irregular curve at Largin, it had not been shored; which supported his opinion that the problem was attributable to the original construction.

The Senior Inspector of Railways at the BoT, Col. W Yolland who, as we have already seen, had been involved with the Inspection of the Cornwall Railway at its inception, was also called to give evidence. He stated that he had noticed when inspecting Largin recently that the rails were very close to the parapet on the right hand side, travelling towards Falmouth; a circumstance which he had noted at the time of his original inspection was prevalent in a number of instances, but he could not be specific if it had applied to Largin on that occasion. He was also concerned regarding the danger that attended the repairing of these viaducts; firstly, to the public through the omission of some operation and, secondly, to the servants of the Company employed theron. He had never expected that there should be a permanent system of:

> '...keeping gangs of men continually employed from the beginning to the end of each year, taking out beams and putting in others..., taking out legs and putting in others, taking up planking and putting in other planking, and so on'.

His comment insofar as Coombe St Stephens was concerned was forthright and to the point — 'I mean to say an 'S' curve, of all places in the world, ought never to be constructed on a viaduct, and the viaduct a wooden viaduct'. This condemnatory statement should be compared with the laudatory remarks, although qualified, of his original Inspection report.

He fully supported the recommendations which Margary had been making to the Cornwall Company over the previous thirteen or fourteen years, that all these viaducts should be replaced by permanent structures in stone, as 'the only recommendation an engineer who values his reputation should think of making'. Interestingly, Mr Clarke, for the Cornwall Company had nothing to ask him.

The evidence presented by T H Gibbons, the Resident Engineer of the Cornwall Railway, responsible for the reconstruction work on the viaducts of the Cornwall and West Cornwall Railways, gave a close insight to the day to day problems associated with these structures. He confirmed that the Cornwall Company employed one inspector and 54 men, in six gangs of nine men each, continuously engaged on viaduct repairs. He outlined the procedure of repair, involving the removal of all the ballast supporting the track and setting it on wooden wedges; this required a passing train to proceed slowly, and there was an attendant risk of the rails spreading and the train dropping down on to the floor of the viaduct. This had happened on two occasions; at Coombe by Saltash in 1876 and then near Menheniot.

He went on to say that having completed the necessary preparations, a team could replace one of the slanting legs within one and a half hours, but because of the irregular running of the trains, they often had to wait for two or three days before there was a sufficient interval between trains to provide the necessary length of time. He also confirmed the failure of members which we have already noted in relation to the viaducts concerned. He expressed his concern of the lateral movement of those structures which were built on a curve, and the necessity to insert shores to counteract that movement, brought about, in his opinion, by the several changes of timbers, leading to a general loosening of the framework. There had been instances where shores had to be replaced because their original support had not been adequate to resist the movement of the whole structure.

The difficulty of successfully fitting replacement timbers into an existing structure, which had been one of the objectives of Brunel's original designs, was emphasised by Mr Rowbotham, the Engineer from the Central Division of the GWR. In particular, he observed that the exact fitting of a new timber into its cast iron shoe was almost an impossibility, as was getting the fastenings as true and tight as the original. With increasing traffic, these problems were further exacerbated with attendant risk of accident, hence the importance of replacing these structures in stone or iron.

Much of this evidence called into question not only the construction, but also the original design of the curved viaducts — Largin and Coombe St Stephens in particular — and thus, was implied criticism of Brunel himself. It is, therefore, surprising that

141. Forder replacement viaduct under construction in October 1906, with Brunel's original route to St Germans in the right background and the new route deviating to the left. The student of naval history will be intrigued by the collection of pre-dreadnought warships at anchor off Devonport. ***From the Clinker Collection, Brunel University Library***

Mr Clarke did not call his own expert witness in defence of the great engineer, and to show from the original calculations, assuming they existed, that the deterioration in the structures was, perhaps, largely brought about by the increase in traffic of heavier and faster trains. Furthermore, Brunel's former assistant, R P Brereton, was present at the Hearing and it is interesting to conjecture how he would have responded in the defence of his late chief, had he had been called to give evidence.

That said, in the face of evidence so critical of the general condition of the timber viaducts, and the ever present anxiety regarding safety, the ruling by the Arbitrator is all the more remarkable. It effectively placed an embargo on any further replacement work for the time being, while perpetuating repair work with its concomitant weakening of the existing structures. At the same time, it should be borne in mind that with the completion of the works at Largin and Coombe St Stephens in 1886, a total of only 14 of the original 34 viaducts between Plymouth and Truro had been rebuilt or replaced. Consequently, apart from Coombe by Saltash, further work on replacing the remaining twenty was not started until after the conversion of the route from broad to narrow gauge in 1892.

Pausing at the year 1886, a pattern is discernable in that all the inland Class E structures had been replaced, together with the viaducts in the Glynn Valley. The same situation applied over the three viaducts in the Liskeard area where inferior workmanship in the piers had been suspected, at Moorswater, Bolitho and Cartuther. The structures at Fal and Coombe St Stephens, with their suspect 'S' configuration, leading to a weakening of the piers had also been replaced. Thus, by this date, of the original Cornwall Railway timber viaducts, those built on the early contracts, between Truro and Lostwithiel, to the lighter Class A1 design, continued in service until their replacement was put in hand from 1893 through to 1904. The remainder of the Class A2 designs east of Liskeard were replaced over the period 1893–1899, with the all timber Class C structures over the tidal creeks seeing service through until 1908.

While in the light of the Arbitration ruling, work on replacing the Cornwall Railway structures had been suspended from 1886, the same situation did not affect the West Cornwall line. There the work continued apace, and between 1883 and 1888 masonry replacements for the six Y class viaducts were put in hand. Penwithers, Chacewater, Blackwater, Redruth, Angarrack and Guildford were all built in granite, by contract. At the same time, the Company progressively rebuilt the Class Z structure at Hayle. Thus, of the original West Cornwall timber viaducts, only Penponds and Penzance then remained still in use after 1888, their replacement being deferred, as we have seen, until 1900 and 1921 respectively.

142. The replacement Nottar viaduct under construction in October 1906, showing the temporary staging required for its building, with coffer dams around the pier foundations in mid stream. Note also the partially excavated cutting in the left background as the route is carved through the inland hills towards St Germans. ***From the Clinker Collection, Brunel University Library***

The fact that reconstruction of the Cornwall viaducts had been suspended from 1886 did not mean that the problem was not receiving attention. In 1888 the Ordinary Shareholders of the Cornwall Company finally accepted the Great Western offer of £8 in cash for each £20 share, and following an Amalgamation Act, the Cornwall Company was dissolved on 1st July 1889. It thus became an integral part of the Great Western Railway. However, the Joint Committee was as concerned as ever regarding viaduct safety. Yet again, Margary responded to a request to report on the condition of Coombe by Saltash which, it will be recalled, had been the subject of his recommendation for action in 1883. His further report of 7th February 1887 (four years later), emphasised the need for attention and finally, in 1889, a contract was placed by the Cornwall Company for a new masonry viaduct, to be built on the downside. This was the Cornwall Company's last act, and, probably, Margary's last involvement in this ongoing saga, since in 1891 he retired and was succeeded as Plymouth Divisional Engineer by T H Gibbons. The new viaduct was completed in 1894.

Following the track conversion from broad gauge in 1892, and with the Cornwall Company now part of the Great Western system, the extensive programme was put in hand to replace all the remaining inland structures on the main line, involving a total of 13 viaducts. The work was completed as follows: Liskeard (1894), Milltown (1896), Coldrennick (1897), Treviddo (1897), St Austell (1898), Gover (1898), Tresulgan (1899), Penponds (1900), Keyham (1900), Tregarne (1902), Tregagle (1902), Truro (1904) and Carvedras (1904). Either new masonry structures were built or the original piers were raised to carry wrought iron or steel girders. All were built of sufficient width to take a double narrow gauge line. The tidal viaduct at Weston Mill, as we have seen, was replaced by a steel structure comprising four bow string girder spans, with masonry approaches, and completed in 1903.

There then remained the five tidal viaducts between Saltash and St Germans; as early as 1880 Margary had given thought to the action necessary in order to replace these structures and had come to the conclusion that it was unlikely the line would be doubled over this length for a number of years. Accordingly, his recommendation had been to rebuild them using cast iron pillars carried on the existing wooden piles of the original structures, the new viaducts to be of width sufficient only for a single line of broad gauge track.

However, with the passage of time, his successors had taken the bold decision to construct a new double narrow gauge line from Saltash. Detouring inland so as to eliminate the viaducts at Wivelscombe and Grove, the deviation would rejoin the original route at St Germans. The works involved were heavy, as apart from the cuttings and embankments, and a tunnel at Shillingham 452 yards long, this plan required the building of three massive new masonry viaducts. These being at Forder, Nottar and St Germans, were completed in 1908; Fig.141 is a view of the constructional work at Forder, taken in 1906, showing Brunel's original route in the background; while Fig.142, also taken in 1906, is of Nottar, giving an excellent appreciation of the temporary staging involved in its construction. With the rebuilding of Stonehouse Pool in that same year, the only timber viaduct then remaining on the main line was the one on the approach to Penzance, which was to remain in service until 1921.

While there appears to be little information available regarding the methods used in the construction of the timber viaducts, we do have a report regarding the procedure generally adopted for their demolition. Whitley[12] gives an outline of the work involved, based on the technique developed by Gibbons, prior to his retirement as Divisional Engineer at Plymouth in 1909. With the original structure taken out of service, the permanent way and ballast were removed from the viaduct, together with the parapets. In their place a three rail track was laid, back to the stacking ground, comprising a standard gauge track to take permanent-way trolleys and a 12ft gauge line for the special demolition wagon, believed originally to have been designed by Gibbons. It comprised a bed carried on four wheels, on which were mounted two long reach jibs, mounted in the form of derrick cranes and operated by long chains controlled by two hand winches, fixed at the rear of the wagon. The equipment and operations involved may be appreciated from the details of Fig.143 which shows the dismantling of Carnon viaduct.

The sets of raking legs were secured by 4in timbers of sufficient length, lashed to both sides, to prevent their falling when the carrying beams and decking were removed. The support structure was then progressively dismantled by attaching a double-legged sling to the first set of legs; a ganger being lowered to the top of the masonry pier so as to free the bottom ends from the cast iron seatings, as the weight of the legs was taken by the wagon. Once lifted clear, the load was hand propelled back to the stacking ground, off loaded and the component parts dismantled.

The demolition gang proceeded across the viaduct in this fashion until the superstructure had been completely broken down, loaded into wagons and sent back to the Engineers' Depot. Some idea of the time involved in these operations may be gathered from Whitley's note that the dismantling of Ponsanooth viaduct occupied 50 working days, including five Sundays. He quotes a timber content of 13,300ft^3 but this figure seems low. Based on the author's analysis and the length of 645ft, the total was over 21,000ft^3.

143. Carnon timber viaduct in the course of dismantling, using the special twin jib crane developed by Gibbons for this work. This illustration shows the detail of construction of a typical Class A viaduct, with the three laminated horizontal carrying beams supporting the cross timbers of the decking and the specially shaped ends of the raking legs fitting their cast iron shoes. ***L G Booth Collection***

144. Nottar old viaduct in the course of dismantling in 1908. The Class C superstructure is being removed, leaving the timber trestles with their corbels in position, later to be cut down and brought ashore for breaking up. ***Courtesy Trustees of the Science Museum***

Depending on their location and structural stability, the masonry piers have, in the main, been left standing; although in the interest of long term safety, some have been demolished or cropped. With the passage of time, they are tending to become a liability but proposals are under consideration to make some at least a lasting memorial to Brunel.

We have no contemporary record regarding the procedure adopted for the demolition of the tidal viaducts, but from a photograph showing Nottar viaduct in a part dismantled condition (Fig.144) we can surmise the methods which were used. Following the removal of the ballast, the track would then be wedged to allow the use of a travelling steam crane. Starting at one end, the track would be progressively lifted, followed by the removal of the parapets, decking and finally the lower horizontal beams of each span, until the whole of the superstructure had been dismantled. This left the trestles, complete with corbels, still standing, presumably to have their legs cut at low water, felled and then floated ashore, to be broken up.

At the sites today, apart from being able to trace the formation of the original line on either side of the tidal inlets, nothing remains of these structures except the piles, buried in the depths of the Tamar or Lynher mud for all time.

Chapter 10

A FINAL BALANCE SHEET

It is some 140 years since Brunel was working on the designs of his Cornish Railway viaducts, and at that distance in time it is possible to make an objective assessment of the contribution which they made, in general to the science of timber engineering and, in particular, to the railways of Cornwall. Insofar as the railways were concerned, there can be no doubt, under the prevailing financial limitations of the times that without his bold designs the rail links between Penzance and Truro and Truro and Plymouth, would not have been completed when they were. But, a price had to be paid; firstly, timber was prone to decay and the Companies were saddled with increasing annual maintenance costs; secondly, the viaduct structures themselves, designed to cater for the traffic conditions of the mid nineteenth century, became progressively overloaded in later years, with the growth in both size and numbers of trains. A further result, according to contemporary newspaper accounts, was their unpopularity with the travelling public.

However, none of these reports indicate the reasons why, and to find an answer we need to consider the prevailing background conditions at that time. Until the coming of the railway, few of the populace had ever travelled far from their native locations and those who had, were used to the relatively slow speed of the stage coach or horse. The railway presented quite a different experience, with speeds of 30 to 40 mph. This factor, coupled with its route curving along hillsides and crossing deep valleys by these timber structures, often over 100ft in height, added to the contrast. Furthermore, these same structures, by virtue of being built from a collection of timber legs, beams, struts and braces, notched and bolted together, inevitably creaked under the influence of the passage of a heavy train. Indeed, we know from Crispin's own experience as a passenger in a train crossing the viaducts west of Saltash, how 'the timber groaned, the passengers groaned and the train groaned'. Thus, to the travelling public accustomed to more leisurely modes of transport, this combination of experiences could well have caused anxiety; but hardly 'alarm', which seemed to be the main criticism. We have, therefore, to look further for the real explanation.

In considering this problem, we are fortunate to have the great advantage of hindsight, with which to examine the available information and evolve an answer. It could well be explained by the note included on the 1941 survey drawing of the Dare viaduct, to the effect that 'there has always been movement of the piers, sideways and vertically up and down, necessitating adjustments to trestles and alignment of track'. This structure was built on a curve and we know from Margary's many reports that the designs lacked lateral strength; we also know that Brunel's original concept of easy replacement of faulty timbers in his fan designs, in practice gave rise to a general weakening of the whole structure. Hence, these two features would have led to a progressive deterioration and allowed movement of the decking and thus disturbed the level and alignment of the track; giving rise to erratic riding of the train and doubtless communicating alarm to its passengers.

However, against this background, it must not be forgotten that throughout their controversial life, there was no fatal accident on any of the Cornish viaducts. Equally, in analysing their overall condition in these circumstances, it is a marvel that they lasted in service as long as they did. It would, therefore, be quite unreasonable to criticise Brunel for these shortcomings. In the face of severe financial limitations in constructing a route through the quite exceptional terrain of Cornwall, he built 43 viaducts in a distance of 80 miles, as cheaply as possible, all of which was accomplished largely within the limitations of technical knowledge then available to him. They were designed to carry the traffic of the 1860s, which by the 1870s had nearly trebled in volume. It must also not be forgotten, that these structures were very much secondary to his main concern which was, of course, the magnificent Royal Albert Bridge across the Tamar, at Saltash. The reader does not need to be reminded that this Brunellian masterpiece, although strengthened in its later life, continues to carry twentieth century traffic loads across the Tamar into Cornwall.

It is also important to stress that much of the detail work on the later timber viaducts would have been delegated to his assistants and site engineers. Therefore, it is sad indeed that Brunel, in the final years of his very full life, was unable to exercise a more searching control over their work, and thus avoid at least some of the problems which came to light in later years. By virtue of the fundamental testwork which he carried out on yellow pine, his experiments with laminated beams and the practical consideration of the use of continuous beams, his fertile mind was well aware of the basic parameters which should govern his designs. Sadly, few records appear to have survived which would indicate the results he obtained from all this investigation. There is no doubt he was also concerned to find an adequate means of protecting timber members in service, and was far from satisfied with the results of his many tests using different processes. This may well have prompted the concept of easy replacement in service of the component members of some of his designs. Hence, his vision of a range of standard structures, using standard components which could easily be replaced. However, different locations called for individual solutions, and the concept of simple interchangability was lost. Consequently, although a practical engineer, he was expecting too much for each replacement member to be made exactly to match its original.

The criticism regarding lateral strength is not entirely merited, since the Class B design, with inverted 'V' struts to the centre beam, proved satisfactory at Largin in countering this weakness, albeit the structure was subject to considerable problems in service. From the available evidence, it is quite apparent that these arose from the initial irregular erection of the superstructure on the masonry piers; not a design fault. Indeed, that the original piers continue in use on the present day structure is tribute indeed to their satisfactory design and construction. Again, with hindsight, we can say he should, perhaps, have applied the Class B design to every curved viaduct but we do not know how much his decision to use the cheaper Class A configuration was influenced by the ever pressing lack of finance.

We must also not lose sight of the generally inadequate level of knowledge available at that time concerning the overall physical properties of timber. These were not adequately defined until late in the nineteenth century, so it is unlikely that Brunel was fully aware of how, among other considerations, the percentage of moisture, the age of the tree, and the method of seasoning all played an important part in producing a product of consistent quality.

Furthermore, when it is realised that over the decade during which these viaducts were being built, nearly a million cubic feet of 'yellow pine' was imported into Cornwall, inevitably, there must have been a wide variation in the quality and suitability of the material that was used. It is quite apparent that the variations in these properties reflected in the life of the component parts of the viaducts — those built in the early 1850s certainly appeared to have a longer life than the viaducts completed just before the opening of the line. Moorswater was surely a classic example in this respect, with some 50% of its timbers replaced within twenty years, while the viaducts at Truro remained in service until 1904.

While these aspects were not fully appreciated until later in the nineteenth century, doubtless engineers took note of the problems which beset the early Cornish viaducts. Brereton in particular, when he came to complete the Falmouth branch, heeded the experience of those viaducts already in service. This led him to use the Class A2 superstructure on all but Ponsanooth where he followed Brunel's original intention to use the Class B, but with the added benefit of a stronger parapet. Even so, for the curved structures he was prepared to continue with the Class A2 configuration, which would indicate that the problem of lateral weakness was not fully appreciated in their early life. It was probably the build up of traffic, with heavier and faster trains, that eventually brought this shortcoming to light.

All this experience proved to highlight the weakness of timber as a principal structural material in these types of application, but Brunel's work did furnish much basic data on some of the properties of the material. It probably influenced those engineers coming after him to undertake more fundamental research into the whole concept of timber as a structural material for general use. Insofar as the Cornish viaducts were concerned, sadly, it was left to one of his original engineering assistants, Margary, to cope with the operational, technical and corporate problems that surrounded them throughout the greater part of their life; and which plagued the whole of his time as Engineer to the Joint Committee, through to his retirement in 1891. Not until July 1934, with the replacement of Collegewood viaduct, was the problem finally brought to a satisfactory conclusion, and with it, the end of a fascinating chapter of Cornish railway history.

As a concluding comment, it is perhaps a salutary reflection to realise that Brunel designed and built the magnificent Royal Albert bridge at Saltash for a cost of £225,000 — a very reasonable sum when it is compared with the £601,865 for Robert Stephenson's Britannia Bridge. It remains in service today, over 130 years after its completion.

Based on their total timber content of 800,000ft^3, costed at 5/7½d/ft^3 as detailed in the Arbitration Report, the cost of his timber viaducts for the Cornwall Railway, designed and built at the same time, amounted to a like total of £225,000. The cost of the masonry piers would have been over and above this figure. Yet, after only 20 years, by 1879, six had been replaced, followed by a further eight in each of the two following decades and by the end of 50 years all had gone from the mainline. The remaining eight on the less heavily loaded Falmouth branch were progressively replaced over the following 25 years.

Because of financial necessity Brunel used timber and there can be no denying that his designs were attractive and fulfilled their original purpose in providing a cheap solution to the problem of crossing the natural hazards in Cornwall, However, compared with his work on the Royal Albert Bridge, they showed a surprising lack of engineering design analysis, which should have been well within the technical competence of the time. How much was due to Brunel's involvement in other major projects and, hence, his delegation of the work to less qualified or experienced staff, or to his intransigence in approaching their construction from a largely practical standpoint as opposed to one of original design, we shall never know.

From this aspect, it is difficult to appreciate the same engineer was involved in their design as well as that of the Royal Albert Bridge. Yet to have built them all from durable materials in the first instance would probably have cost, at the very least, more than double the above figure — a sum which would have been quite unattainable at the time the Railway was being built. On the basis of financial consideration alone, then perhaps that is the real measure of Brunel's vision and courage in his contribution to the railways of Cornwall.

REFERENCES

Abbreviations
PRO Public Record Office, Kew
RO (County) Record Office

Chapter 1 — Historical Background

1. Tyers G — Brunel's Timber Viaducts — Railway Magazine September 1934
2. PRO RAIL 134/36 — Arbitration Hearing 28th April 1884
3. MacDermot E T — *History of the Great Western Railway* Vol 2 pp146, 147, 149 & 161. Ian Alan 1989
4. *West Briton & Cornwall Advertiser* — 6th May 1859
5. Clinker C R — Centenary at Saltash — *Modern Transport* May 1859
6. Simmons J — The Railway in Cornwall 1869-1881 — *Journal of the Royal Institution of Cornwall* Vol IX
7. PRO RAIL 134/36 — Arbitration Hearing 28th April 1884
8. Ibid.
9. Ibid.
10. Booth L G — Timber Works — *Works of I K Brunel* Ed A Pugsley — Cambridge 1980

Chapter 2 — Construction of the Lines

1. *West Briton & Cornwall Advertiser* — 21st February 1851
2. Hagarty D — The Barlow Rail — *Industrial Heritage* Vol 9 No 4
3. *West Briton & Cornwall Advertiser* — 5th March 1852
4. PRO MT 29/12 — West Cornwall Railway Inspection Report — 10th March 1852 and 18th August 1852
5. Ibid.
6. *West Briton & Cornwall Advertiser* — 27th August 1852
7. Ibid. — 5th March 1852
8. Ibid. — 27th August 1847
9. PRO RAIL 134/17 — Letters & Reports from I K Brunel 1853 to 1859
10. Simmons J — The Railway in Cornwall 1835-1914 *Journal of The Royal Institution of Cornwall* Vol IX
11. *West Briton & Cornwall Advertiser* — 2nd September 1853
12. PRO RAIL 134/17 — Letters & Reports from I K Brunel 1853 to 1859
13. Ibid.
14. *West Briton & Cornwall Advertiser* — 2nd September 1853
15. PRO RAIL 134/17 — Letters & Reports from I K Brunel 1853 to 1859
16. Ibid.
17. Ibid.
18. *West Briton & Cornwall Advertiser* — 7th March 1856
19. Ibid. — 4th September 1857
20. PRO RAIL 134/17 — Letters & Reports from I K Brunel 1853 to 1859
21. *Royal Cornwall Gazette* — 5th March 1858
22. PRO RAIL 134/16 — Report etc from H S Bush — 3rd June 1858
23. *Cornwall Times* — 18th December 1858
24. PRO RAIL 134/17 — Letters & Reports from I K Brunel 1853 to 1859
25. *West Briton & Cornwall Advertiser* — 25th February 1859
26. Ibid.
27. *West Briton & Cornwall Advertiser* — 15th April 1859
28. PRO MT29/20 — Cornwall Railway Inspection Report — 25th April 1859
29. *Cornish Times* — 7th May 1859
30. *West Briton & Cornwall Advertiser* — 6th May 1859
31. PRO RAIL 134/17 — Letters & Reports from I K Brunel 1853 to 1859
32. *West Briton & Cornwall Advertiser* — 22nd August 1863
33. PRO RAIL 134/16— Report etc from H S Bush 14th February 1867
34. *West Briton & Cornwall Advertiser* — 5th September 1851

Chapter 3 — Design Considerations

1. Booth L G — Strength & Testing of Timber during the 17th & 18th Centuries *Jour. Inst. Wood Science* — November 1964
2. Rankine W J M — *Introductory Lecture on the Harmony of Theory & Practice in Mechanics* — Griffin 1856
3. Charlton T M — Theoretical Work — *Works of I K Brunel* — Ed A Pugsley Cambridge 1980
4. Frohling W — The Treatise 'On Draught' etc — *Trans. Newcomen Soc. Vol.58* 1986/7
5. Brunel I — *Life of I K Brunel* — Longmans Green 1870
6. Booth L G — Laminated Timber Arch Railway Bridges in England & Scotland *Trans. Newcomen Soc.* Vol.XLIV 1971/2
7. Booth L G — Timber Works — *Works of I K Brunel* — Ed A Pugsley Cambridge 1980
8. Mercer C A — Penadlake Viaduct Built by I K Brunel — University of Surrey 1978
9. PRO RAIL 134/17 — Letters & Reports from I K Brunel 1853 to 1859
10. PRO RAIL 134/34 — Report by P J Margary
11. PRO RAIL 134/36 — Arbitration Hearing 28th April 1884
12. PRO RAIL 1005/80 — Original manuscript undated
13. Booth L G — Laminated Timber Arch Railway Bridges in England & Scotland *Trans. Newcomen Soc.* Vol XLIV 1971/2
14. James J G — Some Steps in the Evolution of Early Iron Arched Bridge Designs — *Trans. Newcomen Soc.* Vol 59 1987/8
15. PRO RAIL 134/36 — Arbitration Hearing 28th April 1884
16. Fletcher L E — Description of the Landore Viaduct — *Proc.Inst.Civ. Engrs.* — Vol 14 1855
17. Brunel I — *Life of I K Brunel* — Longmans Green 1870
18. *Proc.Inst.Civ.Engrs.* — Vol 230 1929-30 p136
19. Brunel I — *Life of I K Brunel* — Longmans Green 1870
20. MacDermot E T — *History of the Great Western Railway* Vol 2 1989
21. GWR Drawing — Wooden Viaducts of Cornwall 1932
22. Brunel I — *Life of I K Brunel* — Longmans Green 1870
23. Ibid.
24. PRO MT 29/20 — Cornwall Railway Inspection Report — 25th April 1859

REFERENCES

Chapter 4 —The Timber of Construction

1. Sutcliffe G L — *Modern Carpenter, Joiner & Cabinet Maker* Gresham Publishing Co
2. Brunel I — *Life of I K Brunel* — Longmans Green 1870
3. Bell W — Stresses of Rigid Arches, Continuous Beams & Curved Structures *Proc.Inst.Civ.Engrs.* Vol 33 1871
4. Booth L G — Timber Works — *Works of I K Brunel* — Ed A Pugsley Cambridge 1980
5. PRO RAIL 134/30 — Report on CR to GWR by J Grierson & M Lane 1865
6. PRO MT29/12 — West Cornwall Railway — Captain Laffen's Report 10th March 1852
7. *West Briton & ornwall Advertiser* — 6th May 1859
8. PRO RAIL 134/36 — Arbitration Hearing 28th April 1884
9. Whitley H S B — Timber Viaducts in South Devon & Cornwall GWR — *Railway Engineer* October 1931
10. Ibid.
11. Ibid.
12. Cornwall CRO AD540/5/6
13. Whitley H S B — Timber Viaducts in South Devon & Cornwall GWR — *Railway Engineer* October 1931
14. PRO RAIL 134/36 — Arbitration Hearing 28th April 1884
15. Cornwall CRO AD540/5/6
16. Ibid.

Chapter 5 — The Viaduct Classes and their Constructional Features

1. *West Briton & Cornwall Advertiser* — 6th May 1859
2. PRO RAIL 257/20 — Report on Timber Viaducts & their Reconstruction by P J Margary 12th February 1880
3. West Cornwall Railway — Penpons to Camborne — Drawing No 11 dated 1851
4. A copy of drawing ref.3 with amendments and dated c1861
5. Whitley H S B — Timber Viaducts in South Devon & Cornwall GWR — *Railway Engineer* October 1931
6. GWR Dare Branch — Demolition drawings of Dare & Gamlyn Viaducts ref C15533 April 1941
7. Cornwall Railway — Drawings of Fal and Carvedras viaducts — Nos 3 & 4 undated
8. Cornwall Railway — Keyham Creek Viaduct — Drawing No 8
9. Cornwall Railway — Keyham Creek Viaduct — Drawing No 6
10. Great Western Railway Drawing — Wooden Viaducts in Cornwall 1932
11. Whitley H S B — Timber Viaducts in South Devon & Cornwall GWR — *Railway Engineer* October 1931
12. Cornwall Railway — Keyham Creek Viaduct — Drawing No 10
13. Cornwall Railway — Keyham Creek Viaduct — Drawing No 6
14. Margary P J — Reconstruction of the St Pinnock & Moorswater Viaducts on the Cornwall Railway — *Proc.Inst.Civ.Engrs.* Vol 69 1882
15. PRO RAIL 134/47— Drawing of Moorswater Viaduct c1860
16. PRO RAIL 257/20 — Report on Timber Viaducts & their Reconstruction by P J Margary 12th February 1880
17. Cornwall Railway — Keyham Creek Viaduct — Drawing No 7
18. PRO RAIL 257/20 — Report on Timber Viaducts & their Reconstruction by P J Margary 12th February 1880
19. Whitley H S B — Timber Viaducts in South Devon & Cornwall GWR — *Railway Engineer* October 1931
20. Cornwall Railway — Wivelscombe Lake Viaduct — Drawing No 13
21. Gibbons T H — Railway Viaducts in Cornwall, Old and New — *Proc.I.Mech.E.* July 1899
22. PRO RAIL 134/34 — Report by P J Margary

Chapter 7 — The Building Testing & Maintenance of the Viaducts

1. PRO RAIL 134/36 — Arbitration Hearing 28th April 1884
2. Ibid.
3. PRO RAIL 134/17 — Letters & Reports from I K Brunel 1853 to 1859
4. PRO MT29/12 — West Cornwall Railway Inspection Reports — 1852
5. *West Briton & Cornwall Advertiser* — 12th March 1852
6. PRO MT29/12 — West Cornwall Railway Inspection Reports — 1852
7. PRO MT29/20 Cornwall Railway Report 25th April 1859
8. Whitley H S B — Timber Viaducts in South Devon & Cornwall GWR — *Railway Engineer* October 1931
9. Ibid.
10. *Proc.Inst.Civ.Engrs.* Vol 230 1929-30 p138
11. Whitley H S B — Timber Viaducts in South Devon & Cornwall GWR — *Railway Engineer* October 1931

REFERENCES

Chapter 8 — The Viaducts Described

1. PRO RAIL 257/20. A Report by P J Margary dated 12th February 1880 on the condition of the Cornwall Railway viaducts which provides much of the information contained in this chapter
2. Crispin S J — unpublished notes
3. PRO RAIL 134/34. A further Report by P J Margary dated 11th February 1887, similar to (1) above, which provides additional information
4. *GWR Magazine* — April 1937
5. Gibbons T H — Railway Viaducts in Cornwall, Old and New — *Proc.I.Mech.E.* July 1899
6. Cornwall Railway — St Germans Contract — Drawing No 14
7. Cornwall Railway — Wivelscombe Lake Viaduct — Drawing No 13
8. *West Briton & Cornwall Advertiser* — 6th May 1859
9. *Cornish Times* — 14th May 1859
10. Messenger M J — Unpublished notes
11. Cornwall Railway — St Germans Viaduct — Drawing No 12
12. *Cornish Times* — 23rd January 1858
13. *West Briton & Cornwall Advertiser* — 1st February 1897
14. Bolitho Papers — Cornwall CRO
15. PRO RAIL 134/47 — Drawing of Moorswater Viaduct
16. Allan J — *History of the Borough of Liskeard* 1856
17. PRO RAIL 134/3 — Cornwall Railway Minute Book 1854-71
18. *West Briton & Cornwall Advertiser* — 7th March 1856
19. PRO RAIL 134/3 — Cornwall Railway Minute Book 1854-71
20. *West Briton & Cornwall Advertiser* — 5th September 1856
21. Ibid. — 6th March 1857
22. PRO RAIL 134/16 — Report by H S Bush
23. PRO RAIL 134/36 — Arbitration Hearing — 28th April 1884
24. Cornwall Railway — Moorswater Viaduct — Plan of Piers at Ground Level 15th December 1876 — MC265/38
25. PRO RAIL 134/9 — Minutes of Joint Committee — 1st November 1867
26. *Cornwall Gazette* — 15th February 1878 — Letter
27. *Cornish Times* — 31st March 1877
28. PRO RAIL 134/10 — Minutes of Joint Committee — 27th February 1878
29. Margary P J — Reconstruction of the St Pinnock and Moorswater Viaducts on the Cornwall Railway — *Proc.Inst.Civ.Engrs.* Vol 69 1882
30. Brunel Archive — University of Bristol — General Notebook 1844-50
31. Cooke R A — *Track Layout Diagrams of the GWR* — Section 11 East Cornwall
32. PRO RAIL 134/10 — Minutes of the Joint Committee
33. Ibid.
34. Margary P J — Reconstruction of the St Pinnock and Moorswater Viaducts on the Cornwall Railway — *Proc.Inst.Civ.Engrs.* Vol 69 1882
35. PRO RAIL 134/10 — Minutes of the Joint Committee
36. PRO MT6/150/1 — Inspection Report — 1st January 1876
37. Crispin S J — Unpublished Notes
38. Cornwall Railway — Crossing of River at Lostwithiel — Viaduct Drawing No 2 — Undated
39. PRO RAIL 134/36 — Arbitration Hearing — 28th April 1884
40. Gibbons T H — Railway Viaducts in Cornwall, Old and New — *Proc.I.Mech.E.* — July 1899
41. PRO RAIL 134/16 — Miscellaneous Reports
42. *West Briton & Cornwall Advertiser* — 22nd September 1881
43. West Cornwall Railway — Penpons to Camborne — Drawing No 11(modified) dated c1861
44. Notes from local history of Angarrack — undated
45. *Royal Cornwall Gazette* — 31st October 1851
46. *West Briton & Cornwall Advertiser* — 5th March 1852
47. Ibid. — 30th March 1882
48. Ibid. — 5th March 1852
49. GWR Proposed Hayle Viaduct Drawing dated 1st November 1880
50. Butland W E — Replacement of Penzance Railway Viaduct — *GWR Magazine* 1922
51. Cornwall Railway — Penwithers Viaduct Drawing dated 27th June 1861
52. Cornwall Railway — Ringwell Viaduct Drawing dated 26th June 1861
53. *West Briton & Cornwall Advertiser* — 22nd August 1863
54. Cornwall Railway — Carnon Viaduct Drawing dated 1st July 1861
55. PRO RAIL 134/5 — Minutes of Joint Committee — 29th November 1861
56. Cornwall Railway — Carnon Viaduct Drawing dated 7th December 1861
57. *West Briton & Cornwall Advertiser* — 22nd August 1863
58. PRO RAIL 1005/80 — Miscelleneous Reports
59. Cornwall Railway — Perran Viaduct Drawing dated 22nd February 1854
60. Cornwall Railway — Perran Viaduct Drawing dated 26th June 1861
61. Cornwall Railway — Ponsanooth Viaduct Drawing dated 22nd February 1854
62. PRO RAIL 1005/80 — Miscellaneous Reports
63. Cornwall Railway — Pascoe Viaduct Drawing dated 28th July 1854
64. Cornwall Railway — Pascoe Viaduct Drawing dated 27th June 1861
65. Cornwall Railway — Penryn Viaduct Drawing dated 27th June 1861
66. Tredgold T — *Elementary Principles of Carpentry* — 5th edn 1870

Chapter 9 — The Pattern of Replacement

1. PRO RAIL 134/36 — Many of the details of this chapter originate from this reference
2. See Appendix 2
3. Cooke R A — *Track Layout Digrams of the GWR* — Section 11 East Cornwall
4. Ibid.
5. Ibid.
6. PRO RAIL 257/20 — Report on Timber Viaducts & their Reconstruction by P J Margary 12th February 1880
7. PRO RAIL 134/13 — Minutes of Joint Committee
8. PRO RAIL 134/36 — Arbitration Hearing 28th April 1884
9. Ibid
10. PRO RAIL 134/13 — Minutes of Joint Committee
11. PRO RAIL 134/36 — Arbitration Hearing 28th April 1884
12. Whitley H S B — Timber Viaducts in South Devon & Cornwall GWR — *Railway Engineer* October 1931

APPENDIX 1

APPROXIMATE ANALYSIS OF TIMBER CONTENT OF SUPERSTRUCTURES

Viaduct Class	A1	A2	B	C	D	E	Y	Z
Span ft. between piers	65ft	66ft	66ft	41ft	66ft	39ft 6in	50ft	21ft
Deck + Carrier	4in deck 3 Hor. Lam. Beams	4in deck 3 Hor. Lam. Beams + Parapets	6in deck 3 Hor. Lam. Beams	8in deck 2 Trussed Parapets	8in deck 2 Trussed Parapets + Lam. Beams	4in deck 3 Hor. Lam. Beams	4in deck 3 Hor. Lam. Beams	4in deck 3 Hor. Lam. Beams
ft^3/span	910	1,320	1,056	902	1,320	553	700	273
ft^3/ft span	14	20	16	22	26	14	14	13
Supports	3 sets of 4 Raking Legs on Masonry Piers	3 sets of 4 Raking Legs on Masonry Piers	4 sets of 4 Raking Legs on Masonry Piers	Timber Trestle on Timber Piles	2 sets of 4 Raking Legs on Trestles	3 sets of 2 Raking Legs on Masonry Plinths	3 sets of 3 Raking Legs on Masonry Piers	Vert'l Struts
ft^3/Span	780	792	924		1,254	356	750	–
ft^3/ft span	12	12	14	–	19	9	15	–
TOTALS								
ft^3/Span	1,690	2,112	1,980	–	2,574	909	1,450	–
ft^3/ft span	26	32	30	–	39	23	29	–
Timber wt. per span tons	28	35	33	15*	43	15	24	5*

* Superstructure only

APPENDIX 2

ANALYSIS OF VIADUCT REPAIR AND REPLACEMENT COSTS

Extracted from Data in PRO RAIL 134/4

Viaduct Name	Period	Cost of Repairs £	Average Cost pa £	Period	Average Cost pa £	Repl'nt Cost £
Stonehouse Pool	1860/82	2,688	122			
Keyham	1860/82	2,242	102			
Weston Mill	1860/82	6,180	281			
Coombe by Saltash	1860/82	4,868	221			
Forder	1860/82	3,839	175			
Wivelscombe	1860/82	1,196	54			
Grove	1860/82	633	29			
Nottar	1860/82	6,046	275			
St Germans	1860/82	8,514	387			
Tresulgan	1860/82	2,316	105			
Coldrenick	1860/82	4,738	215			
Treviddo	1860/82	2,484	113			
Cartuther	1860/82	1,680	78	1869/81	117	7,883
Bolitho	1860/82	2,231	101	1869/81	168	9,188
Liskeard	1860/82	3,349	152			
Moorswater	1860/80	6,560	328	1868/80	497	30,368
Westwood	1860/80	857	43	1868/80	63	3,958
St Pinnock	1860/79	2,246	118	1869/79	205	9,284
Largin	1860/82	2,615	119			
West Largin	1860/75	336	22			
Draw Wood	1860/76	593	37	1869/76	72	11,563
Derrycombe	1860/80	1,058	53	1869/80	86	5,108
Clinnick	1860/80	475	24	1869/79	41	5,020
Penadlake	1860/78	669	37	1869/78	59	4,444
Milltown	1860/82	1,829	83			
St Austell	1860/82	3,489	159			
Gover	1860/82	2,966	135			
Coombe St Stephens	1860/82	3,513	160			
Fal	1860/82	2,886	131	Estimated		12,000
Probus	1860/71	455	41			2,664
Tregarne	1860/82	3,352	152			
Tregagle	1860/82	1,400	64			
Truro	1860/82	5,480	249			
Carvedras	1860/82	4,248	193			
TOTALS		**98,031**				**101,480**

APPENDIX 3 — SCHEDULE OF TIMBER CONTENT & MAINTENANCE COST: £/1,000ft³/year

Viaduct No.	Name	L'th[a] ft	H'ht ft	Class	Unit ft³/ft	Timber Content ft³ Super. Str're	Supports	Total K ft³	Period 1[b] Cost £	Years	£/K ft³	Period 2[c] Cost	Years	£/K ft³
1	Stonehouse Pool	321	57	A2	54	17,334	–	17·33	2,688	22	7·04			
2	Keyham	432	90	A2	32	13,824	–	13·82	2,242	22	7·37			
3	Weston Mill	1,200	46	C	22	26,400	10,771[d]	37·17	6,180	22	7·56			
4	Coombe by Saltash	609	87	D	39	23,751	5,120[d]	28·87	4,868	22	7·65			
5	Forder	696	67	C	22	15,312	8,400[d]	23·71	3,839	22	7·38			
6	Wivelscombe	129	24	C	22	2,838	243[d]	3·08	1,196	22	17·53			
7	Grove	117	28	E	23	2,691	–	2·69	633	22	10·78			
8	Nottar	1,134	67	C	22	24,948	13,854[d]	38·80	6,046	22	7·09			
9	St Germans	945	106	–	34	32,130	28,128[d]	60·26	8,514	22	6·42			
10	Tresulgan	525	93	A2	32	16,800	–	16·80	2,316	22	6·27			
11	Coldrenick	790	134	A2	32	25,280	6,320[e]	31·60	4,738	22	6·80			
12	Treviddo	486	101	A2	32	15,552	–	15·52	2,484	22	7·27			
13	Cartuther	411	89	A2	32	13,152	–	13·15	1,680	22	5·81	1,404	12	8·89
14	Bolitho	546	113	A2	32	17,472	–	17·47	2,331	22	6·06	2,016	12	9·62
15	Liskeard	720	150	A2	32	23,040	–	23·04	3,349	22	6·61			
16	Moorswater	954	147	D	39	37,206	18,240[f]	55·45	6,560	20	5·92	5,964	12	8·96
17	Westwood	372	88	A1	26	9,672	–	9·67	857	20	4·43	756	12	6·51
18	St Pinnock	614	151	B	30	18,420	–	18·42	2,246	19	6·42	2,050	10	11·13
19	Largin	567	130	B	30	17,010	–	17·01	2,615	22	6·99			
20	West Largin	315	75	A1	26	8,190	–	8·19	336	15	2·74			
21	Draw Wood	669	42	E	23	15,387	–	15·39	593	16	2·41	504	7	4·68
22	Derrycombe	369	77	A1	26	9,594	–	9·59	1,058	20	5·52	946	11	8·97
23	Clinnick	330	74	A1	26	8,580	–	8·58	475	20	2·77	410	10	4·78
24	Penadlake	396	42	E	23	9,108	–	9·11	669	18	4·08	531	9	6·48
25	Milltown	484	75	A1	26	12,584	–	12·58	1,829	22	6·61			
26	St Austell	713	109	A1	26	18,538	–	18·54	3,489	22	8·55			
27	Gover	679	95	A1	26	17,654	–	17·65	2,966	22	7·64			
28	Coombe St Stephens	721	70	A1	26	18,746	–	18·74	3,513	22	8·52			
29	Fal	570	90	A1	26	14,820	–	14·82	2,886	22	8·85			
30	Probus	435	43	E	23	10.005	–	10·00	455	11	4·14			
31	Tregarne	584	83	A1	26	15,184	–	15·18	3,352	22	10·04			
32	Tregagle	303	69	A1	26	7,878	–	7·88	1,400	22	8·08			
33	Truro	1,310	92	A1	26	34,060	–	34·06	5,480	22	7·31			
34	Carvedras	969	86	A1	26	25,163	–	25·16	4,248	22	7·38			

Notes: [a]Estimated by Author; [b]Period 1 — Mainly 1860 to 1882; [c]Period 2 — Mainly 1869 to 1881; [d]Trestle Support; [e]Trussed beam; [f]Struts.

APPENDIX 4

Schedule of Important Dates relating ot the Cornwall Railways with particular reference to the viaducts

1826	Redruth & Chasewater Railway opened
1834	Hayle Railway Act granted
1846	Cornwall Railway & West Cornwall Railway Acts granted
1847	Work started on Cornwall Railway near Truro
1849	Work started on West Cornwall Railway
1851	Brunel proposed Cornwall Railway as single line
1852	Work restarted on Cornwall Railway at Truro
	West Cornwall Railway opened
1853	Contract let for Royal Albert Bridge
	Contract let for Falmouth Branch
1855	Cornwall Railway leased to constituent Companies of Joint Committee
1858	Line between South Devon Railway and Royal Albert Bridge completed
1859	Cornwall Railway opened
	Death of I K Brunel
1863	Falmouth Branch opened
1871	Probus viaduct replaced
1875	Draw Wood & West Largin viaducts replaced
1879	Clinnick & Westwood viaducts replaced
1881	Moorswater viaduct replaced
1882	St Pinnock viaduct reconstructed
	Bolitho & Cartuther viaducts replaced
1884	Fal viaduct replaced
	Arbitration Hearing in London
1885	Angarrak viaduct replaced
1886	Coombe St Stephens & Guildford viaducts replaced
	Largin & Hayle viaducts reconstructed.
1887	Penwithers (W Cornwall) viaduct replaced
1888	Chacewater, Blackwater & Redruth viaducts replaced
1894	Coombe by Saltash viaduct replaced.
	Liskeard viaduct reconstructed
1896	Milltown viaduct replaced
1897	Coldrennick viaduct reconstructed
	Treviddo viaduct replaced
1898	St Austell & Gover viaducts replaced
1899	Tresulgan viaduct replaced
1900	Penponds viaduct replaced
	Keyham viaduct reconstructed
1902	Tregarne & Tregagle viaducts replaced
1903	Weston Mill viaduct replaced
1904	Truro & Carvedras viaducts replaced
1908	Stonehouse Pool viaduct reconstructed
	St Germans deviation opened
1921	Penzance viaduct replaced by stone embankment
1923	Penryn & Pascoe viaducts replaced
1926	Penwithers (Falmouth branch) viaduct replaced
1927	Perran viaduct replaced
1930	Ponsanooth viaduct replaced
1933	Ringwell & Carnon viaducts replaced
1934	Collegewood viaduct replaced

APPENDIX 5

COMPARATIVE STRESS CALCULATIONS FOR THE VIADUCT CLASSES

With a view to establishing comparative stress levels in the different classes of viaduct arising from a given loading, simple calculations have been carried out in accordance with the relevant sections of British Standard BS 5268: Part 2: 1984, based on the static loading quoted by Fletcher and using the engineering units current in Brunel's lifetime. No account is taken of rolling or braking loads. This investigation is only intended to compare the relative strength of the viaduct classes, as calculated from a simple method of analysis.

Referring to *Structural Rules of Thumb* by D Beckett[1], the Material properties were taken to be those of Pitch Pine, ref Table 9 of the above Standard, which are considered to approximate those of Brunel's 'Yellow Pine'; grade stress (the stress which can safely be permanently sustained by the material) being that of Grade SS, to give:

1. Bending parallel to grain, 10·50 N/mm^2 or 1,523 lb/in^2
2. Compression " " 11·00 " 1,596 "
3. Density 37 lb/ft^3
4. Modulus of Elasticity 9,000 " (min) 1,305,720 lb/in^2
   ('Yellow Pine' would probably have been higher)

Permissible Stress = Grade Stress factored for Section Depth(k_7); Wet Exposure (k_2); Duration of Loading (k_3).

DECK & CARRYING BEAMS Factor	BS 5268 Table	Section 12"X24"	12"X4"	10"X24"	12"X8"	12"X6"
k_1 Section Modulus	2	1·06	1·06	1·06	1·06	1·06
k_2 Wet Exposure	14	0·80	0·80	0·80	0·80	0·80
k_3 Loading	15	1·25	1·25	1·25	1·25	1·25
k_7 Depth – $(300/d)^{0 \cdot 11}$			1·13		1·04	1·08
or $0 \cdot 81.(d^2+92300)/(d^2+56800)$		0·88		0·88		
Section Modulus $Z = k_1.bd^2/6$		1,221	34	1,018	136	76
Permissible Stress lb/in^2		1,340	1,721	1,340	1,584	1,645

LEGS	BS 5268 Table	Section 12"X12"	14"X14"	24"X12"	E
Factor					
k_1 Cross Sectional Area	2	1·04	1·04	1·04	
k_2 Wet Exposure	14	0·60	0·60	0·60	·80
k_3 Loading	15	1·25	1·25	1·25	
Moment of Inertia in^4		1,728	3,201	3,456	
Permissible Stress lb/in^2		1,245	1,245	1,245	

Assume Fletcher's loading of 1 ton per ft. per rail, as a distributed load of 2 tons on each deck member, plus self weight. The parapet rails, posts, ballast boards with fenders etc, are added according to location. The deck member is treated as a continuous beam (other than for Class D), so as to establish the reaction on each of the carrying beams. This calculation, and those that follow, are based on the relevant formulae by G Lister Sutcliffe[2].

Of the three carrying beams, it will be seen that the centre one is the more heavily loaded, and this reaction load from each deck member is then considered as being applied as a distributed load along the laminated beam, together with the weight of the beam and, as necessary, that of the parapet, treating it as a continuous beam. The supports are assumed to be equally spaced according to viaduct class across the fan. In order to take account of the reaction due to the linking span between fans, it is treated as a simply supported beam and its reaction added to that of the outer leg. These calculations enable comparative stress levels to be established for the various viaduct classes, together with the reactions at the leg supports. The corresponding load in each leg can then be calculated, in relation to the critical load of that leg when considered as a pin jointed strut.

A perfect structure is assumed with a 100% effective laminated joint in the carrying beam. As we are concerned only in establishing comparative data between the different viaduct classes, the affect of inevitable slip at the interface is ignored.

The accompanying analyses show examples of these calculations for three of the viaduct classes while the Table summarises the results of such simple structural analysis, applied to each of the inland viaduct classes.

References

1 *Structural Rules of Thumb (Aspects of the History and Design of Structures)* Issue No 2 June 1990 by D Beckett — School of Land & Construction Management — Thames Polytechnic.

2 *The Modern Carpenter Joiner & Cabinet Maker* — G Lister Sutcliffe — Gresham 1904.

Consider Viaduct Class A1

1. DECK LOADING

1 ton/ft/Rail Loading considered as 4,4801b distributed load over 15ft span or 2991b/ft acting on a Continuous Beam having three supports, equally spaced at 7·08ft centres.

Weight of deck Timber 13 lb/ft
So total loading will be 312 lb/ft

Then
MAXIMUM BENDING MOMENT in Deck Timber

$M = 0{\cdot}125wl^2$
$= 0{\cdot}125.312.7{\cdot}08^2 = 1{,}955$ lb.ft

Maximum Bending STRESS
$f_m = M/Z$
$= 1{,}955.12/34 = 690$ lb/in^2
Compared with Permissible Stress 1,721 lb/in^2

and
REACTIONS on Carrying Beams will be:

On Outer Beams
$R_o = 0{\cdot}375wl$
$= 0{\cdot}375.312.7{\cdot}08 = 829$ lb

On Centre Beam
$R_c = 1{\cdot}25wl$
$= 1{\cdot}25.312.7{\cdot}08 = 2{,}761$ lb

The Centre Beam is thus the more heavily loaded and will be considered for further analysis. The weight of the Ballast Boards, Fenders and Handrailing are assumed to be carried by the Outer Beams.

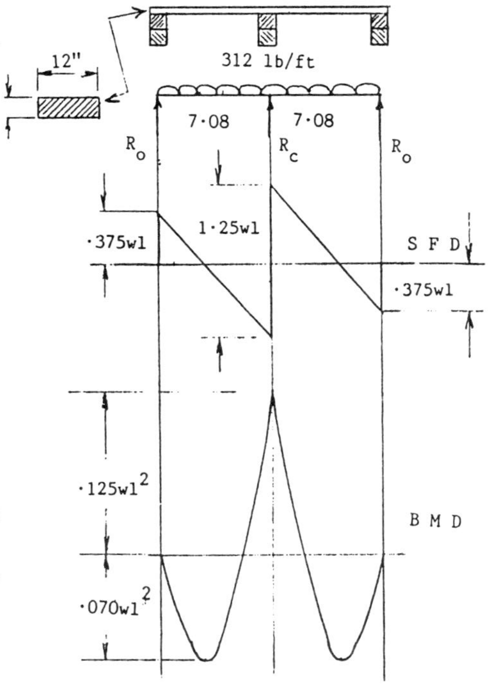

2. CENTRE BEAM

From the above analysis
Distributed Load on Carrying Beam = 2,761 lb/ft
Weight of Beam = 74 lb/ft
Total Distributed Loading = 2,835 lb/ft

Then
Assume a Continuous Beam over four equally spaced Fan Supports at 15ft cts

MAXIMUM BENDING MOMENT

$M = 0{\cdot}10wl^2$
$= 0{\cdot}10.2{,}835.15^2 = 63{,}788$ lb.ft

Maximum Bending STRESS
$f_m = M/Z$
$= 63{,}788.12/1{,}221 = 627$ lb/in^2
Compared with Permissible Stress 1,340 lb/in^2

and
REACTIONS at Fan Supports will be:

On Outer Struts
$R_o = 0{\cdot}40wl$
$= 0{\cdot}40.2{,}835.15 = 17{,}010$ lb

On Inner Struts
$R_i = 1{\cdot}10wl$
$= 1{\cdot}10.2{,}835.15 = 46{,}778$ lb

Allow for Reactions of Centre Beam of LINKING SPAN at Outer Struts, when treated as simply supported Beam, ignoring affect of Crown Piece.
MAXIMUM BENDING MOMENT

$M = 0{\cdot}125wl^2$
$= 0{\cdot}125.2{,}835.20^2 = 141{,}750$ lb.ft

Maximum Bending STRESS
$f_m = M/Z$
$= 141{,}750.12/1{,}221 = 1{,}393$ lb/in^2
Compared with Permissible Stress 1,340 lb/in^2

REACTION at each support will be
$R = 0{\cdot}50wl$
$= 0{\cdot}50.2{,}835.20 = 28{,}350$ lb

Hence total Reaction on Outer Strut will be 17,010 + 28,350 = 45,360 lb

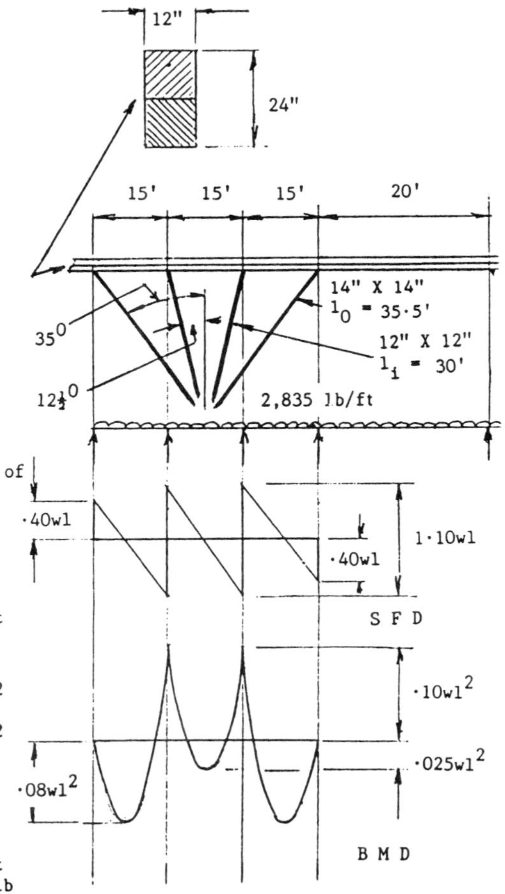

3. LOADING OF STRUTS OR RAKING LEGS

Inner Leg, section 12"X12"
l_i = 30ft @ 12½°
Load in Leg P_m = 46,778/cos 12½°
= 46,778/·9763 = 47,914 lb

Compressive STRESS in Leg f_m = 47,914/144 = 333 lb/in^2
Compared with Permissible Stress 1,245 lb/in^2
and Fletcher permitted value of 373 lb/in^2

Critical Load of Strut (Euler) $P_c = \pi^2 EIk_2/l_i^2$
$= 9{\cdot}87.1,305,720.1,728.{\cdot}80/(12.30)^2$
= 137,461 lb

and ratio P_c/P_m = 2·87

Outer Leg, section 14"X14"
l_o = 35·5ft @ 35°
Load in Leg = 45,360/cos 35°
= 45,360/·8192 = 55,371 lb

Compressive STRESS in Leg f_m = 55,371/196 = 283 lb/in^2
Compared with Permissible Stress 1,245 lb/in^2
and Fletcher permitted value of 373 lb/in^2

Critical Load of Strut (Euler) $P_c = 9{\cdot}87.1,305,720.3,201.{\cdot}80/(12.35{\cdot}5)^2$
= 181,848 lb

and ratio P_c/P_m = 3·28

Consider Viaduct Class D
1. DECK LOADING

1 ton/ft/Rail Loading considered as 4,480lb distributed load over an equivalent 15ft span or 299lb/ft acting on a simply supported beam at 15ft centres.

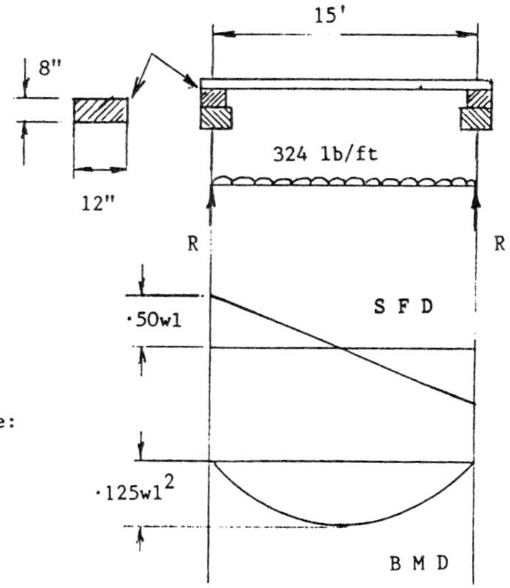

Weight of beam 25lb/ft
So total loading will be 324lb/ft

Then
MAXIMUM BENDING MOMENT in Deck Timber

$M = 0{\cdot}125wl^2$
$= 0{\cdot}125.324.15^2$ = 9,113 lb.ft

Maximum Bending STRESS
f_m = M/Z
= 9,113.12/136 = 804 lb/in^2
Compared with Permissible Stress
1,584 lb/in^2

and
REACTION on each Carrying Beam will be:

R = 0·50wl
= 0·50.324.15 = 2,430 lb

2.LOADING OF OUTER CARRYING BEAMS

Consider Loading per ft run on each Beam.
The weight of Ballast Boards, Parapets etc must be included as follows;

Ballast Board	2½"X18"	12 lb
Fender	8"X6"	13
Parapet Rail	12"X10"	31
Posts, Straining Pieces etc	12"X12" sections over 36ft	42
Coffin Pieces	12"X12" sections over 36ft	42
Carrying Beam	12"X12"	37
	12"X14"	43
Total Structural Weight		220
Reaction from loading of Deck timber		2,430
Thus TOTAL Loading		2,650 lb/ft

REACTIONS at Fan Supports will be:

On Outer Struts
$R_o = 0{\cdot}40wl$
$= 0{\cdot}40.2{,}650.12 = 12{,}72C$ lb

On Inner Struts
$R_i = 1{\cdot}10wl$
$= 1{\cdot}10.2{,}650.12 = 34{,}980$ lb

Allow for Reactions from LINKING SPAN at Outer Struts, treating Span as simply supported Beam of similar construction.

REACTION at each support will be
$R = 0{\cdot}50wl$
$= 0{\cdot}50.2{,}650.30 = 39{,}750$ lb

Hence total Reaction on Outer Strut will be 12,720 + 39,750 = 52,470 lb

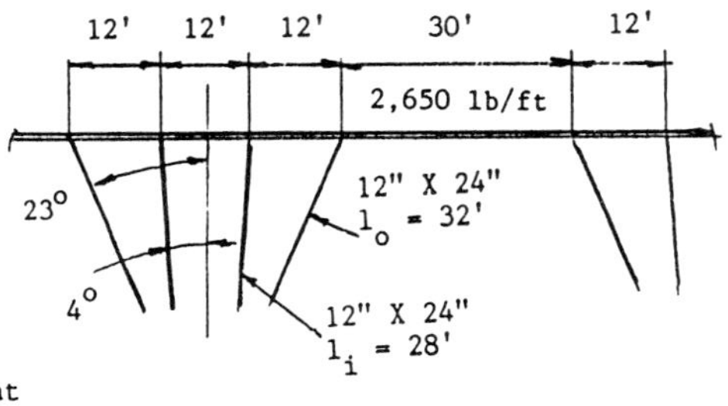

3. LOADING OF STRUTS OR RAKING LEGS

Inner Leg, section 12"X24" @ 4°
$l_i = 28$ft
Load in Leg $\quad P_m = 34{,}980/\cos 4^\circ$
$= 34{,}980/{\cdot}9976 = 35{,}064$ lb

Compressive STRESS in Leg $\quad f_m = 35{,}064/(12.24) = 122$ lb/in^2
Compared with Permissible Stress $= 1{,}245$ lb/in^2
and Fletcher permitted value of 373 lb/in^2

Critical Load of Strut (Euler) $\quad P_c = \pi^2 EIk_2/l_i^2$
$= 9{\cdot}87.1{,}305{,}720.3{,}456.{\cdot}80/(12.28)^2$
$= 315{,}611$ lb

and ratio $\quad P_c/P_m = 9{\cdot}00$

Outer Leg, section 12"X24" @ 23°
$l_o = 32$ft
Load in Leg $\quad P_m = 52{,}470/\cos 23^\circ$
$= 52{,}470/{\cdot}9205 = 57{,}002$ lb

Compressive STRESS in Leg $\quad f_m = 57{,}002/(12.24) = 198$ lb/in^2
Compared with Permissible Stress 1,245 lb/in^2
and Fletcher permitted value of 373

Critical Load of Strut (Euler) $\quad P_c = 9{\cdot}87.1{,}305{,}720.3{,}456.{\cdot}80/(12.32)^2$
$= 241{,}640$ lb

and ratio $\quad P_C/P_m = 4{\cdot}24$

However, the foregoing assumes a perfect structure with both components of each Leg equally sharing the total load. Assuming only one component takes the full load, then
$f_m = 57{,}002/(12.12) = 396$ lb/in^2

compared with the above noted permissible stress levels - 6% above the Fletcher value.

Critical Load of Strut (Euler) $\quad P_c = 9{\cdot}87{\cdot}1{,}305{,}720.1{,}728.{\cdot}80/(12.32)^2$
$= 120{,}820$

and ratio $\quad P_c/P_m = 2{\cdot}12$

This result represents the worst condition under the assumed static loading.

Consider Viaduct Class E

1. DECK LOADING
This will be the same as for Class A1 or 312 lb/ft, to give similar Stress levels in the Deck Timber and Reactions at the Outer and Centre Carrying Beams - ie $R_o = 829$ lb and $R_i = 2{,}761$ lb.

2. Consider the CENTRE BEAM
As for Class A1 the Total Distributed Loading = 2,835 lb/ft
Then
Assume a Continuous Beam extending over a spread of three pairs of struts ie. over six equally spaced Supports at 19·80ft cts

MAXIMUM BENDING MOMENT

$M = {\cdot}11wl^2$
$= {\cdot}11.2{,}835.19{\cdot}80^2 = 122{,}258$ lb.ft

Maximum Bending STRESS
$f_m = M/Z = 122{,}258.12/1{,}221 = $ 1,202 lb/in^2
Compared with Permissible Stress of 1,340 lb/in^2

and
REACTIONS at Fan Supports of Centre Beam within this spread will be:

On Outer Struts
$R_o = {\cdot}39wl = {\cdot}39.2{,}835.19{\cdot}80 = $ 21,892 lb

On Inner Struts
$R_i = 1{\cdot}13wl = 1{\cdot}13.2{,}835.19{\cdot}80 = $ 63,430 lb

On Central Struts
$R_c = {\cdot}97wl = {\cdot}97.2{,}835.19{\cdot}80 = $ 54,449 lb

3. LOADING OF STRUTS OR RAKING LEGS

Consider the worst case
ie. Inner Leg of spread, of section 12"X12"
l = 34 ft @ 17½°
Load in Leg
P_m = 63,430/cos 17½° = 63,430/·9537 = 66,509 lb

Compressive STRESS in Leg f_m = 66,509/144 = 462 lb/in²
Compared with Permissible Stress 1,245 lb/in²
and Fletcher permitted value of 373 lb/in²

Critical Load of Strut (Euler) $P_c = \pi^2 EIK_2/l_i^2$
= $9{\cdot}87.1{,}305{,}720.1{,}728.{\cdot}80/(12.34)^2$
= 107,024 lb

and Critical ratio P_c/P_m = 1·61

CLASS	MEMBER	LOAD	SPAN	SECT'N	M_{max}	f_{max}	f_{perm}	REACTIONS					
		lb/ft	ft	inXin	lb.ft	lb/in²	lb/in²	lb	lb	lb	lb	lb	lb
								On Carrying Beams					
					·125wl²	M/Z		·375wl	1·25wl	·375wl			
A1.E.	DECK	312	7·08	12X4	1955	690	1721	829	2761	829			
A2.		312	7·50	12X4	2194	774	1721	878	2925	878			
B.		318	7·08	12X6	1993	315	1645	844	2814	844			
Z.Y.		333	6·50	12X4	1759	621	1721	812	2706	812			
								·50wl	·50wl				
D.		324	15	12X8	9113	804	1584	2430	2430				
	CENTRE BEAM							At Supports					
					·10wl²			·40wl	1·10wl	1·10wl	·40wl		
A1.		2835	15	12X24	63788	627	1340	17010	46778	46778	17010		
B.		2888	15·3	12X24	67605	664	1340	17675	48605	48605	17675		
A2.		2999	15·3	12X24	70510	693	1340	18390	50572	50572	18390		
					·11wl²			·39wl	1·13wl	·97wl	·97wl	1·13wl	·39wl
E.		2835	19·8	12X24	122258	1202	1340	21892	63430	54449	54449	63430	21892
Z.		2780	21	12X24	134858	1325	1340	22768	65969	56629	56629	65969	22768
					·125wl²			·375wl	1·25wl	·375wl			
Y.		2780	15	12X24	78188	768	1340	15638	52125	15638			
								·40wl	1·10wl	1·10wl	·40wl		
D.	OUTER BEAM	2650	12	12X24	–	–	–	12720	34980	34980	12720		

LEGS (Outer Raking Struts)

	Reac'n	Slope Deg	L'th l ft	Sect'n inXin	Max Load P_m lb	f_{max} lb/in²	f_{perm} lb/in²	Load P_c lb	P_c/P_m	L/t	Ult.Res. lb/in²
A1.	45360*	35	35·5	14X14	55371	283	1245	181854	3·28	32	1500
A2.	48380*	34	37·5	14X14	58357	298	1245	162974	2·79	34	1350
D.	52470*	23	32	12X24	57002	198	1245	241640	4·24	32	1500
Y.	43988*	20	40	14X14	46811	239	1245	143239	3·06	34	1350
E.	63430	17½	34	12X12	66509	462	1245	107024	1·61	34	1350
Z.	65969	0	39	14X14	65969	336	1245	150678	2·28	39	1100
	Alternative			13X13		390		112032	1·70		

* Continuous Beam Reaction at Outer Support plus Reaction from Linking Span

BIBLIOGRAPHY

Primary and documentary sources and articles in magazines and journals are given as references in the text.

Anthony, G H. *The Hayle West Cornwall & Helston Railways*, 1968.
Beckett, D. *Brunel's Britain*, 1980 — ISBN 0 7153 7973 9.
Beckett, D. *Aspects of the History and Design of Structures*, 1990.
Biddle, G. *The Railway Surveyors*, 1990 — ISBN 0 7110 1954 1.
Bennett, A. *The Great Western Railway in West Cornwall*, 1988 — ISBN 0 946184 35 3.
Bennett, A. *The Great Western Railway in Mid Cornwall*, 1988 — ISBN 0 946184 53 4.
Bennett, A. *The Great Western Railway in East Cornwall*, 1990 — ISBN 1 870754 11 5.
Brunel, I. *Life of Isambard Kingdom Brunel*, 1870.
Conder, F. R. *The Men who Built Railways* (ed J. Simmons), 1983 — ISBN 0 7266 9173 5.
MacDermot E. T. *History of the Great Western Railway* Vol.2 — ISBN 0 7110 0412 9.
Moseley, H. *Mechanical Principles of Engineering & Architecture*, 1843.
Nock. O. S. *Railway Archaeology*, 1981.
Pugsley, A. *Works of Isambard Kingdom Brunel* (edited), 1976 — ISBN 0 521 23239 2.
Rankine, W. J. M. *Introductory Lecture on the Harmony of Theory & Practice in Mechanics*, 1856.
Rolt, L. T. C. *Isambard Kingdom Brunel*, 1957 — ISBN 0 582 10774 X.
Sutcliffe, G. L. *The Modern Carpenter, Joiner & Cabinet Maker*, 1904.
Vaughan, A. *Pictorial History of Great Western Railway Architecture*, 1977 — ISBN 0 902888 22 6.
Vaughan, A. *Isambard Kingdom Brunel — Engineering Knight Errant*, 1991 — ISBN 0 7195 4636 2.
Woodfin, R. J. *The Cornwall Railway*, 1972.

GLOSSARY OF TECHNICAL TERMS

Ballast Board — Vertical board fixed on either side of a viaduct to contain the ballast.
Batter — The slope of a structure, slightly out of the vertical.
Broad Gauge — The distance between the rails, of 7ft 0¼in, of Brunel's original permanent way.
Cill Timber — A cross timber seated on the top of a trestle or pier used to carry the legs or supports of the superstructure.
Coffin Piece — A timber which linked the radial legs of the viaduct to the horizontal timber of the parapet or handrail, and was shaped like a coffin.
Corbel or Bolster — A short piece of timber capping a strut or leg and offering a larger bearing to the supported beam. Also known as a Corbel-Piece.
Decking — The timber planks which formed the floor of the viaduct and carried ballast and permanent way.
Fender — Timber capping pieces fixed to the top of a Ballast Board.
Inclined Bolts — The bolts used to clamp the component members of a Laminated Beam.
Joggle — An Insert (usually of Hardwood) 12in × 6¼/5½in (tapered) × 1¾in thick let into a recess in each of the mating faces of the members forming a laminated beam which thus prevented movement between the mating surfaces of the two members; a wrought iron tapered wedge being driven into the assembly to ensure a tight fit of the joggle in the recess.
Laminated Beam — A composite beam composed of two (or more) members, secured together with inclined bolts and incorporating joggles to prevent slippage between their mating faces under load.
Landward Span — The span which joined the end fan of a viaduct to the adjacent embankment or abutment.
Linking Span — The short span which joined two adjacent fans of an inland viaduct, generally not greater than 20ft in length.
Narrow Gauge — The distance between the rails of 4ft 8½in which was the width normally considered 'standard' but which Brunel and his engineers referred to as 'narrow'.
Plinth — A shallow masonry construction used to carry the supports of the timber superstructure.
Queen Post Truss — a truss which incorporated two vertical struts within its framework together with diagonal straining pieces.
Tie Beam — A horizontal timber located on either side of a pier or trestle at cill level to link it to its neighbour.
Tie Bar — A wrought iron member which formed a tension link between various parts of the structure, particularly between adjacent piers.
Trestle — A timber framework used as an alternative to a masonry pier to carry the supports for the viaduct superstructure.
Trough — The arrangement formed from the ballast board and fender on each side of the viaduct and the decking which thus retained the ballast.
Waling — Horizontal timber used to brace the radial legs or struts of the viaducts.
Wedge — A wrought iron piece tapered 1¼in × 1¾in thick × 13in long which was driven between a joggle and its recess to ensure a tight fit.

The engineering units used throughout this book are those current in Brunel's lifetime. They may be converted to SI units as follows:

Length	1 foot = 12 inches = 0·3048 metres
Force	1 ton = 2,240 pounds (lb) = 9964 newtons
Stress	1 ton/in^2 = 2,240 lb/in^2 = 15·44 newtons/mm^2
Speed	1 mile per hour = 1·609 km per hour

Other units involved were:

Weight	1 ton = 20 cwt
	1 cwt = 112 pounds (lb)
Money	£1 = 20 shillings = 100p
	1 shilling = 12 pence (d)

Throughout the text the dimensions of beams are referred to as 'Width' × 'Depth'.

INDEX

Numbers in *italics* refer to illustrations